An Investigation of the Evidence

Colin Wilson's *After Life* provides you with a rare theoretical examination of spirits, parapsychological abilities, and the nature of human personality. Explore a rich collection of case studies documenting evidence for the validity of near-death experiences, reincarnation, and the survival of the soul:

- The soldier who found himself outside his earthly body
- A séance in a Parisian drawing room
- An apparition delivers a warning
- Psychic powers of primitive peoples
- The famous Bridey Murphy case
- The girl who was "possessed" by Elizabeth Barrett Browning
- The ghost of chimney sweep Samuel Bull
- A "psychic double" goes to church
- And many more

About the Author

Colin Wilson was born in Leicester in 1931. He left school at sixteen and took various jobs before he became a full-time writer with the publication of *The Outsider*. He is the author of many books with subjects ranging from mysticism to criminology. He has also written articles and plays and is a contributor to several newspapers and journals. He regards himself primarily as a philosopher concerned with the meaning of human existence. Unlike many "existentialists," his outlook is basically optimistic. Colin Wilson still lives in Cornwall with his wife. His recreations are collecting gramophone records, mainly opera, and mathematic.

After Life

Survival of the Soul

Colin Wilson

2000
Llewellyn Publications
St. Paul, Minnesota, 55164-0383, U.S.A.

SECOND EDITION
First printing, 2000

First edition, two printings, Harrap Ltd., 1985

Cover design: William Cannon
Editing and book design: Christine Snow

Library of Congress Cataloging-in-Publication Data
Wilson, Colin, 1931–
After life: survival of the soul / Colin Wilson. — 2nd ed.
p. cm.
Rev. ed. of: Afterlife. London: Harrap, 1985.
Includes bibliographical references and index.
ISBN: 1-56718-817-6
1. Parasychology. 2. Future life. I. Wilson, colin, 1931–
Afterlife. II. Title.
BF1040W65 2000 99-41158
133.9'01'3–dc21 CIP

Llewellyn Publications
A Division of Llewellyn Worldwide, Ltd.
P.O. Box 64383, Dept. K817-6
St. Paul, MN 55164-0383
www.llewellyn.com

Printed in the United States of America on recycled paper

Other Books by the Author

Philosophical Books

The Outsider (1956)
Religion and the Rebel (1957)
The Stature of Man (or *The Age of Defeat*) (1959)
The Strength to Dream: Literature and the Imagination (1962)
Origins of the Sexual Impulse (1963)
Beyond the Outsider: The Philosophy of the Future (1965)
Introduction to the New Existentialism (1966)
(Republished as *The New Existentialism*)
Sex and the Intelligent Teenager (1966)
The Strange Genius of David Lindsay (1970)
Chords and Discords (1964) (Also published as *The Brandy of the Damned: Discoveries of a Musical Eclectic*)
Eagle and Earwig (Essays in Literary Criticism) (1965)
Poetry and Mysticism (1970)
A Book of Booze (1974)
The Craft of the Novel (1975)
Frankenstein's Castle (1980)
Starseekers (1980)
Access to Inner Worlds: The Story of Brad Absetz (1983)
The Bicameral Critic (Essays in Literature and Philosophy) (1985)
The Essential Colin Wilson (1985)
Marx Refuted (Edited by Colin Wilson and Ronald Duncan) (1987)
The Misfits: A Study of Sexual Outsiders (1988)
Existentially Speaking: Essays on Literature and Philosophy (1989)
An Atlas of Holy Places and Sacred Sites (1996)
From Atlantis to the Sphinx (1996)
Alien Dawn (1998)
The Books in My Life (1998)

Biographies

Rasputin and the Fall of the Romanovs (1964)
Bernard Shaw: A Reassessment (1969)

Voyage to a Beginning (1969)
New Pathways in Psychology: Abraham Maslow and the Post-Freudian Revolution (1972)
Gurdjieff: The War Against Sleep (1980)
The Quest for Wilhelm Reich (1981)
Jung: The Lord of the Underworld (1984)
Steiner: The Man and his Vision (1985)
Aleister Crowley: The Image of the Beast (1987)
The Strange Life of P.D. Ouspensky (1993)

Occult
The Occult: A History (1971)
Strange Powers (1973)
Men of Strange Powers (also *Mysterious Powers*) (1975)
Enigmas and Mysteries (1976)
The Geller Phenomenon (1976)
Mysteries: An Investigation into the Occult (1978)
Poltergeist: A Study in Destructive Haunting (1981)
The Psychic Detectives: The Story of Psychometry (1984)
Beyond the Occult (1988)
The Supernatural (edited by Damon Wilson) (1991)

Criminology
An Encyclopedia of Murder (with Patricia Pitman) (1961)
A Casebook of Murder (1969)
Order of Assassins (1972)
An Encyclopedia of Modern Murder (with Donald Seaman) (1983)
A Criminal History of Mankind (1984)
An Encyclopedia of Scandal (with Donald Seaman) (1987)
Jack the Ripper: Summing Up and Verdict (with Robin Odell) (1988)
The Mammoth Book of True Crime (edited by Howard Dossor) (1988)
Clues (1989)(also *Written in Blood: A History of Forensic Detection*)

The Second Mammoth Book of True Crime (edited by Damon Wilson) (1990)
The Serial Killers (with Donald Seaman) (1990)
A Plague of Murder (with Damon Wilson) (1995)
The Corpse Garden: The Crimes of Fred and Rose West (1997)

Novels

Ritual in the Dark (1960)
Adrift in Soho (1961)
The Sex Diary of a Metaphysician (1963) (also *The Man Without a Shadow*)
The Violent World of Hugh Greene (1963) (also *The World of Violence*)
Necessary Doubt (1964)
The Glass Cage (1966)
The Mind Parasites (1967)
The God of the Labyrinth (1970)
The Killer (1970) (In America, *Lingard*)
The Black Room (1971)
The Return of the Lloigor (1974)
The Schoolgirl Murder Case (1974)
The Space Vampires (1976)
The Janus Murder Case (1984)
The Personality Surgeon (1985)
Spider World: The Tower (1986)
Spider World: The Delta (1987)
The Magician From Siberia (1988)
The Philosophers Stone (1989)
Spider World: The Magician (1992)

For Simon Scott
with affection and gratitude

Acknowledgments

As usual, I owe a considerable debt of gratitude to the Society for Psychical Research, and its librarian Nick Clarke Lowes, and to the College of Psychic Studies, and its librarian Bernadette Giblin. Both provided me with many books that would otherwise have been quite unobtainable.

I am grateful to Dr. Adam Crabtree, Dr. Wilson Van Dusen, and to Margot Grey for allowing me to quote from unpublished material, and to the late Anita Gregory for some valuable comments. I also wish to thank Joe Keeton, Ray Bryant, Andrew and Marguerite Selby, and Ian Wilson, for invaluable material for the reincarnation chapter; and Julie Peters for drawing my attention to the case of the calculating twins.

Finally, I should like to thank Simon Scott, at whose suggestion this book was written.

Contents

Preface xvii

Chapter One **Voices in the Head** 1

Adam Crabtree's patients who heard "voices inside their heads"; Julian Jaynes and auditory hallucinations; case of Sarah Worthington; case of Susan: possession by a sexually obsessed father; case of Art: possession by a living woman; Julian Jaynes and split-brain research; Wilson Van Dusen on "The Presence of Spirits in Madness"; two types of voices: "higher order" and "lower order"; Van Dusen's discovery of Swedenborg; Swedenborg's description of "possession"; "Angels possess the interior of man"; Crabtree's case of the girl "possessed" by Elizabeth Barrett Browning; Alan Vaughan possessed after playing with an ouija board; Brad Absetz contacts his "other self"; Swedenborg's views on life after death; Bertrand Russell on survival; Alfred Sutro's psychic experience; The Rev. Bertrand's near-death experience; near-death experience: "passing down a tunnel"; death of Dr. Karl Novotny; emergence of an "overall pattern."

Chapter Two **The World of the Clairvoyant** 35

Darwin arrives in Tierra del Fuego; the clairvoyant as a different species; development of Rosalind Heywood's psychic abilities; telepathy with a sleeping patient; Rosalind Heywood's "Orders"; case of Julia; case of Vivian Usborne; Jaynes' theory of how man became a "left-brainer"; Ramakrishna's experience of "samadhi"; magic of primitive man; porpoise-callers of the Gilbert Islands; how we lost our psychic powers; Rosalind Heywood and "The Singing"; Lethbridge's theory of apparitions as "tape recordings"; Mrs. Willett's experience of "two minds"; case of the soldier who found himself

Preface

THIS WAS A BOOK THAT I HAD NEVER INTENDED to write.

As a child, I read books on ghosts and spirits from the local library, and had no doubt whatsoever of their existence. My grandmother attended the local Spiritualist church, and we often talked about the reality of life after death. Then, at the age of ten, I discovered chemistry and astronomy, and the belief in ghosts seemed to evaporate like a bad dream.

In his autobiography *The Invisible Writing*, Arthur Koestler describes how he was reading a pamphlet about the persecution of the Jews, and experiencing a feeling of helpless rage. Then he opened a book on relativity, and read a sentence about Einstein leading the human spirit "across the peaks of glaciers never explored before by any human being." Suddenly, he seemed to see Einstein's energy-mass formula hanging above mountain tops, surrounded by mist, and immediately experienced a sense of overwhelming happiness. At the age of twelve, I felt much the same, not just about Einstein, but about the whole concept of science. It seemed to me then that there was no secret of the universe that would not one day be revealed.

Then, one day in our clay modeling class, we began to talk about the mystery of where space comes to an end. What lay beyond the outer edges of the universe? As I thought about it, it suddenly struck me that this contradicts all our human feelings of certainty. It is impossible for anything to go on forever, yet equally impossible to imagine space coming to an end. I suddenly began to feel dizzy, as if standing on the edge of a precipice. As I made my way home that afternoon, I experienced a strange sensation of fear and insecurity. It suddenly seemed to me that human reason, which I had regarded as the answer to all problems, was laughably feeble and inexact.

In spite of this sense of insecurity, which was like a nagging toothache, I experienced no temptation to return to the comforts of spiritualism. It simply seemed a pleasant delusion.

What really bothered me was that, even if there *was* life after death, this would not make any difference to this apparently impenetrable mystery of human existence. I saw clearly that human beings live by habit, craving a sense of familiarity. When young children go on holiday, they experience a feeling of homesickness, no matter how pleasant they find their new surroundings. We *need* to feel that life is predictable and repetitious, and that all mysteries can eventually be solved, just as we need to feel the solid ground under our feet.

As I grew up, and made my first hesitant attempts to become a writer, I continued to feel a kind of irritable contempt for people who believed in life after death. They wanted simple certainties and I could see that these did not exist. In one of my later novels, I expressed this in a simple image. The hero of the novel, a professor of philosophy, dreams that he is standing at one end of a chessboard, and that his opponent stands at the other end. Both know the rules ey are surrounded by a wall of impenetrable mist, ossible to see what lies beyond the limits of the

' not believe in ghosts. A friend told me that he ı Sussex, where the ghost of an old man was ı, standing by the manure heap; local people er tenant of the cottage. But if ghosts exist- hessboard, not in the mist beyond it.

ıgent asked me if I would like to write a ır an American publisher, and I agreed I was fairly sure that the whole subject illusions and old wives' tales, like fairy ers.

the book, my wife read me an anec- of Sir Osbert Sitwell. Sitwell's father one of his escapades in "unmasking" a ook. His son tells how, just before the brother officers went to see a famous ı looked at their hands, and was obvi- went back to her when the others had he matter. She told him: "I could see months later, the war started, and

a skeptic impressed me. As I went on npses of the future, second-sight, and began to see that these were not fan- nt. A few of them might be lies or bviously true. Long before I had fin- totally convinced of the reality of so-

ction on life after death, I must admit ır perhaps it would be more accurate ed. What if human beings *did* survive n who we are, why we are alive, what lives.

ot
cil h
ors w
nendous
ıd that it

were due
paranor-
nd-over-
how this
ng black
t Diane's

such an
ng down
them as
clusions,
rivileged
t polter-
ter, on a
chology,
a shrug:
ologist I

ople had
nd there
far from
searcher
ce been

In 1980, I suggested to my British publisher that I shoul book about poltergeists—the "banging ghosts" who thro around the room and make a general nuisance of thems wife and I had been up to Pontefract to study the evidence tergeist that had smashed every breakable item in the coun belonging to a couple named Pritchard. We spoke to neigh described the "haunting," and listened to tapes of the tre racket the "spook" had made—a banging and crashing so lo could be heard two streets away.

I was convinced at that time that poltergeist phenomena to the unconscious minds of disturbed adolescents—what mal researchers call "spontaneous psychokinesis," or mi matter. But when the daughter of the house, Diane, told me poltergeist had dragged her upstairs by her throat, leavi bruises, I suddenly knew beyond all doubt that this was no own unconscious mind. This was a spirit.

Most paranormal researchers would be disturbed by admission—to begin with, expressing these views would bri on them the contempt of their colleagues, who would regar gullible idiots. But I have no difficulty admitting my con since I hold no academic post, and writers are regarded as p eccentrics. So, in *Poltergeist*, I admitted my conviction tha geists are spirits, very often of dead people. (A few years la television program, I met a German professor of parapsy and when I asked him what poltergeists were, he said with "Why, spirits, of course." But he is so far the only parapsych have met who has been willing to admit it.)

Now this case has an important postscript. Several pe seen the shadowy form of a monk in the Pritchard's house, had once been a gallows on the hilltop where it stood. Not the hilltop there were the ruins of a monastery. A local r had uncovered a story to the effect that a monk had o hanged on the gallows for rape.

I have no idea whether this is true. But it seems to add substance to the notion that the "spirit" that haunted the Pritchard's house was that of someone who had died.

In other words, the case seemed to demonstrate the reality of life after death.

Yet although I wrote about it in *Poltergeist*, there was still a sense in which it did not "sink in." If you had asked me in 1983, "Do you believe in life after death?" I would have replied, "I suppose I think it likely, but frankly I don't really care."

That was how I continued to feel until a British publisher asked me to write this book.

I was, of course, already familiar with much of its material, having been reading and writing about "the paranormal" for more than a decade. Yet it was not until I took a deep breath and plunged into the subject that the sheer overwhelming weight of the evidence really began to impress me.

Fortunately, my friend Adam Crabtree had asked me to write an introduction to a book of his cases about "possession." I was glad to be able to start on this scientific note, quoting a psychiatrist, for I had always felt a kind of uneasy distaste for the subject of life after death. I can understand why nineteenth-century scientists got so angry about it. Religion always brings out this feeling in me. It is not that I am specifically antireligious—the religion of the great saints and mystics has always fascinated me. But whenever I am—on rare occasions—forced to sit through a church service, I find myself thinking: My God, how I detest Christianity. Talk of "Spiritualism" produces much the same effect, a mixture of boredom and irritation.

As I continued to tell the story of Adam Crabtree's cases of "possession," and the experience of another psychiatrist with whom I had corresponded, Wilson Van Dusen, I had the feeling that I was dealing with solid fact, not vague religious hopes for an afterlife. Then, of course, the whole history of Spiritualism, from the rapping noises in the Fox household in New York State, is such a superb story. I realized that again during the past week as I reread the proof of this new second edition.

Oddly enough, I had not actually *read* this book. When you write a book, you are too close to it to see it as a whole. Even when you reread it for the first time in proof, you are still too close to it. Now, reading it after more than ten years, it is as if I am reading someone else's book. As I become aware of the sheer consistency of the evidence, I recognize just how powerful is the case for human survival of physical death.

Dostoevsky once said that if it is true that human beings survive death, this is the most important thing we can ever know. I am not sure I agree with him. In my book *New Pathways in Psychology*, I commented: "There's something bloody fishy about human existence." I have always been inclined to Descartes method of radical doubt. He said, in effect: Suppose God is a confidence trickster, who is intent on deceiving us. Suppose a kettle ought to turn to ice when you put it on the stove, or suppose objects ought to fall upward instead of downward. How could we use our power of reason to see through this grand deception?

As I look at this apparently normal, solid world around me, I feel an odd kind of suspicion that someone is pulling my leg. I can so easily imagine it other than it is. Human beings are immensely complicated machines, yet we are thrown into the world without an instruction book. I do not seem to be able to share the view of the majority of my fellow human beings, that the world is a fairly straightforward place. So even if I convince myself that life after death is a proven fact, I cannot accept that this has in any way "solved" the riddle of human existence. It seems to me obvious that we are like blinkered horses, totally unaware of the reality that surrounds us. I *still* feel "there's something bloody fishy about human existence."

Having said which, I feel that the facts I have presented in this book are basically solid and dependable, and that anyone who takes the trouble to study them will feel, as I do, that death is probably an even stranger adventure than being alive.

—Cornwall, 1999

Chapter One

Voices in the Head

Dr. Adam Crabtree is a psychotherapist who lives and works in Toronto, Canada. He began to practice in 1966, and, like most psychiatrists, soon began to encounter cases in which patients heard "voices" inside their heads.

Now such cases are not particularly rare, and "hearing voices" is certainly not a sign of madness. Dr. Julian Jaynes, a Princeton psychologist, began to make a study of auditory hallucinations after experiencing one himself. He was lying on a couch when he heard a voice speaking from the air above his head. Naturally concerned about his sanity, Jaynes discovered, to his relief, that about 10 percent of people have had hallucinations of some sort, and that about a third of these take the form of "phantom voices." One perfectly normal young housewife told him that she held long conversations with her dead grandmother every morning when she made the beds.

Jaynes, of course, takes it for granted that such experiences *are* hallucinations, and for a long time, Adam Crabtree shared that belief. Then he encountered a case that raised some basic doubts. It concerned a young woman named Sarah Worthington, who was the patient of a colleague of Crabtree's. After a treatment that had been initially successful, Sarah Worthington had suddenly plunged into moods of depression in which she was tempted to commit suicide.

The three of them met in Crabtree's office, and he began to probe her difficulties. One of his questions was whether she had ever heard voices inside her head, and she admitted that she had. Crabtree asked her to lie down and relax, and to do her best to try to recall these inner conversations. Almost immediately, the girl's body tensed and she exclaimed: "Oh, the heat! I'm hot!" She went on speaking, both psychiatrists observed the change in her voice. Sarah lacked confidence; this new personality had the voice of someone who was used to exercising authority. When they asked the woman what she wanted to do, she replied: "Help Sarah." It was a clear indication that this was *not* Sarah. They asked the woman her name, and she replied: "Sarah Jackson." She identified herself as Sarah's grandmother. Crabtree explained that he and Jenny were also trying to help Sarah, and asked the "grandmother" if she would be willing to help. She replied: "Yes." This ended the first session.

At the next session, the grandmother soon came back. She was still talking about a fire, and at one point she asked, "Where is Jason?" Jason, it transpired, was her son, and the fire she was referring to had taken place in 1910. Sarah Jackson had rushed home as soon as she heard that there was a fire in her street—her seven-year-old son had been left in the house alone. The whole neighborhood was ablaze. In fact, Jason had been moved to safety by neighbors, but it took Sarah Jackson another hour to discover this, and in the meantime, she had rushed around the streets in a frenzy, stifling in the heat. The experience had imprinted itself deep in her consciousness.

According to the grandmother, she had "taken possession" of Sarah Worthington when her granddaughter was playing the piano—both of them loved music. It soon became clear that, in spite of her avowed intention of helping her granddaughter, it was Sarah Jackson herself who was in need of help. She was tormented by guilt about her own life—particularly about how badly she had treated her daughter Elizabeth, Sarah's mother. Elizabeth had developed into an unhappy, neurotic girl, who had in turn treated her own daughter badly. Sarah's relations with her mother were a strange duplicate of Elizabeth's relations with *her* mother. Both mothers had greatly preferred their son to their daughter, and had taught the daughter that men were everything and women nothing. The grandmother had become fully aware of all this by the time she died, which is why she now felt that she had to help her granddaughter. Instead of helping, she had made things worse; Sarah was frightened and confused by the voice inside her, and was becoming desperate.

Now grandmother Jackson was "out in the open," things became much easier. She was able to give the psychiatrists invaluable information about Sarah's family background. Although Sarah was at first astonished to realize that her grandmother was speaking through her, she gradually learned to accept it, and began to achieve deeper insight into her problems. At the end of two months she was cured. The grandmother remained a "possessive presence," but now that Sarah understood it, she was no longer afraid. In fact, it gave her a sense of comfort to feel that her grandmother was a vaguely beneficent presence in the background of her life.

The reader's reaction to this story is probably much the same as my own when I first read it in the typescript of Adam Crabtree's *Multiple Man*: that there must be some purely psychological explanation. Sarah had known her grandmother as a child; perhaps she had heard the story about the fire from her own lips. Perhaps she recognized how similar her mother's problems had been to her own. Her unconscious mind had "re-told" her the story as a rationalization of her own sufferings. But the more I read of Crabtree's book (which his publishers had sent to me, asking if I would write an introduction), the more I saw that such explanations are unacceptable. He goes on to recount another eight cases from his practice, each one involving some type of "possession." After the third or fourth case, the unconscious mind explanation had begun to wear very thin.

A social worker named Susan was unable to sustain any normal relationship with a male, and recognized, correctly, that this was due to some deep resentment towards her father. Crabtree was able to speak to her father—who had died in a car crash—just as he spoke to Sarah's grandmother, and he learned that he had been sexually obsessed with his daughter. Until she was sixteen, he had crept into her bedroom after she was asleep and had fondled her genitals. On some unconscious level, she was aware of what was happening. She recognized his desire for her, and treated him with contempt, behaving provocatively and exercising her new-found sexual power to make him squirm. The contempt spread into her relations with boyfriends and caused problems. When her father died in the car crash, he was drawn to his daughter as a "place of refuge," and she was vulnerable to him because of the sexual interference. Once "inside her," he was in a condition of "foggy sleep," unaware of his identity or his present position. Crabtree patiently explained to Susan's father that he was actually dead, and that he ought to leave his daughter alone. One day, he simply failed to appear at the therapeutic session; Susan experienced a sense of relief and freedom.

I found one case particularly fascinating and intriguing. It concerned a university professor named Art, whose first marriage had been unsuccessful, and who was about to embark on a second. He was beginning to experience a deep reluctance to go through with the marriage, and he associated this with "inner storms" in which a censorious voice criticized him and various people he knew. He was vaguely aware that the voice sounded like his mother—who was living in Detroit—and he had arrived at the common sense explanation that the voice was some negative aspect of himself, and that he had somehow incorporated elements of his mother, who had always been intensely possessive toward him.

Crabtree followed his usual procedure, placing Art in a state of deep relaxation, and then opening a dialogue with the mother, who was called "Veronica." Veronica was perfectly willing to talk at length about her relation to her son, and about why she disapproved of so many of his friends. "Veronica came across as blatantly, almost naively, self-centered. . . ." She explained that she simply wanted to make her son recognize that many people he trusted, including his future wife, were stupid and scheming and not worthy of his respect.

Crabtree asked her if she thought all this interference could be good for her son, or even good for herself, and she finally admitted that the answer was probably no. In Detroit she was living a drab and boring life, and Crabtree pointed out that if she paid more attention to her own affairs and less to her son's, things might improve.

During the therapy, Art's mother discovered that she had a cancerous growth, and had to have an operation. The Veronica who spoke through Art's mouth agreed that this might be because she was robbing herself of vitality by "possessing" her son. At this point, Art's "inner voice" began to fade, until he finally ceased to hear it, but there was a remarkable change in his mother in Detroit. She had been experiencing a slow deterioration, and emotional withdrawal from life. Now, suddenly, her vitality began to return; she started going out and making new friends. "She seemed to have gained the proverbial 'new lease' on life."

Crabtree insists that his own attitude toward such cases is not that of a believer in the paranormal; he claims to be merely an observer, a phenomenologist, who simply treats each case *as if* it were possession. Clearly, there is nothing contradictory in such an attitude. Susan and Sarah and Art *could* have been manufacturing the voices themselves; the unconscious mind is capable of far more remarkable feats. Still, the fact remains that most readers will feel that, taken all together, these cases make an overwhelming impression of being something more than unconscious self-deception.

I turned back to Julian Jaynes to see what he had to say about "disembodied voices." He outlines his theory in a remarkable work called *The Origin of Consciousness in the Breakdown of the Bicameral Mind*, published in 1976 ("bicameral" means simply having two compartments). Jaynes advances the extraordinary theory that our remote ancestors heard "voices" all the time, the reason being that—according to Jaynes—early man lacked all self-awareness in our modern sense of the word. Jaynes believes that our caveman ancestors could not look inside themselves and say: "Now let me think . . .", because they had no "inner me." Their eyes were like a car's headlamps, directed permanently toward the outside world. So if one of these men was ordered to go and build a dam down the river, he would find it extremely difficult to remember why he was ambling along the river bank. But his sense of purpose would be refreshed by a voice—the voice of his chief—which seemed to come from the air above his head, and which would repeat his instructions.

Where would that voice come from? According to Jaynes, from the right-hand side of the brain. Jaynes' theory depends heavily on the science of "split-brain" research, which has made such remarkable advances since the mid-1950s.

For some reason no one yet understands, the brain consists of two identical halves, as if a mirror had been placed down the middle. (It has even been suggested that one of them is intended as a "spare" in case the other half gets damaged.) The top part of the brain, the part immediately below the skull, is the specifically human part; it is called the cerebrum, or cerebral hemispheres, and it has developed at a phenomenal speed over the past half-million years (which, in evolutionary terms, is the mere bat of an eyelid). If you could remove the top of the skull, the two halves of the brain would look rather like a walnut. The bridge that joins them together is a bunch of nerves called the *corpus callosum*.

For more than a century it has been known that the left hemisphere deals with language and logical thinking, while the right seems to deal with patterns and intuitions. The left enables us to add up a column of figures, the right to recognize somebody's face. You could say that the left is a scientist and the right is an artist. A man with left-brain damage will probably develop a speech impediment, but he could still draw a picture or hum a tune. A woman with right-brain damage will sound perfectly logical and coherent, but she will probably not even be able to draw a matchstick man.

The strangest thing is that if the bridge joining the two halves, the corpus callosum, is severed (as it sometimes is to prevent epilepsy), the patient literally becomes *two* people. One "split-brain" patient tried to unzip his pant's zipper with one hand while the other tried to zip it back up; another tried to hit his wife with one hand, while the other held it back. Another tried to do a jigsaw puzzle with his right hand, and his left hand kept trying to interfere, so that he had to sit on it. (It should be added that the right brain controls the left side of the body, and vice versa—once again the reason is a mystery.)

The most significant discovery is that the person you call "you" lives in the left brain; the person who lives in the right seems to be a stranger. One split-brain patient whose right brain was shown a dirty picture (i.e., with her left eye) blushed; when asked why she was blushing, she replied: "I don't know." Jaynes believes that "disembodied voices" come from this "other person" in the right side, and that they sound in the left brain—the "you"—as if through a loudspeaker.

There is one obvious objection to this theory. Jaynes is not a split-brain patient, yet he had an auditory hallucination. The same applies to Adam Crabtree's patients. The curious answer is that, to some extent, we are *all* split-brain patients. Every one of us is more or less out of touch with that deeper intuitive self. Mozart once remarked that tunes were always walking into his head fully fledged. What he meant, obviously, was that tunes came into his left brain—the "I" from the other half, the half that creates tunes and pictures. If Mozart is, in some sense, a split-brain patient, then even the rest of us most certainly are.

According to Jaynes, it was voices that walked, fully fledged, into the left brain of our remote ancestors. They assumed, understandably, that these were the voices of the gods—or of God—and this is why people in the Old Testament or the *Iliad* are always being told what to do by divine voices.

This particular aspect of Jaynes' theory is irrelevant to our present discussion; all that concerns us here is his belief that "voices" originate in the right brain, and that men have been hearing them since the beginning of human history. If that is correct, it certainly offers a plausible explanation for the voice of Sarah's grandmother and Susan's father and Art's mother. In fact, in the latter case, it sounds far more convincing than the notion that a living woman in Detroit could somehow "get inside" her son's head in distant Toronto.

It is when Jaynes goes on to discuss the voices heard by mental patients that certain doubts begin to arise. He points out that most of the cases that have been studied involve schizophrenics, and says:

> *They converse, threaten, curse, criticize, consult, often in short sentences. They admonish, console, mock, command, or sometimes simply announce everything that's happening. They yell, whine, sneer, and vary from the slightest whisper to a thunderous shout. Often the voices take on some special peculiarity, such as speaking very slowly, scanning, rhyming, or in rhythms, or even foreign languages. There may be one particular voice, more often a few voices, and occasionally many. . . .*

The voices described by Crabtree do not sound in the least like this bewildering babble; they apparently conversed like any normal person. The same applies to the housewife who held long conversations with her grandmother as she was making the beds. There is no reason, of course, why "phantom voices" should not sound like those of a normal person; but it seems to be a fact that most of them don't.

This is confirmed by a study made by another clinical psychologist, Dr. Wilson Van Dusen, formerly of the Mendocino State Hospital in California. Van Dusen spent sixteen years observing the effect of hallucinations, and he describes his findings in a chapter called "The Presence of Spirits in Madness" in his book *The Presence of Other Worlds.* His conclusions are, perhaps, even more startling than those of Julian Jaynes.

Van Dusen explains that most patients who are hallucinating prefer to keep their experiences to themselves, since they know it will be taken as a proof that they are mad. However, one unusually cooperative patient asked him if he would mind talking directly with her hallucinations, and he did. Naturally, the hallucination could not answer Van Dusen directly; he had to ask the patient to give an account of what he could hear and see. There was nothing to stop Van Dusen addressing the hallucination directly though. "In this way I could hold long dialogues with a patient's hallucinations and record both my questions and their answers." Like Adam Crabtree, he insists he was using the phenomenology method. "My only purpose was to describe the patient's experiences as accurately as possible . . . I treat the hallucinations as realities—that is what they are to the patient."

One consistent finding, says Van Dusen, was that the patients felt as if they had contact with another world or order of beings. "Most thought these other persons were living. All objected to the term 'hallucination.'"

> *For most individuals the hallucinations came on quite suddenly. One woman was working in the garden when an unseen man addressed her. Another man described sudden loud noises and voices he heard when riding in a bus. Most were frightened, and adjusted with difficulty to this new experience. All the patients described voices as having the quality of a real voice, sometimes louder, sometimes softer, than normal voices. The experience they described was quite unlike thoughts or fantasies; when things are seen they appear fully real. For instance, a patient described being awakened one night by air force officers calling him to the service of his country. He got up and was dressing when he noticed their insignia wasn't quite right, then their faces altered. With this he*

knew they were of the Other Order and struck one hard in the face. He hit the wall and injured his hand. He could not distinguish them from reality until he noticed the insignia. . . .

Most patients soon realize that they are having experiences that others do not share, and for this reason learn to keep quiet about them. Many suffer insults, threats and attacks for years from voices with no one around them aware of it.

Perhaps Van Dusen's most significant finding is that he learned that his patients seemed to experience two distinct kinds of "voices"; he speaks of these as the "higher order" and the "lower order."

Lower order voices are similar to drunken bums at a bar who like to tease and torment just for the fun of it. They find a weak point of conscience, and work on it interminably. For instance, one man heard voices teasing him for three years over a ten cent debt he had already paid. They call the patient every conceivable name, suggest every lewd act, steal memories or ideas right out of consciousness, threaten death, and work on the patient's credibility in every way. For instance, they brag that they will produce some disaster on the morrow and then claim credit for one in the daily paper. They suggest foolish acts, such as raise your right hand in the air and stay that way, and tease if he does it and threaten him if he doesn't.

In fact, it seems clear that these lower order hallucinations behave exactly like bored children with nothing better to do.

The vocabulary and range of ideas of the lower order is limited, but they have a persistent will to destroy. They invade every nook and cranny of privacy, work on every weakness and belief, claim awesome powers, make promises, and then undermine the patient's will. . . .

A few ideas can be repeated endlessly. One voice just said "hey" for months while the patient tried to figure out whether "hey" or "hay" was meant. Even when I was supposedly speaking to an engineer . . . the engineer was unable to do any more arith-

> *metic than simple sums. . . . The lower order voices seem incapable of sequential reasoning. Though they often claim to be in some distant city, they cannot report more than the patient hears, sees or remembers. They seem imprisoned in the lowest level of the patient's mind. . . .*

The lower order, then, are basically tormenters. About one-fifth of the hallucinations seem to be of a higher order, and they, on the other hand, seem concerned with helping the patient. The higher order is much more likely to be symbolic, religious, supportive, and genuinely instructive; it can communicate directly with the inner feelings of the patient. It is similar to Jung's archetypes, whereas the lower order is like Freud's id. Van Dusen mentions a case of a gaspipe fitter who experienced a higher order hallucination of a lovely woman who entertained him while showing him thousands of symbols. "[H]is female vision showed a knowledge of religion and myth far beyond the patient's comprehension." After Van Dusen had been holding a dialogue with this "higher order" hallucination, the gaspipe fitter asked for just one clue to what they had been talking about.

Van Dusen reports that he has been told by these higher order beings "that the purpose of the lower order is to illuminate all of the person's weaknesses." The purpose—or one of the purposes—of the higher order seems to be to protect people against the lower order.

> *This contrast may be illustrated by the experiences of one man. He had heard the lower order arguing for a long while about how they would murder him. He also had a light come to him at night, like the sun. He knew it was a different order because the light respected his freedom and would withdraw if it frightened him. In contrast, the lower order worked against his will, and would attack if it could sense fear in him. This rarer higher order seldom speaks, whereas the lower order can talk endlessly.*

While the lower order "is consistently nonreligious and antireligious," jeering angrily at the least mention of religion, the higher order "appeared strangely gifted, sensitive, wise, and religious."

Van Dusen made one extremely striking observation about the hallucinations. Although he was able to observe a very large number of them over the years, he soon realized that "after twenty patients, there wasn't much to be learned" because the hallucinations were all so similar. This in itself seems baffling. After all, one would expect to find as many different types of hallucinations as there are people. For example, one might expect veterinarians to have hallucinations that claim to be talking animals, engineers to be tormented by talking machines, gardeners to be haunted by talking plants or trees, librarians by talking books, or dentists by talking sets of false teeth. Nothing of the sort. The lower order hallucinations were all strikingly similar; so were those of the higher order. This either implies some basic similarity in the part of our minds that create hallucinations, or something far stranger.

Van Dusen is inclined to believe in something far stranger. Through his interest in "hypnogogic phenomena"—the odd dreams and visions we sometimes experience on the edge of sleep—Van Dusen seems to have turned to the writings of the Swedish religious mystic Emanuel Swedenborg, whose *Journal of Dreams* is full of fascinating raw material for the psychiatrist. After a career as a highly successful engineer and geologist, Swedenborg went through a mental crisis at the age of fifty-six—in 1744—during which he experienced horrifying nightmares: being caught in the wheel of a huge machine; feeling between a woman's thighs to find that her vagina was full of teeth; finally, he dreamed he was holding a conversation with Jesus. He abandoned science and became an obsessive student of the scriptures. The result was a series of remarkable works containing his own theology. He became one of the most powerful influences on the religious thought of his time.

What made his works so unusual was that he claimed to have actually visited heaven and hell, and to have held long theological discussions with angels and deceased religious teachers. (He actually claimed to have converted Martin Luther to his own theology, but was unable to make John Calvin see reason.) This again might be dismissed as the fairly typical delusion of a religious crank, except that he was able to offer some impressive evidence that he really *had* been in touch with the dead. The queen of Sweden asked Swedenborg to give her greetings to her dead brother—probably in a spirit of mild mockery. At the next court reception, Swedenborg greeted the queen for her brother, and said that he wanted to send his apologies for not answering her last letter; he would now do so through Swedenborg. The queen turned pale and said: "No one but God knows this secret." The widow of the Dutch ambassador asked Swedenborg to contact her deceased husband because she had received a huge bill from a goldsmith, and she was convinced that her husband had already paid it. Swedenborg came to see her a few days later, and told her that he had talked with her husband, and the goldsmith's receipt was in a secret compartment in a bureau. The widow knew nothing about any such compartment: but that is precisely where the receipt turned out to be.

Swedenborg also described at some length what it was like to be "possessed" by spirits, and Van Dusen was struck by the extraordinary similarity between Swedenborg's accounts and the hallucinations described by patients in the Mendocino State Hospital. Swedenborg says that spirits and angels can converse with man directly by entering "by an internal way into his organ of hearing, thus affecting it from within." Swedenborg goes on: "To speak with spirits at this day is rarely granted because it is dangerous . . . ," which clearly seems to imply that there was some past age in which men could converse more directly with spirits. The explanation Swedenborg gives is that spirits do not normally know "they are with man," because there is a kind of barrier between these entities and a human's own consciousness. If spirits get through this barrier—or are allowed through because a human has dabbled in "the occult," they are likely to become a nuisance: "Evil spirits are such that they regard man with deadly hatred, and desire nothing more than to destroy him, both body and soul." Swedenborg also mentions that the barrier between spirits and human consciousness may be broken by people who "indulge much in fantasies, so as to remove themselves from the delights proper to the natural man." This, says Van Dusen, is a pretty good description of what we now call schizophrenia. (We should note that schizophrenia does not mean "split personality"—as the modern misconception has it—but simply a withdrawal from reality.)

"All of Swedenborg's observations on the effect of evil spirits entering man's consciousness conform to my findings," says Van Dusen. He mentions passages in Swedenborg in which the characteristics of the lower order are described: their determination to destroy a man, their ability to cause anxiety or pain, their desire to destroy conscience, their hatred of religion, their tendency to bully, threaten, deceive, and lie, and their curious skill at mimicry. All these characteristics of the lower order, as experienced by mental patients, are specifically described in the writings of Swedenborg. Van Dusen was particularly struck by their hatred of religion: "If voices are merely the patient's unconscious coming forth, I would have no reason to expect them to be particularly for or against religion. Yet the lower order can be counted on to give its most scurrilous comments to any suggestion of religion." Swedenborg also notes the obsession of the lower order with filth and obscenity, another point noted by Van Dusen.

Van Dusen also observed that although the lower order claim to be individuals, they seldom reveal any trace of real personal identity. Swedenborg explains that the personal memory is taken from them at death, so they are forced to rely on the memory and abilities of the person they are possessing. Another striking similarity between Swedenborg's spirits and the lower order is the attempt to possess some organ or part of the patient's body. "Several worked on one patient's ear, and he seemed to grow deafer. One voice worked for two years to capture a patient's eye, which went visibly out of alignment." They often set out to possess the genitals. "One female patient described her sexual relations with her male spirit as both more pleasurable and more inward than normal intercourse."

There is an equally striking correspondence between the higher order described by mental patients and the entities Swedenborg calls "angels." The angels are kind, helpful, and wise. The reason that they are so sparing of words is that a human's "interior mind" does not think in words, but in "universals which comprise many particulars"—that is to say, in intuitive insights. They are, in short, a right-brain function. Or, to put it another way, angels communicate through the right cerebral hemisphere, and prefer symbols (we may recollect Van Dusen's gaspipe fitter who was shown hundreds of universal symbols in an hour by his higher order mentor). Swedenborg also notes that higher order spirits can see the lower ones, but not vice versa—which again corresponded to Van Dusen's own experience.

Van Dusen was inclined to wonder why higher order hallucinations are so much rarer than those of the lower order (approximately one-fifth as many). Swedenborg suggests an answer. Angels, he says, possess the very interior of man, and their "influx is tacit." So they are simply less apparent than the hostile spirits, who make sure their presence is recognized.

What are we to make of all this? Both Crabtree and Van Dusen insist that they try to function solely as observers, implying that the reader can choose which explanation he prefers—spirits or the unconscious mind. We have seen that Van Dusen is inclined to wonder why, if the lower order is merely the patient's unconscious, they should show such consistent hostility to religion. Also, how can we explain the following story from Crabtree's book? An acquaintance of Crabtree's called Pat was invited by a girlfriend to spend a weekend at her grandparent's farm. The grandparents turned out to be dabblers in the occult, and parts of the house, such as the attic, gave Pat peculiar feelings of uneasiness. Later, the grandparents suggested that Pat should try automatic writing, which she did with some misgivings. The moment she took the pen in her hand and relaxed, she slipped into a drugged, trance-like state, and experienced a numbness in her hand and arm. She seemed to see a woman who appeared behind her; the woman had a doll-like face, and wore a long mauve gown. Pat felt as though her energies were being usurped by this woman, and suddenly her hand wrote: "Elizabeth Barrett Browning here." (Her hosts had earlier mentioned Elizabeth Barrett Browning.)

There followed a long message that included the information that Elizabeth and Robert Browning were having difficulty getting used to their "new surroundings." Slowly, the energy seemed to diminish until the writing stopped, but Pat felt oddly dissociated for the rest of the day.

Later that evening a second session was held. This time several different entities used Pat's hand to write, and the messages were of a "coarse nature." At a third session, Elizabeth Browning answered the question of where she lived now. She replied: "Everywhere . . . nowhere. We are you and you are us." After that she seemed to become very cagey.

Then the handwriting changed to that of Pat's deceased brother, Tom, and there was a message of love and comfort. When Pat said how moved she felt, her girlfriend snapped: "That wasn't Tom. They'll pretend to be anyone." Evidently she knew a great deal about lower order entities.

Later, one of the grandparents remarked that some entity no longer seemed to be in the house; it had left because it was attracted to Pat's aura. Pat was disturbed at the thought that she had been used as a kind of sponge to soak up some dubious force.

Back home again, Pat began to hear Elizabeth's voice inside her head, and she felt oddly detached from reality. Elizabeth tried to persuade her to do more automatic writing, but she felt that if she did this, she would only be consolidating the spirit's hold. "We need you," said Elizabeth. "If you refuse to speak to us we shall live in your room, in your walls."

Pat's girlfriend had told her that if she ignored the entity, it would soon go away. She found that it was not as easy as that. She tried reading a trashy novel and ignoring the voice, but a sensation that someone was pressing her face against her own made it hard to concentrate. In bed she tossed and turned so violently that she had to remake the bed several times, but she felt that her "starvation" technique was the right one. After a few days, her ability to concentrate began to return; slowly, little by little, the influence of the entities (for she felt there was more than one) began to diminish. Finally, she had the impression that she could actually see the woman in the mauve dress receding, turning first into a mauve mass, then into a "low grade vibration."

Pat may have been very suggestible, and her unconscious mind may have created the woman in mauve, but it must be admitted that this explanation seems less convincing than the alternative—that Pat had willingly opened herself to one of the lower order, and had to extricate herself as best she could. Descriptions of this type of possession are familiar in occult literature. The American researcher Alan Vaughan describes how he himself became "possessed" for a time. He had bought himself a ouija board to amuse a friend who was convalescing. Soon he was receiving all kinds of messages, some of which seemed to convey information that was not available to Vaughan's own unconscious mind—for example, when the radio announced the death of newspaper columnist Dorothy Kilgallen from a heart attack, they asked the board if this was true; it replied that she had actually died of poison. Ten days later, this proved to be true. (It was suspected—and still is—that she died because she knew too much about the John F. Kennedy assassination.) Then, to his alarm, Vaughan found that a spirit who called itself "Nada" (as in "nothing"—recalling Elizabeth's answer to the question about where she lived) had "got inside his head." "I could hear her voice repeating the same phrases over and over again"—in the typical manner of the lower order. When asked about this, the board replied: "Awful consequences—possession."

A friend who understood such matters undertook to help Vaughan, and another spirit took possession of his hand and made him write a message: "Each of us has a spirit while living. Do not meddle with the spirits of the dead." Then the spirit seemed to cause an uprising of energy in Vaughan's body which pushed both Nada and the helpful entity out of the top of Vaughan's head:

> *I felt a tremendous sense of elation and physical wellbeing. . . . My mind began to race in some extended dimension that knew no confines of time or space. For the first time, I began to sense what*

was going on in other people's minds, and, to my astonishment, I began to sense the future through some kind of extended awareness. . . .[1]

Here again, we can see that Vaughan's account seems to tally closely with what Swedenborg had to say about angels and spirits. Nada repeated the same phrases over and over again, as the lower order always do. She identified herself as the wife of a Nantucket sea captain, and Vaughan remarks that she seemed to resent the fact that he was alive and she was dead. The entity that helped to push Nada out of Vaughan's head sounds very much like one of Swedenborg's angels.

Could not both entities have been a product of Vaughan's right brain, as Julian Jaynes suggests? This is conceivable; yet again, there *does* seem to be a distinction between the manifestations of the right brain and lower order entities. The right brain is the intuitive self—the aspect of us that provides insight and "inspiration"—such as the tunes that "walked into" Mozart's head. It has better things to do than repeat the same stupid phrase over and over again.

The distinction can be seen clearly in a case I have described elsewhere,[2] that of Brad Absetz, an American teacher living in Finland, who accidentally stumbled upon the trick of establishing contact with his "other self." After the death of their child from cancer, Brad Absetz's wife retreated into a state of schizophrenia. For hours at a time, she would lie on the bed, her eyes closed, struggling with guilt and depression. Brad would lie there beside her, waiting for her to emerge from these sessions of gloomy introspection so he could comfort and encourage her. He lay totally alert, waiting for the slightest movement that would indicate she was returning to normal awareness. Yet clearly, a man who lies on a bed for hours at a time will drift into a state of relaxation. One day, as he lay there in this combined state of relaxation and alertness, he experienced a curious sense of

1. Alan Vaughan, *Patterns of Prophecy* (1973), p. 4.
2. *Access to Inner Worlds: The Story of Brad Absetz* (1983).

inner freedom, of release from the body, almost as if floating clear of the bed. Then he noticed an impulse in the muscles of his arm, as if it wanted to move. Brad mentally gave his arm "permission to move," and it floated up into the air. Soon both arms were making spontaneous movements, while he looked on as a bystander.

In the dining hall, where buffet meals were served, his hands showed a disposition to select food for themselves. For several weeks, he allowed them to select the food they preferred—it was seldom what he would have chosen himself—and noticed that he began to lose weight, and to feel fitter than ever before. His "hand" later used crayons and paints to create an extraordinary series of paintings and to make metal sculptures. It also began to write poems in free-verse form, and these poems were remarkable for a certain clarity and purity of language.

What had happened is that the right-brain self had begun to express itself; we might say that in the parliament of his mind, the member for the unconscious had worked up the courage to start making speeches. Psychologists refer to the right brain as the "non-dominant hemisphere"; in most of us, it behaves like a suppressed housewife who never dares to utter her own opinion. Brad's hours of quiescence had taught "her" to overcome her shyness.

One day when he took up a pencil to allow his hand to write, the handwriting was quite different from his own. A woman named herself and briefly introduced herself. Brad's immediate reaction was a powerful sense of rejection. He pushed the paper away, and said forcefully: "I will not be a mouthpiece for anyone but myself." The "communicator" went away and did not return. Here we seem to have a clear distinction between the "voice" of the right brain and some external communicator or spirit.

In short, whether we can accept it or not, it seems that there is a *prima facie* case for the existence of disembodied entities with which we can, under certain circumstances, communicate.

Let us, for the moment, give Swedenborg the benefit of the doubt on these matters, and consider what else he has to say. His views are very simple. According to Swedenborg, man is a spirit who inhabits a body, in precisely the same way that a driver sits in an automobile. The body is no more the man than the automobile is. At death, the man leaves his body behind, and continues to exist in an incorporeal form. When the heartbeat ceases, the spirit—that is, the man himself—passes on to another plane of existence, and this is described by Swedenborg at some length in his book *Heaven and Hell.*

Our first reaction to this is that it reveals a certain naiveté. We are aware of personality as something that changes and develops over the course of a lifetime. H. G. Wells points out that every single cell in our body changes every seven years, so a man of forty is totally different from the same man at thirty or fifty. Moreover, personality can alter through some accident; for example, people who have received violent blows to the head may seem to turn into another personality. One leading investigator of the paranormal, Professor John Taylor, writes in *The Shape of Minds to Come*: "We recognize personality as a summation of the different contributions to behavior from the various control units of the brain." So to assume that the personality can survive death is a little like assuming that a house will somehow go on existing after it has been demolished, or that the "spirit" of a ship will live on after it has been dismantled in the breaker's yard. My personality wilts visibly when I get tired, and it goes out like a light when I fall asleep. So the very idea of its surviving death seems a logical absurdity.

All these objections were beautifully summarized in an article Bertrand Russell wrote in the 1930s on "Do We Survive Death?"[3] A person, he says, is simply a series of mental occurrences and habits, and if we believe in life after death, we must believe that the memories and habits that constitute the person will somehow continue to exist. This leads him to state flatly: "It is not rational arguments, but emotions, that cause belief in a future life." He goes on to say that one feeling that encourages the belief in survival is admiration for

3. Russell, *The Mysteries of Life and Death* (no date).

the excellence of man. He quotes the Bishop of Birmingham on the subject. Man knows right and wrong. He can build Westminster Abbey. He can make an aeroplane. He can calculate the distance to the sun. So how can we believe that he will perish utterly at death?

This, says Russell (in effect), is emotional rubbish, the same kind of rubbish that stood in the way of Galileo and Newton and other great scientists when they wanted to investigate the universe. People like the Bishop of Birmingham said that the planets must move in circles, because the circle is the most perfect curve, and that all species must be immutable because God would not bother to create something that was imperfect. They were, of course, quite wrong.

Anyway, says Russell, it is only when we think abstractly that we have a high opinion of man. Civilized states spend half their revenue on murdering one another. Think of all the horrors that human beings have committed on one another. Surely if our world is the outcome of deliberate purpose, the purpose must have been that of a fiend.

These last arguments are actually as emotional and illogical as those Russell attributes to the Bishop. The heart of his argument lies in his assertion that a person is simply a series of mental occurrences and habits. My own experience contradicts this. I feel a strong conviction that the being who looks out from behind my eyes is the same person as the baby who opened his eyes on the world fifty-odd years ago. It is true that he drove a Mini, and I drive a rather heavy saloon model. It is also true that I have almost entirely forgotten what it felt like to be that baby. All the same, I feel that we are fundamentally the same person.

Moreover, I have noticed that my own children began to reveal their personalities when they were very small, indeed, so small that they could do little but drink milk and sleep. If John Taylor and Bertrand Russell are correct, and personality has its source in the control units of the brain, then we must all be born with remarkably individual control units.

We could go on arguing like this until the cows come home. Nothing will convince Russell that human beings are more than a series of mental occurrences and habits, and nothing will convince the Bishop that we are not immortal souls. Let us, instead, turn to a different type of testimony: that which claims to be personal experience. The trouble with such stories is that most of them are uncheckable, so whether you can accept them or not depends on your credulity threshold—or what Renee Haynes called the "boggle threshold." What it boils down to, eventually, is how far we feel we can trust the individual concerned.

Consider, for example, the following story told by the well-known playwright Alfred Sutro, in his reminiscences *Celebrities and Simple Souls* (1933). Sutro says that he has only had one single psychic experience in his whole life. He was being driven along a country road by his chauffeur when he thought he heard the wail of a child. He asked the chauffeur to stop. The man said he could hear nothing, but Sutro followed the sound behind some trees, and down a slope to a river bank. There he found a pretty child of three or four, crying and sobbing. She was soaking wet, and had obviously fallen into the water. He carried her back to the car, but was unable to make her stop crying long enough to tell him what had happened. He asked her where she lived and pointed ahead; the girl nodded, so the chauffeur drove on. Not far away they came to a gate, and the girl signaled toward it. They drove along a drive to the front door of a "largish house." As the car pulled up, a man and woman rushed out to meet Sutro: "Have you any news of the child?" "She's in the car," said Sutro, and went back to it. But the car was empty. "Where's the little girl?" he asked the chauffeur, but the man looked blank. "The child I brought to the car." "You didn't bring any child into the car," the chauffeur replied.

They drove back to the river bank; the body of the child was lying in a few feet of water.

An extraordinary story, certainly one which most people would dismiss as preposterous, but there is a certain amount of circumstantial evidence in its favor. Sutro was a famous playwright of his time, and would presumably not tell lies for the fun of it. The fact that it was his only psychic experience also suggests that it was genuine.

It was not. Sutro states that he has told the story to various people who dabble in the psychic and occult, and has been offered various explanations, but he has never been offered the true one—which is that he has made it up. It was evidently intended to demonstrate the gullibility of people who believe in life after death.

Once we know that, we can begin to see the weaknesses in the story. Would a man driving in a car hear the crying of a child? Even if he did, would he bother to stop to investigate—crying children are not all that rare. Would the chauffeur not have asked him what on earth he was doing, as he talked to the empty seat next to him and asked it where it lived? Would Sutro have gotten out of the car at the front door, leaving the child behind in the car?

These are the sort of questions we have to ask of any "supernatural" experience if we wish to avoid being taken in. This was recognized by the early investigators of the Society for Psychical Research (SPR) when it was formed in 1882. They saw that it was necessary to get the corroboration of as many people as possible, and to get them to make sworn statements. Even that, of course, would not guarantee that a story was not bogus, but in a few cases, the circumstantial evidence and the corroboration of witnesses would combine to make this highly unlikely. One such story is told in the *Proceedings* of the SPR (Volume 8, 1892), and it can serve as an example of a story that bears all the hallmarks of truth. It was told by the Rev. J. L. Bertrand, the Protestant pastor of Neuilly-sur-Seine, and corroborated by the other people concerned. Bertrand was in Switzerland, leading a party of young men in the ascent of a mountain called the Titlis. When they were not far from the summit, Bertrand felt too tired to go on, so he asked the rest of the party, led by a guide, to go on without him, and pick him up on their way down.

I sat down, my legs hanging over a dangerous slope or precipice, my back leaning on a rock as big as an armchair. I chose that brink because there was no snow, and because I could face better the magnificent panorama of the Alpes Bernoises. I at once remembered that in my pocket there were two cigars, and put one between my teeth, lighted a match and considered myself the happiest of men. Suddenly I felt as if thunderstruck by apoplexy, and though the match burned my fingers, I could not throw it down. My head was perfectly clear and healthy, but my body was as powerless and motionless as a rock. There was for me no hesitation. "This," I thought, "is the sleep of the snows! If I move I shall roll down in the abyss; if I do not move I shall be a dead man in twenty-five or thirty minutes." A kind of prayer was sent to God, and then I resolved to study quietly the progress of death. My feet and hands were first frozen, and little by little death reached my knees and elbows. The sensation was not painful, and mv mind felt quite easy. But when death had been all over my body my head became unbearably cold, and it seemed to me that concave pincers squeezed my heart, so as to extract my life. I never felt such an acute pain, but it lasted only a second or a minute, and my life went out. "Well," thought I, "at last I am what they call a dead man, and here I am, a ball of air in the air, a captive balloon still attached to earth by a kind of elastic string, and going up and always up. How strange! I see better than ever, and I am dead. . . . Where is my last body?" Looking down, I was astounded to recognize my own envelope. "Strange," said I to myself. "There is the corpse in which I lived and which I called me, as if the coat were the body, as if the body were the soul! What a horrid thing is that body—deadly pale, with a yellowish-blue colour, holding a cigar in its mouth and a match in its two burned fingers. Well, I hope that you shall never smoke again, dirty rag! Ah! if only I had a hand and scissors to cut the thread which ties me still to it! When my companions return they will look at that and exclaim "The Professor is dead." Poor young friends! They do not know that I never was as alive as I am, and the proof is that I see the guide going up rather by the right, when he promised me to go by the left; W— was to be the last one on the rope, and he is neither the first nor the last, but alone, away from the rope. Now the guide thinks that I do not see him because he hides himself behind the young men whilst drinking at my bottle of Madeira. Well, go on, poor man, I hope that my body will never drink of it again. Ah! there he is stealing a leg of chicken. Go on, old fellow, eat the whole of the chicken if you choose, for I hope that my miserable corpse will never eat or drink again." I felt neither surprise nor vexation; I simply stated the facts with indifference. "Hullo!" said I, "there is my wife going to Lucerne, and she told me that she would not leave before tomorrow, or after tomorrow. . . . They are five before the hotel at Lungern. Well, wife, I am a dead man. Goodbye." My only regret was that I could not cut the string. In vain I travelled through so many beautiful worlds that earth became insignificant. I had only two wishes: the certitude of not returning to earth, and the discovery of my next glorious body, without which I felt powerless. I could not be happy because the thread, though thinner than ever, was not cut, and the wished-for body was still invisible to my searching looks.

Suddenly a shock stopped my ascension, and I felt that somebody was pulling and pulling the balloon down. My grief was measureless. The fact was that . . . our guide had discovered and administered to my body the well-known remedy, rubbing with snow. . . . Here is for me an obscurity. I remember only that all seemed to me confusion and chaos, and I felt disdain for the guide who, expecting a good reward, tried to make me understand that he had done wonders . . . I never felt a more violent irritation. At last I could say to my poor guide, "Because you are a fool you take me for a fool, whilst my body alone is sick. Ah! If you had simply cut the string."

"The string? What string? You were nearly dead."

"Dead! I was less dead than you are now, and the proof is that I saw you going up the Titlis by the right, whilst you promised me to go by the left."

The man staggered before replying, "Because the snow was soft and there was no danger of slipping."

"You say that because you thought me far away. You went up by the right, and allowed two young men to put aside the rope. Who is a fool? You—not I. Now show me my bottle of Madeira and we will see if it is full."

The blow was such that his hands left my body and he fell down, saying, evidently to himself, "Did he follow us? No, we should have seen him. Could he see through the mountain? Is his body dead, and does his ghost reproach me for what I did?"

"Oh," said I brutally, "you may fall down and stare at me as much as you please, and give your poor explanations, but you cannot prove that my chicken has two legs because you stole one."

This was too much for the good man. He got up, emptied his knapsack while muttering a kind of confession, and then fled.

The Rev. Bertrand's observation that his wife had gone to Lucerne a day earlier than intended also proved to be correct.

In a case like this, we have not only the corroboration of the other people concerned, but also the Rev. Bertrand's apparently "impossible" knowledge of what the guide had been doing while his back was turned. If he was mistaken to believe that he experienced death, then he certainly had some strange experience of extrasensory perception.

There are a number of interesting points about this account. One is the "string" that Bertrand keeps wishing was cut. He does not explain what he means by a string, but, as we shall see, it can be found again and again in accounts of so-called "out-of-the-body experiences" (OBEs for short), in which people have "floated" out of their bodies and had a sensation of looking down on their physical body, connected to it by a kind of shining cord. Another is Bertrand's ability to perceive things that were happening elsewhere—what the guide was doing, his wife preparing to visit Lucerne, and so on. Again, this has been described repeatedly by people who claim to have had out-of-the-body experiences. Yet another point to note is Bertrand's feeling of relief at being out of his body, and the subsequent feeling of reluctance—in fact, of rage—when he was drawn back into it. This is again a familiar feature of such accounts.

And *this*, basically, is what distinguishes the Rev. Bertrand's story from the one invented by Alfred Sutro. Sutro's tale is the kind of thing that people who know very little about psychical research imagine to be a typical ghost story. It is not. If we are to judge by the thousands of records in the annals of the SPR, or its American or European equivalents, "real" ghosts do not sit around on river banks, a few yards from their drowned bodies, making sobbing noises loud enough to be heard over a car engine. They do not allow themselves to be picked up or point out the houses where they live. Neither, for that matter, do they walk around with their heads underneath their arms, wailing or clanking chains. The typical apparition, as described in report after report, looks quite like a normal person. One lady was sitting reading when a tall, thin old man entered the room; when she looked more closely she recognized him as her great uncle. He looked agitated, and was carrying a roll of paper. He made no reply when she spoke to him, but walked out of a half-open door. She was not in the least alarmed because she made the natural assumption that her great uncle had come to see her. By the next post she received a letter from her father asking her to go and see the great uncle, who was seriously ill. She went, but found that he had died the previous afternoon, at exactly the time she had seen him. A roll of paper was found under the dead man's pillow, and his niece concluded that he had wanted to change his will in her father's favor, but had been overtaken by death. This story is taken from one of the classic volumes of early research undertaken by founder members of the SPR: *Phantasms of the Living*, by Gurney, Myers, and Podmore (Volume 1, p. 559). It follows basically the same *pattern* as hundreds of similar accounts. (This particular book is well over a thousand pages long.) The story told by the Rev. Bertrand follows the same kind of pattern as hundreds of similar records of near-death or after-death experiences.

It is always possible to pick holes in each individual account. For example, the case of the great uncle was passed on to the SPR by a certain Major Taylor, who explained that the lady who wrote it, "Miss L," wished to withhold her name in deference to the views of a near relative. The whole thing could have been invented by Miss L, or by Major Taylor or, for that matter, by the authors of the book. But then, there are hundreds of cases in *Phantasms of the Living*, and most of them show the same basic similarities; it seems unlikely that they were all invented.

This is finally the most convincing argument for the view of life after death put forward by Swedenborg: there is such an enormous body of similar evidence to support it. There are literally hundreds of reports of life after death that display the same pattern. That pattern is roughly as follows. After the death experience, which may be accompanied by a sense of pain or suffocation, there is a sudden sensation of freedom. In many cases, the person has a sense of passing down a long tunnel, and seeing a light at the end. Then he is looking at his own body. This is usually accompanied by a feeling of deep peace, and a certain relief at having done with physical existence. The person may find it impossible to accept the idea that he is dead, and tries to talk to other people, but is ignored—although animals sometimes seem to be aware of the person. He tries to touch them, but the hand goes right through. Again and again in these accounts, the "dead person" is met by relatives who have already died; this happens only when the person acknowledges that he is dead. There seem to be many cases in which the dead person is in a state of confusion, rather like being in a fever, and fails to grasp that he is no longer alive. In that case, the person may remain trapped on earth—an "earth-bound" spirit—indefinitely.

The obvious objection to the Rev. Bertrand case, as evidence of life after death, is that there is no real evidence that he *did* experience death. He may only have passed into a dream-like state. Even his accurate knowledge of the guide's misdemeanors is not proof that he experienced death; it may have been some kind of "dream clairvoyance." But there have been many cases in which "spirit mediums" have relayed messages that claim to come from the dead, and which describe the death process in some detail. Here is a typical case from the records of a modern researcher, Dr. Robert Crookall. It concerns the death of Dr. Karl Novotny, a pupil of psychologist Alfred Adler. His friend Grete Schröder had dreamed of Novotny two days before his death at Easter in 1965, and in her dream he announced his forthcoming death. When this actually happened, she was so impressed that she went to consult a medium—although before this she had taken no interest in such matters. The medium transcribed an account of Novotny's death by means of automatic writing, in a hand which Grete Schröder recognized as Novotny's own.

"Novotny" described how, when he was spending Easter at his country home, he agreed to go for a walk with some friends. He had been feeling ill for some time, and seems to have had doubts about whether to accompany them.

> *However, I forced myself to go. Then I felt completely free and well. I went ahead and drew deep breaths of the fresh evening air, and was happier than I had been for a long time. How was it, I wondered, that I suddenly had no more difficulties, and was neither tired nor out of breath.*
>
> *I turned back to my companions and found myself looking down at my own body on the ground. My friends were in despair, calling for a doctor, and trying to get a car to take me home. But I was well and felt no pains, I couldn't understand what had happened. I bent down and felt the heart of the body lying on the ground. Yes—it had ceased to beat—I was dead. But I was still alive! I spoke to my friends, but they neither saw me nor answered me. I was most annoyed and left them. . . .*
>
> *And then there was my dog, who kept whining pitifully, unable to decide to which of me he should go, for he saw me in two places at once, standing up and lying down on the ground.*
>
> *When all the formalities were concluded and my body had been put in a coffin, I realized that I must be dead. But I wouldn't*

acknowledge the fact; for like my teacher Alfred Adler, I did not believe in after-life. . . . I went up the hill to where Grete lives. She was sitting alone and appeared very unhappy. But she did not seem to hear me either.

It was no use, I had to recognize the truth. When finally I did so, I saw my dear mother coming to meet me with open arms, telling me that I had passed into the next world—not in words, of course, since these only belong to the earth. Even so, I couldn't credit her statement and thought I must be dreaming. This belief continued for a long time. I fought against the truth and was most unhappy. . . .[4]

It is easy to sympathize with Bertrand Russell's mistrust of this kind of "evidence." It *sounds* like wishful thinking. It also contradicts our common-sense assumptions. For example, he describes himself taking deep breaths of the evening air. Do the dead breathe like the living, converting oxygen to carbon dioxide? Presumably he found himself fully dressed as he stood beside his own body—if he had suddenly found himself naked, he would have noticed sooner that something odd was going on. Does this mean that our clothes also survive death? The account sounds so disappointingly factual. If he had described a whirlpool of colored lights and a sensation like expanding like a ripple across the surface of a pond, we might find it more convincing. This utterly commonplace description of trying to feel his own heartbeat and getting angry with his friends sounds like the invention of someone with a poor imagination.

Against these objections, we must place the simple fact that there are so many reports of the death experience that follow roughly the same pattern. Any scientist would admit that this makes the evidence more convincing. If one sailor came back reporting that he had been shipwrecked on an island where the natives had green hair and long tails, it would probably be safe to assume either that he was a liar or

4. Robert Crookall, *What Happens When You Die*, p. 63.

that he was suffering from delirium tremens. If hundreds of sailors report the same experience over many years, it would be downright stupid not to give it careful consideration. There must be something behind it, if only a conspiracy among the sailors. In the same way, when report after report of people in sudden danger contains the phrase "my whole life flashed in front of my eyes," it looks probable that the brain has some curious "rapid playback" mechanism that is activated by the threat of death. Those who believe in an afterlife may speculate that the purpose of this mechanism is to "remind" the person of his identity, so that he does not enter the "next world" in a state of total confusion. Those who take a more skeptical view may regard it as a natural phenomenon, perhaps due to a flood of adrenaline, or to some electrical discharge caused by an emergency. But in view of the number of reports of this sensation, the most indefensible attitude would be to dismiss it as an old wives' tale.

Does this mean that Bertrand Russell is wilfully blinding himself to the facts when he says that "it is not rational arguments but emotions that cause belief in a future life"? Not necessarily. We have to recognize that the world is full of millions of facts, and that everyone has to choose which ones he finds interesting. Even the greatest intellects can never hope to know more than a tiny fraction of all the facts about the world we live in. Russell chose to devote his life to trying to establish the basic "facts" about logic and mathematics; no one can blame him for not being curious about the existence of an afterlife. In view of that lack of curiosity, it is also hard to blame him for concluding that "when you're dead you're dead."

Where Russell does deserve a certain amount of criticism is in the shallow nature of his assumptions about *why* people can believe in an afterlife. He takes it for granted that there is no solid scientific evidence for life after death, and that therefore it must be wishful thinking. To the objection that he has failed to consider the facts, he would probably reply that he doesn't have the time—but that if someone could present him with one solid, incontrovertible fact to prove life after death, he might be ready to be convinced.

The simple truth is that this is *not* the way we build up our convictions. I do not decide that a person is trustworthy because I have solid, incontrovertible proof of it. I decide it on the basis of dozens of experiences of that person, which finally fit together like a mosaic, giving me an overall picture of his character. It could be compared to a newspaper photograph which, when looked at through a magnifying glass, turns into a series of black and gray dots. Nobody looking at those individual dots could believe that they would really build up into a recognizable face. The strange thing is that when we look at the picture at a distance, the dots vanish, and we cannot only see a recognizable face, but even the expression in the eyes. If we look at the same eyes through the magnifying glass, it is quite impossible to see how the dots create an "expression."

All this applies particularly to the problems of the paranormal. I had experience of this a few years ago, when writing a book about the poltergeist—the "noisy ghost" that has been recorded down the ages.[5] My ex-publisher called on me one day and asked me what I was writing. I had just returned from Pontefract, where I had been investigating a case of an apparent "haunting" by a black monk, and I began telling him about it. "Surely you don't really believe in all that stuff?" he asked. He began to raise all the usual objections: inaccurate reporting, mischievous children, seismic disturbances, lying witnesses. I countered each objection by describing some other case in which it could not possibly apply, and he immediately thought up some new objections. After half an hour or so, I saw that nothing I could say would alter his mind. As far as he was concerned, ghosts and poltergeists were a regrettable remnant of superstition, and that was that. Every case I described to him was just another dot on the newspaper photograph. Looking at it through his magnifying glass, he could not see that it proved anything.

---

5. See my *Poltergeist, A Study in Destructive Haunting* (1981).

I had spent months studying hundreds of cases, from ancient Rome to modern London, from medieval France to present-day Brazil. I had come to recognize all the basic characteristics of the poltergeist, and to see that they never seem to change. In short, they formed a *pattern*. Unless my friend could be persuaded to spend a few weeks studying the same cases, he would continue to believe that each one could be explained away as fraud or deception. If I had actually *said* that to him, he would have felt that I was being patronizing. He was convinced—quite correctly—that his powers of reasoning were as good as mine. What he could not see was that, if reason is to be effective, it has to operate on a broad range of facts. Without facts to work on, the most brilliant deductive mind in the world is spinning in a vacuum.

This book is not an attempt to convince anyone of the reality of life after death. It is simply an attempt to present the facts in an orderly manner. At the end, the reader should be in a position to make up his or her own mind.

Chapter Two

The World of the Clairvoyant

WHEN I OPEN MY EYES IN THE MORNING, I TAKE it for granted that I am looking at the same world that you see when you open your eyes. On the whole, this is probably a fair assumption, but it can blind me to some important differences between myself and my fellow human beings.

When Charles Darwin arrived in Tierra del Fuego on the *Beagle* in December 1832, he was astounded that the natives were such excellent mimics. Although they knew no English, they could repeat a whole sentence with a good English accent. Moreover, they could join in sea shanties as they sat around the fire with the crew of the *Beagle*, by the simple expedient of repeating each word a moment after the English sailors had sung it.

(Darwin said "the manner in which they were invariably a little behindhand was quite ludicrous.") Darwin was baffled. "How can this faculty be explained?" he asked. "Is it a consequence of the more practiced habits of perception and keener senses, common to all men in a savage state, as compared with those long civilized?"

Darwin is on the right track; but his essentially English habits of thought make him incapable of going to the heart of the matter. A later zoologist, Lyall Watson, understood it:

> *A pygmy from the dense forests of the Ituri, where it is never possible to see very far, is astonished by the tiny antelope he sees in the distance when taken out on to the plain for the first time. In the perpetual gloom of the forest floor, sound is more important than sight, and the pygmy's experience is arranged in a different kind of sense life. His is a separate reality.*

In other words, the pygmy's culture is auditory, not visual. In our culture, sight is more important than sound. A city dweller hardly notices the continuous flood of sound that batters his ears, but has to notice buses and cars because they may run him down. The primitive has to pay the same attention to sounds, because they may indicate the presence of a dangerous wild animal or an enemy. If Darwin could have got inside the head of a Tierra del Fuegan, he would probably have felt as confused as if he was looking through the eyes of a Martian.

The psychologist William James made the same point in his important essay "On a Certain Blindness in Human Beings." He showed that we tend to be blind to things that do not interest us; they are simply "not there." Since each of us is interested in different things, each sees a different world. A man sitting on a bus or tube thinks he is surrounded by other members of the same species; in fact, he is among troglodytes, Martians, Venusians, Tierra del Fuegans, Patagonians, and a dozen other outlandish tribes.

Among civilized human beings, there is a species whose outlook is as strange and "different" as that of a Tierra del Fuegan. They are called psychics or clairvoyants, and they are far more common than the rest of us realize. Yet when a psychic describes an experience that he takes for granted, it may strike the rest of us as either slightly insane or some kind of silly affectation.

Rosalind Heywood describes such an experience. It involved herself and her husband as they went out to watch the sunset at Okehampton.

> *Suddenly, without warning, the incredible beauty swept me through a barrier. I was no longer looking at Nature. Nature was looking at me. And she did not like what she saw . . . numberless unoffending creatures were shrinking back offended by our invasion . . . [they] swung round as a unit to inspect us, and I seemed to feel their sigh of relief as they came to a group decision. We were not dangerous or cruel. Our apology was accepted. We might come on—and "in."*

She writes of an aftermath a few days later.

> *Then I, too, suffered an invasion, a delightful one. It was as if, like ebullient children, a covey of little invisibles floated in at the window to say "Hullo!" and coax me to play with them. For a moment their visit seemed perfectly normal, but then my analytical mind got going, and at once, for me, they ceased to exist.*

If this account conveys the impression that its author is some slightly dotty "psychic," like Noel Coward's Madame Arcati (as played by Margaret Rutherford), then it is thoroughly misleading. The author, Rosalind Heywood, was a lifelong member of the Society for Psychical Research, a lady of formidable intellect, whose standards of investigation were as rigorous as those of the most thorough skeptic. In fact, her attitude toward her own experiences is curiously mistrustful and suspicious. When writing about matters of psychical research—as in her book *The Sixth Sense*—she maintains an attitude of logical detachment that makes her sound rather like Bertrand Russell. In her autobiography, *The Infinite Hive*, she then adopts a more personal tone to describe her own experiences, and the result is one of the most convincing of all insights into the strange, Tierra-del-Fuegan world of a clairvoyant.

It is worth noting her comment: "then my analytical mind got going, and at once, for me, they ceased to exist." Clearly, we are talking about the difference between analysis and intuition—that is, between the left and the right brain. This, in turn, suggests that the psychic is closely related to an artist like Mozart, into whose head tunes kept walking unannounced. (The composer Saint-Saens also said that in order to compose, he merely had to listen.) Civilized humans have developed the left brain until it completely dominates and overawes the right. A psychic like Rosalind Heywood is probably closer to our ancestors of ten thousand years ago (or, if Julian Jaynes is correct, much more recently than that).

It is worth looking more closely into the development of Rosalind Heywood's psychic abilities, because it enables us to see that she is not really so very different from the rest of us, and that, therefore, the same faculty must lie latent in all of us.

Born into a fairly typical late-Victorian household, she does not seem to have suspected that she was psychic until she was nearing adulthood. Before that, she seems to have assumed that it was simply imagination. She writes that at thirteen, she was aware of "lesser presences."

> *Once was in my bedroom in my grandfather's house . . . a mysterious invisible Somebody shared it with me. . . . Had the Somebody been mentionable to a grown-up I might have learnt that my mother and aunt had both independently seen the apparition of an old woman standing at the foot of the bed. . . .*

Any developing recognition of her psychic abilities was halted abruptly when, at the age of seventeen, she bought at a station bookstall a copy of *The Riddle of the Universe* by Ernst Haeckel. Haeckel was a materialist philosopher, and *The Riddle of the Universe* is a brilliantly lucid account of the discoveries of modern science that became an immediate bestseller in the early years of the twentieth century. He studies the evolution of the body, the evolution of the mind, the evolution of the universe, in the light of modern biology and astronomy, and claims to prove that there is no such thing as a personal God, that free will is an illusion, and that life after death is the grossest kind of superstition.

Rosalind Heywood was shattered.

> *My poor mother! No bomb could have smashed more effectively the framework on which she had so carefully moulded her daughter's life. Here at last was the truth. There was no God. . . . Gone was any hope of finding that Central Something, and—my all-wise parents lived in a fool's paradise.*

Soon after this, the 1914 war began, and Rosalind Heywood became a nurse. Her first suspicion of extrasensory perception came when she was sitting in the room of an unconscious woman, reading *The Brothers Karamazov*. As she read the section in which Ivan has a discussion with the Devil, the sick woman sat up, pointed her finger at the foot of the bed, and proceeded to talk to the Devil. It could have been coincidence, but it seemed oddly like telepathy.

A few weeks later, she sat watching a man who was gravely ill and delirious. He seemed to be unaware of her presence. Suddenly she experienced a kind of inner "Order": "*Think* him quiet." Recalling the previous experience of telepathy, she decided to give it a try and at once, the man fell into a peaceful sleep. When, later, a Staff Nurse woke him up by moving the screens, she "thought" him asleep again. When the Ward Sister had awakened him for the third time, it no longer worked. Suddenly his tossing stopped and he said calmly, "It's no use concentrating any longer, Nurse. I shall not be going to sleep again." Then the delirium began again as he cried out in joy, "It's Annie! . . . And John! . . . Oh, the Light!"

What Rosalind Heywood has recorded here is, in fact, an extremely common death-bed experience. In 1960, Dr. Karlis Osis of the New York Parapsychology Foundation, sent out ten thousand questionnaires to nurses, asking about their patients' death-bed visions, and discovered that in a large number of cases, the dying believed they saw a deceased relative on the point of death. Sir William Barrett, the founder of the Society for Psychical Research, had already made the same discovery when he was gathering material for his own book *Death-bed Visions*.

Oddly enough, this experience did nothing to shake the skepticism Rosalind Heywood had imbibed from Haeckel's *Riddle of the Universe*. Neither did a great many experiences of "Orders," which led her to take a number of apparently irrational decisions. When a soldier was dying of blackwater fever, and had been given up for lost by the doctors, "Orders" told her to ask him what he would like most in all the world. He replied: "A red rose, Sister." She heard herself promise him one for the next day. It seemed a mad thing to do in a hospital in Macedonia, but the next day she asked the dispatch rider to take a message to GHQ asking for a red rose. Back came a whole bunch of them from the garden of a Greek magnate. The dying soldier recovered. When badly wounded men were unable to sleep, "Orders" told her to make her own sedative and to make it as nasty as possible; she made a random mixture of medicines and added a teaspoonful of salt for good measure. It worked perfectly; after that, the men had no problem sleeping. When a drug addict was refusing to take nourishment, "Orders" told her: "Nag him! Nag! NAG!" It was entirely contrary to her instinct, but she obeyed; finally, he groaned: "I'll eat anything if you'll only go away," and was soon eating normally again.

Most of these examples could, of course, be explained in terms of the subconscious mind, but there are others in Rosalind Heywood's book that are harder to explain. She tells how, about to shut up her house for a month to go away for a midsummer holiday, "Orders" told her that the water must be turned off because a pipe was going to burst. When she mentioned this to her husband, he told her all the technical reasons why pipes do not burst in midsummer. Rather than override his objection, she decided to give a spare key to the builder to use when the pipe burst. He also explained why pipes did not burst in July. In due course, the pipe did burst and the builder was able to use the key to repair it. Here it is altogether more difficult to explain "Orders" in terms of subconscious insight, particularly in view of her insistence that all such matters as plumbing are a mystery to her.

Other examples in *The Infinite Hive* make it seem highly probable that she was exercising a faculty of "precognition," the ability to foresee the future. This is quite clearly a faculty that simply should not exist. For most other so-called psychic faculties—telepathy, clairvoyance, mediumship, psychokinesis—we can advance more-or-less scientific explanations. But for foreknowledge of the future there is no possible explanation; it is simply illogical and absurd—in short, an impossibility, since the future has not yet arrived. Yet Rosalind Heywood's book has several examples of foreknowledge of the future, and most of them defy all rational explanation. She tells, for example, of how her husband met an inventor who seemed incapable of marketing his invention; her husband, who was involved in that line of business, offered to do it for him. When he told her about it, she thought it an excellent idea—until her husband mentioned the man's name. Then she experienced "a wave of dread and repulsion." "Don't, don't have anything to do with that man." Her husband insisted that it was too late to back out of the deal. He went ahead—and in due course, the man swindled them, was arrested, and committed suicide when on bail.

Her own explanation is that her husband was subconsciously aware that the man was a crook, and that she picked this up telepathically. Since she gives many examples demonstrating her husband's psychic abilities, it seems odd that he should dismiss her pleas, and insist on entering into a business partnership with a swindler.

She cites the following example of her husband's psychic faculty. When their car was hit by a limousine, her husband said calmly that he had dreamt about this event last night so he "knew" that only the wheel needed to be changed. When he got out of the car and looked at the damage, he said, "It's as I thought," and changed the wheel.

The common sense explanation here is coincidence, but this cannot be applied to the examples she cites of the same ability in her younger son. When he came from England to America to join his parents for the summer holidays, he told her that he already knew the village they were in because he had dreamed about it. "If you do," said his mother, "lead us down to the sea." He led them down to the beach, then threaded his way among hundreds of sun umbrellas to the one they owned. "How did you know this was ours?" she asked. "I dreamt the pattern on it." Rosalind Heywood agrees that this might have been telepathy. Another episode occurred when her son looked up the name of a London street on a map. He needed to know, he told her later, because he knew someone was going to ask him where it was.

Here, if we rule out the very far-fetched explanation of coincidence, or some complex telepathy with a total stranger, the only other explanation seems to be that in some odd sense, the event her son "precognized" had already taken place, and he was somehow receiving a "memory of the future." In that case, the explanation of her sudden foreboding when her husband mentioned the name of the swindler was that she somehow recognized it as that of a man who had *already* swindled them.

Obviously, this totally contradicts our notion of time as something that flows only one way, but then, the experiences of psychics often seem to contradict our orderly notions of space as well. One of the basic laws of our world is that no one can be in two different places at the same time. Rosalind Heywood was also able to contradict this from personal experience. When she couldn't sleep one night, she thought about waking up her husband to make love to her.

> *Before I could carry out this egotistic idea I did something very odd—I split in two. One Me in its pink nightie continued to toss . . . but another, clad in a long, very white, hooded garment, was now standing, calm, immobile and impersonally outward-looking, at the foot of the bed. This White Me seemed just as actual as Pink Me and I was equally conscious in both places at the same time.*

Pink Me and White Me then began to argue if she should wake her husband up.

> *Pink Me was a totally self-regarding little animal, entirely composed of "appetites" . . . "I shall do what I like," she retorted furiously, "and you can't stop me, you pious white prig!" She was particularly furious because she knew very well that White Me was the stronger and could stop her.*
>
> *A moment or two later—I felt no transition—White Me was once more imprisoned with Pink Me in one body, and there they have dwelt as oil and water ever since. It is only quite lately that I have become aware . . . that I can deliberately identify myself with White Me and watch without feeling them . . . the desires and repulsions that must inevitably toss all Pink Mes around.*

In case the reader assumes this experience to be symbolic rather than real, she goes on to cite a case of a woman who had "split" after the birth of a baby. One of her continued to lie in the bed while the other stood by its side. When questioned about the attitude of these two "selves" to one another, she replied: "The Me outside looked on the Me in bed with profound contempt devoid of all feeling."

Experiences like these did nothing to shake Rosalind Heywood's basic agnosticism, imbibed from Haeckel; in a sense, there is no reason why they should. The existence of telepathy and clairvoyance is not in itself a contradiction of the "materialist" viewpoint. Even experiences of precognition constitute no challenge to materialism. It may prove that our view of time as a one-way street is somehow mistaken, but the truth about time may be as logical and scientific as our present notions about it.

What finally undermined Rosalind Heywood's agnosticism were two experiences of apparent contact with the dead. The first took place in Washington D.C. in the 1930s. Rosalind's husband Frank was in the diplomatic service there. At parties they often met an attractive woman called Julia. One day, she suddenly asked Rosalind to read her hands (she dabbled in palmistry). As she took Julia's hands, Rosalind Heywood found herself saying gravely: "You will never find what you are looking for in this world, will you?" Julia replied, just as gravely: "No."

Some weeks later, Julia presented Rosalind Heywood with a snapshot of herself; she was just about to set out for a trip to Peru. "Orders" told Rosalind Heywood that this was important so she accepted the photograph. On the journey to Perú, the plane crashed in the Andes and there were no survivors.

She found that Julia's name was stuck in her head, being repeated over and over again. Two days later, she wrote a letter of condolence to Julia's mother, then lay down on a settee to rest. A Viennese woodcut suddenly fell off the wall on to the floor. The woodcut was undamaged; its cord was intact; so was the nail on the wall. "I was standing by my desk trying to puzzle out this conundrum when my eye caught the letter to Julia's mother, and at that moment I heard Julia speak." "Don't send that silly letter," Julia said. "Go to my mother now, straightaway, and tell her to stop all this ridiculous mourning at once. I'm very happy and I can't stand it."

She experienced an understandable hesitancy; if, as the wife of a British diplomat, she went around delivering messages from the dead, she might get a reputation for eccentricity. "The more I hesitated, the more insistent 'Julia' became." At last, she went to America to visit Julia's mother, feeling foolish and concerned about how she would be perceived; to ask the mother to stop mourning seemed rude. When she arrived at the house, it was full of mourners who would not let her see Julia's mother. When she insisted, they took her up to the woman's bedroom where she found the mother "alone, in the dark, in bed." Rosalind Heywood repeated Julia's message, waiting for the woman to call her mad:

> *But her face lit up. "I knew it," she cried, "I knew she'd hate it, and I didn't want it. I shall get up and stop it at once!"*

After that, Julia's presence was gone.

Rosalind Heywood's second experience of contact with the dead occurred some twenty years later in London. An old friend, Vivian Usborne, had died after a long illness. Toward the end, he expressed a certain amount of bitterness at the idea that death snuffs out man like a candle and leaves nothing behind. When she went to retrieve a painting he had given her,

> *I ran slap into "Vivian" himself, most joyfully and most vividly alive . . . then came an experience which is extremely hard to describe. . . . I felt "Vivian" communicate inside my mind . . . he had been entirely mistaken in expecting extinction at death. On the contrary, he now had scope, freedom and opportunity beyond his wildest dreams.*
>
> *For a few moments I stood very still, acutely aware of the striking contrast between the smell of death and "Vivian's intensity of life . . . and then I remembered my duty and "said" to him, "This is wonderful, but you've given me no evidence. What can I say to the SPR?"*
>
> *Vivian's response to my question was emphatic and immediate. "I cannot give you evidence. You have no concepts for these conditions. I can only give you poetic images."*

She goes on to add that she has had several other experiences of contact with the dead, but that they were more fleeting than the contacts with Julia and Vivian, and that it would be monotonous to describe them. They all had either a sense of purpose on behalf of the dead or urged her to take action. This, she said, was what made them different from a haunting.

In other words, these experiences of contact with the recently dead were due to a desire on the part of the deceased to "get in touch." Rosalind Heywood merely happened to be "open" enough for them to communicate.

I have considered her experiences at some length because it is important to realize that the experiences of a clairvoyant are not a series of weird occurrences that interrupt the normal flow of everyday life, but a part of its pattern, its fundamental texture. In fact, as a psychic, Rosalind Heywood is not particularly gifted. On the scale of a Daniel Dunglas Home or Eusapia Palladino—or even of a Gerard Croiset or Robert Cracknell—she hardly rates at all. She could be described as "mildly psychic," which is why she forms such an excellent subject for study. She is an ordinary housewife, a typical upper-middle-class Edwardian lady who shares most of the values of her class, and thinks that being psychic is slightly discreditable. This is why she is always looking for other explanations for her experiences—so that, for example, when she feels foreboding at hearing the name of the swindler, she is inclined to wonder if it is some form of telepathy with her husband. She even wonders whether, as primitives believe, the name itself could have linked her with the swindler telepathically—then has to regretfully admit that this is impossible because it was an assumed name. She is unwilling to accept the obvious, if equally baffling, explanation that she recognized the swindler's name because, in some sense, the fraud had "already happened." That is to say, her experience was an example of what Professor Joad once called "the undoubted queerness of time." In spite of her own abundant experience of clairvoyance, Rosalind Heywood was the sort of person who was unwilling to believe in the "undoubted queerness" of anything. She had a strong Victorian prejudice in favor of order and tidiness.

There is, of course, one other possible explanation of her precognition—which she is equally unwilling to entertain: that the information came to her from a spirit. Yet she has just told an anecdote that brings her face to face with that possibility. In the early days of World War II, she tried using a ouija board, consisting of a pointer on which the operator rested his fingers, and a semicircle of cards containing letters of the alphabet. When a doctor friend asked her to demonstrate the board, she decided to rule out the possibility that her unconscious mind was dictating the message by sitting on the floor under the table, with her fingers resting on the pointer above her head. The doctor wrote down the message, and told her that someone called "George" had warned Frank to drive with exaggerated care for the next two days. Frank was Rosalind Heywood's husband, and his brother George had been killed not long before. The doctor was not even aware that Frank was his hostess' husband. At this time, she explains, she was extremely skeptical about the possibility of life after death (in spite of the experience in Washington with Julia; another example of her reluctance to join the ranks of the "believers"), and was inclined to wonder if her own unconscious mind was pulling her leg. With considerable embarrassment, she passed on the message to her husband. The next day he told her: "If I hadn't driven with extreme care, as you asked me to, I should have had no less than three major accidents today."

Although the "spirit" explanation might provide an acceptable alternative to precognition in the case of the swindler—presumably a friendly spirit would know he was a swindler—it still fails to explain how brother George knew in advance that Frank was in danger of having three car accidents during the next forty-eight hours. Here, as in the case of her youngest son's foreknowledge that someone was going to ask him to find a certain street, we have to fall back on Joad's "undoubted queerness of time."

Is it possible, considering Rosalind Heywood's experience as a whole, to discern some pattern that might help to provide a basic explanation?

She herself provides one interesting clue. She seems to have had an unusual susceptibility to beauty. As a child, she spent some time in India. She describes her father pointing up to the snow on the mountain tops.

> *For a long time we could not see them. We had not looked high enough. Then at last, towering against the cobalt sky, we saw Kanchenjunga, white, shining, inviolate, all but the highest mountain in the world. I could not—and cannot—formulate what moved me almost beyond bearing in the Hills. It was as if some wind of the spirit blew down on the childish creature and touched something in it awake, so that it could never be quite childish again. . . .*

Back at home in England, she often cried when remembering the Hills. Years later, at a dinner party, she sat next to a Tibetan explorer, and tried to tell him something of what the Hills had meant to her: "After a pause he said the two words that of all others I would have chosen to hear. They were 'those presences.'"

It was after her return from India that she first became aware of "lesser presences," like the old woman in the bedroom of her grandfather's house.

She describes a number of these experiences of beauty, and their obvious sincerity robs them of any suggestion of "aestheticism"; how, for example, after a fine rendering of Chopin's A-flat Ballade, she experienced a kind of hallucination of "a vast marble hall, oblong, with painted walls and the whole of the east end open to the night sky and the stars." She also mentions that a very gentle touch on her back—by her husband—brought her back to earth as violently as if she had been kicked.

Her experiences bring to mind an event in the childhood of the modern Hindu saint Ramakrishna. One day, as a child, Ramakrishna was crossing a paddy field holding a large bowl of rice, when a flock of white cranes flew across a black storm cloud; the sense of beauty was so overwhelming that he fainted, and the rice flew all over the place. Later in life, Ramakrishna became subject to moods of "God-intoxication"—*samadhi*—in which he was overwhelmed by ecstasy, and would lose consciousness.

The obvious comment to make about such an experience is that it would be highly inconvenient if it happened in the middle of Piccadilly Circus. We are back to Julian Jaynes' theory about the "bicameral mind." Jaynes believes that civilized man *had* to cease being bicameral—hearing the voices of the gods—when life became so dangerous and complicated that his chief concern was to keep his wits about him. Jaynes suggests that this happened as recently as 1200 B. C., after a series of catastrophes in the Mediterranean world, such as the explosion of the volcano of Santorini, which practically destroyed Greek civilization, and the invasion of the destructive barbarians known as the Sea Peoples. There certainly seems to be a certain amount of evidence for Jaynes' belief that it was only after this period that cruelty appeared for the first time in human history.[1]

Even if we find it impossible to swallow Jaynes' belief that the men who built Stonehenge and the Great Pyramid totally lacked what we would call "self-consciousness," it seems clear that he is correct in believing that, at some point in the history of civilization, man was forced to become a "left-brainer"—that is, to deliberately abandon the warmer, gentler consciousness of the animal and the child, and develop a ruthless "eye to business." We might say that ancient man looked at the universe through a kind of telescope, which showed him distant horizons. Then the increasing problems of survival forced him to develop an instrument much more like a microscope or a watchmaker's eyeglass, which would enable him to concentrate on tiny particulars. The result is that he has become shortsighted. He has ceased to be aware of the horizons.

In fact, he is still capable of this wider awareness—but only in certain moments of deep relaxation. When this happens, the left and right halves of the brain seem to merge together, and he experiences a sense of peace and serenity, the "all is well" feeling. But modern man has to *start* from left-brain awareness—our narrow ego-consciousness. Our remote ancestors could probably plunge straight into "cosmic consciousness" by merely relaxing.

As a result of these evolutionary developments, modern man has a high "beauty threshold." "Threshold" is a psychological term, meaning how much stimulus it takes to arouse someone to awareness. A man with a high noise threshold can ignore a racket that would drive a more sensitive person mad. A woman with a high pain threshold can have her teeth filled without a local anaesthetic. Ramakrishna's low beauty threshold meant that any kind of beauty was likely to

1. See my *Criminal History of Mankind*, chapter 2.

plunge him into a trance of ecstasy. To a modern city dweller, this would be as undesirable as permanent diarrhea.

Now Rosalind Heywood was very much a product of British civilization: stiff upper lip, dislike of emotion, cast-iron self-control. Such characteristics usually entail a high beauty threshold—the English take pride in being artistically insensitive. In her case, we can see that this was not so, and that she associated her first psychic experiences with the "wind of the spirit" that "blew down on the childish creature" from Kanchenjunga, and "touched something in it awake."

It may also be significant that when her husband gently touched her back—after hearing the Chopin Ballade—she experienced a shock out of all proportion to the stimulus. Most people have probably noticed the same thing if they are awakened on the verge of sleep. In that midway state between sleep and waking—the state in which we begin to experience hypnogogic hallucinations—the slightest sound, the mere click of a door closing, produces a pattern of light inside the brain, and a sensation like an explosion.

Rosalind Heywood also describes how she tried one morning to practice a little mind-reading, by floating into a state of deep relaxation and trying to contact the mind of another person in the house. She describes the sensation as "a glorified version of a phase of going under an anaesthetic." Then the peace was shattered by "agonizing thunderous bangs which crashed right through me." The bangs continued, and she felt herself returning to physical awareness. It was her husband tapping on the door to say that breakfast was ready. When she asked indignantly why he was battering the house down, he answered that he had only tapped gently. With her lowered sensitivity threshold, she had heard each tap as an explosion like a bomb. She goes on to speculate whether this is why it is so dangerous to "awaken" a medium from a state of trance—it has been known to cause heart failure.

After his first experience of samadhi or "God-ecstasy," Ramakrishna could induce the state at will; he merely had to hear the name of Krishna or Kali to sink into the "God-trance." We can observe something analogous if we react deeply to a certain piece of music; the first notes of the Liebestod from *Tristan* or the opening notes of a Bruckner symphony can induce a tingling sensation in the scalp, followed by a sudden flood of delight. Physiologically speaking, it is merely a habit pattern, like a Pavlov dog salivating at the sound of a bell. What is interesting is that once the brain has learned the "trick"—the route to ecstasy, so to speak—it can repeat it at will. It entails a certain act of will—a deliberate focusing on the source of pleasure. If you listen to the music while reading a newspaper or thinking of something else, it doesn't work, or is appreciably less powerful. But when the brain and the stimulus cooperate, there is instant relaxation, followed by contact with the inner source of pleasure.

What is beginning to emerge, then, is a theory about psychic sensitivity. It runs as follows. When I relax deeply, it is as if someone opened up the partition between the two compartments of my brain, turning them into a single large room. I experience a sense of mental freedom, as if I can suddenly breathe more deeply, and a feeling of *contact* with things. Everyone has had the experience of being in a state of hurry or excitement, and failing to notice that they have bruised or scratched themselves—until the excitement evaporates and the pain makes itself known. Hurry and tension raise our sensitivity threshold, and at the same time, erect a glass wall between us and reality. In the "unicameral" state, this wall vanishes, and everything seems more real.

No doubt dogs and cats are in this state most of the time; they lack any sustained power of concentration. It seems highly probable that our caveman ancestors of forty thousand years ago also spent much of their time in this state. When drawings of animals were discovered in the caves of Cro-Magnon man, scientists concluded that our ancestors whiled away their winter evenings with a lump of charcoal and a pot of red ochre. Then it gradually became clear that this was not an early example of "art for art's sake." It was art for the sake of magic. It was the *shaman* who drew the bison and reindeer, because the men were going out to hunt them the next day; the drawings were supposed to link the minds of the hunters and their prey. To us, with our abnormally high sensitivity thresholds, such an idea seems absurd; to primitives, it must have been a matter of common sense, like dowsing for water. Moreover, there is evidence that such "magic" worked. Sir Arthur Grimble, who was commissioner of the Gilbert Islands, has described how a hereditary porpoise-caller established a mental link with the porpoises, so that they swam into the beach in a kind of trance, and the natives were able to wade into the water and club them to death.[2] Manuel Cordova-Rios, a Peruvian who was kidnapped by Amazonian Indians in 1902, and who spent several years living among them, has descriptions of hunting magic that makes it clear that it actually worked.[3]

As man developed the complexities of civilization, he had to develop a complexity of mind to go with it. The unicameral mind was lost, and replaced by the present version with two compartments—in which the living room is situated to the left. Yet it would be incorrect to believe that it is lost beyond recall. We can, if we want to, deliberately lower the sensitivity threshold. The tiger hunter Jim Corbett, author of *Man Eaters of Kumaon*, described how he developed what he called "jungle sensitiveness," so that he knew intuitively when a tiger was lying in wait for him. (Presumably he would also be able to use the same faculty when he was hunting tigers.) Self-preservation had taught him to drop his sensitivity threshold, so his right brain would give him warnings of danger. We have seen that Rosalind Heywood apparently developed the same faculty accidentally through her sensitivity to the "presence" of the Hills. She also suggests that she developed her telepathic linkage with her husband because he was a nonverbal type, a man of a few words, and she had a "life-long exaggerated need for communication."

---

2. Griable, *Pattern of Island*, chapter 6.
3. F. Bruce Lamb, *Wizard of the Upper Amazon* (1971).

The most peculiar chapter of her book *The Infinite Hive*, called "The Singing," provides interesting support for this primitive, right-brain theory of psychic powers. "Singing" is a sensation that she hears more-or-less all the time (although more at some times than others), and she describes it as,

> *a kind of continuous vibrant inner quasi-sound, to which the nearest analogy is the noise induced by pressing a seashell against the ear, or perhaps the hum of a distant dynamo. . . . Rather, like light, it pervades the whole atmosphere. . . .*

It sounds rather like the noise that—according to the composer John Cage—is made by the nervous system, and which can be heard under conditions of total sensory deprivation, for example, in a deep mine. But in that case, it would always be more or less the same. Rosalind Heywood claims that it varies. The only time she failed to hear it under conditions of silence was while waiting for a train at night on the Hampstead tube station (which is one of the deepest in London, and where, if the nerve theory is correct, it ought to have been particularly evident). She says, that the sound is more prevalent in quiet places like the woods or on a mountain, or in church or library where "thought and devotion have been intense for years."

She adds: "Although the Singing seems to differ according to its apparent origin I cannot formulate in what this difference lies. I can only say that mountain Singing conveys a different 'atmosphere' from church Singing, as an oboe conveys a different 'atmosphere' from a trumpet . . . ." She goes on to speak about "church Singing." "I listened for the Christian note in several quiet empty churches and found that in some it would pass over into a more intense experience, as if—I repeat, as if—an inner force were streaming from the altar."

A young engineer to whom she described the Singing—in the hope of shocking him—replied placidly: "Oh, yes, I hear that too, in places where there have been strong emotions." This comment provides an interesting clue.

As early as 1908, Sir Oliver Lodge, one of the most distinguished members of the Society for Psychical Research, made the interesting suggestion that ghosts may be a kind of tape recording—"as if strong emotions could be unconsciously recorded in matter." He gives the example of a haunted house, where one particular room is the scene of some tragedy long ago.

> *Take, for example, a haunted house . . . wherein some one room is the scene of a ghostly representation of some long past tragedy. On a psychometric hypothesis*[4] *the original tragedy has been literally* photographed *on its material surroundings, nay, even on the ether itself, by reason of the intensity of emotion felt by those who enacted it; and thenceforth in certain persons an hallucinatory effect is experienced corresponding to such an impression. It is this theory that is made to account for the feeling one has on entering certain rooms, that there is an alien presence therein. . . .*[5]

Lodge says that this is why some people have a "feeling" when entering certain rooms, "that there is an alien presence therein." The phrase "nay, even on the ether itself" may seem to be going too far; yet in the second half of the twentieth century this has, in fact, been one of the most widely held theories about the nature of apparitions. The late T. C. Lethbridge, whose contribution I have discussed at length elsewhere,[6] came to believe that a type of manifestation he called a "ghoul"—meaning the kind of creepy sensation described by Lodge—is an emotion "tape recorded" on some kind of electrical field. He even became convinced that there are different types of fields connected with woodlands, mountains, and open spaces, exactly as Rosalind Heywood noted about the Singing. According to Lethbridge, she would simply be "picking up" some form of electrical vibration—a vibration, presumably, that cannot penetrate as deep as the Hampstead underground, or which is somehow insulated by it.

---

4. Psychometry is the ability to "read" the history of an object by touching it or holding it in the hand—or, in the case of a room, sensing some event that has taken place there. See my book *The Psychic Detective* (1984).

5. Lodge, *Man and the Universe* (1908).

6. See my *Mysteries* (1978), chapters 1 to 4.

If there is anything in this theory, and feelings or mental states can be recorded on matter (or its field), this would also explain why she observed a quite different kind of Singing in university libraries or in Christian churches; the "vibration" would be different. It is particularly interesting that she noted an "inner force" streaming from church altars. Christian churches are frequently built on pagan sites; in fact, there was a directive from the Vatican in the Middle Ages that churches should be built on such sites. Any dowser will verify that the "field" around ancient sites—for example, standing stones like those of Stonehenge and Carnac—is unusually powerful. Christian churches, like pagan religious sites, usually face east, and the altar is located at the east end. What Rosalind Heywood sensed streaming from the altar may have been precisely the quality for which the site was chosen in the first place.

According to this theory, the "lesser presence" that Rosalind Heywood sensed in the bedroom of her grandfather's house was not really an old woman, but a tape recording of some past event. (Lethbridge believed that the "recording" can often be seen as well as felt—especially by good dowsers.)

Yet although this explanation has a pleasingly scientific ring, it still fails to account for many of Rosalind Heywood's experiences. It is quite clear that when she experienced Julia and Vivian, she did not feel that she was picking up a tape recording, and that on Dartmoor, she and her husband felt that they had really encountered invisible natural presences, and not some kind of electrical field. Also, how can the sensitivity threshold theory of clairvoyance account for the curious episode of "splitting" into two people?

Where the latter is concerned, we can turn for aid to Rosalind Heywood's friend G. N. M. Tyrrell, whose book *The Personality of Man* has become a classic of psychical research. (It was, in fact, written in her house; she describes how, when left alone in the house during the war, "Orders" told her to write to Tyrrell asking him if he wanted to move to London, and against all the odds—he eagerly accepted.) Tyrrell also cites her story of "splitting" (although he omits to mention her name), and then goes on to mention various parallel cases. There was Mrs. Willett (the pseudonym of Winifred Coombe-Tennant), an automatic writing medium, who in August 1913, received a letter from Sir Oliver Lodge containing certain enclosures. About to take out these enclosures, she experienced a "*thundering* sort of knock-down blow conviction that I must not do so." While she hesitated, wondering whether to overrule this feeling, she divided into two. "Mind No. 1 got my body up and walked it across the room to the door . . . But Mind No. 2 (which was 'me' as I know myself) couldn't make out why it was that I was there." Then Mind No. 1 made her put the letter back in its envelope, walk to her husband's room, and hand it to him. (It was important, from the point of view of evidence, that she should not read the enclosures.)

Tyrrell also cites the case of a soldier in the trenches during World War I who, frozen and miserable, suddenly split and found himself outside his "earthly body." His earthly body went on talking to a companion, who later reported that he had chatted with great wit and humor, as if sitting in front of a comfortable fire.

The third case he cites concerned Sir Auckland Geddes, Professor of Anatomy at Dublin, and it bears a strong resemblance to the case of the Rev. Bertrand quoted in chapter one. Geddes describes how he began to feel very ill from acute gastroenteritis, and when he tried to ring for help, found himself unable to move. As he sat there, he realized that "*my* consciousness was separating from another consciousness which was also me." He calls them A-consciousness and B-consciousness, and says that B-consciousness was attached to his body, sitting in the chair, while A-consciousness was attached to his ego. (We should note that he says "attached" to the ego—not that it was identical with it.)

> *as my physical condition grew worse and the heart was fibrillating rather than beating, I realize that the B-consciousness belonging to the body was beginning to show signs of being composite, that is, built up of "consciousness" from the head, the heart and the viscera. These components became more individual and B-consciousness began to disintegrate, while the A-consciousness, which was now me, seemed to be altogether outside my body. . . .*

He suddenly became aware that he could not only see the room he was in, but the whole house and garden, and then things in London and Scotland. He makes the odd comment that he felt he was now "free in a time dimension of space, wherein 'now' was in some way equivalent to 'here' in the ordinary three-dimensional space of everyday life." In other words, he seemed to be one dimension higher than in the physical world—an observation that may explain Alan Vaughan's experience of precognition as he "left" his body, cited in chapter 1.

Geddes was discovered a few minutes later, and given a powerful camphor injection, which started his heart beating again. Like the Rev. Bertrand, he felt "intensely annoyed" at being drawn back to his body, because he felt that he was finally beginning to understand. (When Geddes described this experience, in a lecture to the Royal Medical Society, he claimed that it was of a friend whose word he could trust implicitly, but he later confessed that it was his own.) He emphasized that, when the experience was over, it had no tendency to fade like a dream.

There is one very obvious difference between this experience of Geddes and that of the Rev. Bertrand on the Titlis. When Bertrand experienced the "separation," his conscious ego looked down on his lifeless body. This seems to be what happens in most out-of-body experiences. Geddes, like Rosalind Heywood, experienced *divided consciousness*; he became two people, both conscious. This is something we find impossible to envisage; we can only imagine consciousness being in one place at once, so to speak. But Rosalind Heywood told Tyrrell: "I was definitely both 'mes,' and conscious in both places simultaneously. There was no sense of a third 'me' linking the two."

This point can be underlined by another case cited by Tyrrell—a more typical example of an out-of-body experience. During the Boer War, Sir Alexander Ogston was admitted to the Bloemfontein Hospital suffering from typhoid fever, and he says that in his delirium "mind and body seemed to be dual . . . I was conscious of the body as an inert, tumbled mass near the door; it belonged to me but it was not I." He speaks of his "mental self" leaving the body and wandering along, "seeing other dark shades gliding silently by," until he felt rapidly drawn back to his body. It sounds as if all this could be easily explained in terms of delirium. But that fails to explain the following incident:

> *I saw plainly . . . a poor R. A. M. C. surgeon, of whose existence I had not known, and who was in quite another part of the hospital, grow very ill and scream and die. I saw them cover his corpse and carry him softly out on shoeless feet. . . . Afterwards when I told these happenings to the sisters, they informed me that all this had happened. . . .*

Ogston experienced no sense of double consciousness, like Rosalind Heywood and Geddes. "He" moved around the hospital while his body lay inert on the bed. This is true of the majority of reported cases. Dr Celia Green, head of the Oxford Institute of Psychophysical Research, made a public appeal for cases of out-of-body experiences in 1966, and received more than four hundred replies. She published the result of her statistical studies in *Out-of-the-Body Experiences* in 1968. In most cases, the subject found himself outside the physical body, usually looking down on it from above. There was usually a sense of total detachment, as if the body belonged to someone else.

Yet the first case in the book suggests that this is slightly more complicated than a straightforward separation of body and soul. A waitress walking home after a twelve-hour stint, in a state of total exhaustion, suddenly found herself looking down on her physical body—still walking along the street—and thinking: "So that's how I look to other people." This seems to suggest that her physical body had a consciousness of its own. Another subject who "separated" during illness, reported "the top 'me' was feeling very relaxed and comfortable but quite aware of the suffering of the other 'me,'" which clearly suggests a double consciousness.

Standard reference works seem to display a certain basic agreement about out-of-the-body experiences. The general view seems to be that such experiences involve a separation of the physical body and what is referred to as the "astral body." C. Nelson Stewart writes as follows:

> *For centuries it has been a common idea that man is made of two components—a soul or spirit which comes from God, and a material body of flesh and blood. But some philosophers and occult theorists have suggested that each man has a third component, an astral body, meaning literally "starry body," and sometimes called "the body of light." This astral body is an exact copy of the flesh and blood body and is made of finer material. . . .*[7]

This, admittedly, sounds typical of the muddled beliefs of occultism, and it is easy to understand why many orthodox researchers, like Antony Flew and D. J. West, regard the astral body as something of a joke. Others, like Professor Jean Lhermitte of the Paris Medical Faculty, are willing to accept the genuineness of out-of-the-body experiences, but regard them as some kind of hallucination, or a trick played by the unconscious mind on our sensory apparatus. But then, cases like that of Sir Alexander Ogston raise the question of how a man suffering from hallucinations could obtain accurate knowledge of something happening elsewhere—such as a patient dying in another part of the hospital. Anyone who takes the trouble to examine the evidence will probably end by agreeing—like Celia Green—that out-of-the-body experiences are more than delusions, and that, therefore, the astral body probably exists.

The problem then is to find a theory that explains how Rosalind Heywood or Sir Auckland Geddes were able to experience double consciousness, and how the soldier mentioned by Tyrrell could carry on a conversation with his companion while his consciousness looked down on himself from above. Even the standard encyclopedias of the occult and paranormal fail to offer an explanation.

---

7. *Man, Myth and Magic* (1972-73).

One of the few occultists who can offer a satisfactory and comprehensive theory is Rudolf Steiner, the founder of the Anthroposophical movement, whose views on life after death will be considered later. Steiner would, in fact, have objected to being labeled an occultist, for he regarded himself as a scientist, and his basic training was in science and mathematics.

Steiner taught that a human consists of four components: body, etheric body, astral body and ego body. When a person sleeps, he splits into two, with the astral body and ego separating from the physical and etheric body.

These views are worth examining more closely. According to Steiner, the etheric body (sometimes called the "aura") interpenetrates the physical body, and may be regarded as its architect. He says: "All the physical organs are maintained in their form and shape by the currents and movements of the etheric body."

The word "currents" offers an interesting clue. Since the eighteenth century—when Galvani discovered that the leg of a dead frog could be made to kick when an electric current was passed through it—it has been recognized that, in some respects, human beings are electrical machines. Every time we think, the brain discharges electric currents.

One of the more baffling things about living matter is what holds it together. This was underlined in the late nineteenth century by a young biologist named Hans Driesch. Driesch waited until the fertilized egg of a sea urchin divided, and then killed off a half of it with a hot needle. He expected the other half to develop into half a sea urchin. To his surprise, it developed into a complete but half-sized sea urchin. He tried fusing two eggs together; the result was a double-size sea urchin. Clearly, some force was actively *shaping* the whole thing. Until then, it had been assumed that an embryo contains a lot of tiny labeled parts, like some do-it-yourself piece of furniture. Driesch's experiment offered a surprising new picture—as if a do-it-yourself wardrobe came with a tiny dwarf whose business is to put it together.

Across the Atlantic, a professor of anatomy, Harold Saxton Burr, was interested in Driesch's results, and particularly in this idea of a "shaping field" or blueprint. Burr pointed out that if a salamander embryo is placed in an alkaline solution, its individual cells "disaggregate" and turn into something like a bag full of marbles. But if these are placed in a slightly acid solution, they come together again and re-form into an embryo. Burr compared this to what happens when a magnet is held underneath iron filings on a sheet of paper—they form into a pattern following the lines of magnetic force. Burr and his colleague F. S. C. Northrop attached delicate voltmeters to trees, embryos, and other forms of living matter, and showed that seasonal changes are accompanied by a change in a weak electric field. This electric field is characteristic of all living creatures. It is the shaping force of life, the dwarf who comes with the do-it-yourself wardrobe. So Steiner's remarks about the etheric body—that it is the architect of the physical body, and that organs maintain their shape through its currents—proves to be a precise and accurate scientific description. Since Steiner wrote these words in 1910 (in *An Outline of Occult Science*)—a quarter of a century before Burr and Northrop began experimenting at Yale—it must be admitted that he showed remarkable prescience.

But, according to Steiner, a human being who consisted only of a physical body held together by an etheric body would be literally a vegetable. In fact, a human being during sleep *is* a kind of vegetable. When he wakes up, consciousness has been added to the mixture and, according to Steiner, consciousness is the astral body—or at least, its most important effect. Just as man shares the etheric body in common with vegetables, so he shares the astral body in common with animals.

In humans, says Steiner, there is yet another principle over and above these. An animal's choices are dictated by its sensations: heat and cold, hunger and thirst, pleasure and pain. A human is able to develop desires and wishes that go beyond these. An obvious example is a man with an interest in mathematics, which seems to have no possible connection with his physical appetites. (Throughout his life,

Steiner maintained an interest in mathematics.) This higher level of choice man calls the ego. The ego, says Steiner, is a principle of continuity. The animal self forgets quickly and easily (everyone has noticed how easily we forget the miseries of physical illness, for example). The ego attempts to provide a certain lasting element in human life.

These observations will strike a chord in every intelligent person. Nietzsche once remarked that we would like to ask the cows the secret of their happiness, but it would be pointless because they would have forgotten the question before they could give an answer. They have no continuity of consciousness. H. G. Wells made the same point in his *Experiment in Autobiography*; that since the beginning of time most living creatures have been "up against it," so their lives have been basically a struggle against circumstance. Now, says Wells, for the first time in history, you can say to a man: Yes, you earn a living, you support a family, you love and hate, but—*what do you do*? It applies to all kinds of humans, from scientists to artists, from mathematicians to religious thinkers. Take away that central preoccupation of their lives, and condemn them to mere "living," and they would want to commit suicide.

So Steiner's fourfold division of humans makes practical sense on at least three of its levels: the physical (obviously), the etheric level and the ego level. If we are willing to concede the evidence for out-of-the-body experiences, then we could say that his fourfold division appeals to common sense on every level.

Another occult system that bears a close resemblance to Steiner's is that of the Kahunas of Hawaii, as described by the anthropologist Max Freedom Long in works such as *The Huna Code in Religion*. The Kahunas (priests of the Huna religion) also believe that man consists of a physical body and three "spirits" or selves. These consist of the "low self," man's instinctive being, which corresponds roughly to the Freudian "unconscious"; the "middle self," man's conscious ego or "everyday self"; and the "high self," a superconscious ego, which possesses greater powers than the other two. The everyday self is ignorant of the existence of the other two. He fails to recognize the existence of the high self because it is as far above ordinary consciousness as the unconscious mind is below it. Moreover, the low self and the middle self intermingle, so that man assumes they are one and the same.

This low self sounds very much like Steiner's etheric body. It interpenetrates every cell and tissue of the body, and is the manufacturer of vital force. It is also the seat of the emotions of love, hate, fear, and desire. Its center of gravity, according to the Kahunas, is the solar plexus. It is naturally violent and emotional, and often behaves like a spoiled child. The middle self should attempt to discipline it and raise it to its own level; regrettably, many people give way to the demands of the low self and descend to its level.

All this begins to answer the question of how Rosalind Heywood could experience herself as White Me and Pink Me, with White Me feeling a certain contempt for Pink Me and its selfish desires. In Steiner's terminology, the ego was looking down on the etheric body; in Kahuna terminology, the low self was Pink Me and the high self was White Me. This seems confirmed by Rosalind Heywood's comments that the White Me and Pink Me dwell within her as oil and water. She identifies with White Me and can "watch without feeling them . . . the desires and repulsions that must inevitably toss all Pink Mes around."

Heywood adds the interesting comment: "If Freud ever struck such cases perhaps they helped to lead him towards the concepts of Id and Superego." In Freud, the Superego is, of course, another name for conscience, not for some higher ego, as Rosalind Heywood here implies. But her own analysis of the situation fits in perfectly with the views of the Kahunas on the low self and the high self.

All this makes it clear that Rosalind Heywood is not, as we might at first have suspected, an egotistic female who has invented a lot of psychic experiences to make herself sound interesting. She is simply describing the world as it is seen through the eyes of a typical clairvoyant. This world certainly differs from the world as described by modern science; yet it has its own inner consistency. If the sensitivity threshold theory is correct, it is certainly not in any way a contradiction of science. In fact, as we have seen, many of Rosalind Heywood's experiences could be explained in terms of the right and left hemispheres of the brain.

Having said which, it is necessary to admit that she says many things that most scientists would find quite unacceptable—like her experiences with Julia and Vivian—the second of which finally convinced her of the reality of life after death. What then are we to make of her experience on the edge of Dartmoor, when she claims to have sensed various nonhuman presences, some of which came to visit her ("a covey of little invisibles") as she sat at her writing desk the next day?

Here it is only possible to repeat that the experience is not peculiar to Rosalind Heywood. The entities she describes are usually known as nature spirits or elementals, and most "sensitives" claim to have seen them. Steiner speaks of them as a matter of fact, and comments:

> *We can lay hold of nature with ideas that assume a monistic (i.e., material) reality because sense perception allows us normally to experience only as much of nature as is in accord with that principle. Everything contradictory is filtered out, and nature is communicated to us in the guise of a monistic system.*

He goes on: "In the elemental world we find earth spirits (gnomes), water spirits (undines), air spirits (sylphs) and fire spirits (salamanders). . . ."[8]

W. Y. Evans Wentz, an authority on Eastern religions, states in his classic study *The Fairy Faith in Celtic Countries*: "we can postulate scientifically . . . the existence of such invisible intelligences as gods, genii, daemons, all kinds of true fairies, and disembodied man." He arrived at this conclusion as a result of years of study of "fairy faith" and the gathering of hundreds of depositions.

---

8. "Right and Wrong Use of Esoteric Knowledge." Lecture delivered at Dornach in November 1917.

By far the strangest story in Adam Crabtree's *Multiple Man* concerns possession by an apparently nonhuman entity. Crabtree admits to having his doubts about including it because it sounds so preposterous, but adds: "The fact remains, however, that it occurred as I have described it (if anything I have toned down some of the more dramatic elements of the experience)." It concerned a man called Marius, who taught history in a university and held a good position with a government health agency. He had been a happily married man until, for no reason he could understand, he suddenly began to experience murderous impulses toward his wife. He seemed to be driven by "some relentless inner compulsion to see blood." These impulses were so strong that he believed he might lose control and kill her.

His dreams seemed to provide a clue—dreams of living among cavemen who wore skins, and of crouching in a crude hut where strips of meat hung up to dry. He had also dreamt of meeting a powerfully built, primitive man coming up from his basement. Soon after this dream he was looking through his collection of coins when he found that one had been displaced and put on a shelf. He had no memory of doing this. A window screen that he had repaired was torn, and again he could find no explanation. It was after this that he began to hear a voice in his head. It told him that he—the voice—was the man he had seen in his dream, and that he was permanently inside Marius. To prove it, he had twice taken possession of him, moving the coin and tearing the screen. He could, he said, possess him whenever he liked.

Marius also seemed to believe that he was possessed by some curious entity called "the Bear." He seemed to have his own ideas about how to exorcise it. He felt that he needed to lie in front of a large wood fire, to absorb its warmth, and that this would strengthen him enough to allow the Bear to reveal itself.

For this therapeutic session, Crabtree and his patient moved to a country retreat, and five strong men also came along, in case Marius should give way to the urge to violence. A huge wood fire was built in the fireplace, and Marius lay in front of it, stripped to the waist.

After half an hour, he began howling and tearing at the floor. When he relaxed and returned to normal, he told them that he now understood about the Bear. It was a huge bear that had been captured by a band of hunters, and then killed slowly—no doubt as part of some ritual. Its spirit had entered one of the hunters, and had then moved down the generations, passing from father to son until it reached Marius. Now it had left.

But the entity that was driving Marius to violence was still inside him. According to Marius, this was a "round hole in space," and it absorbed violence. It had been present when the bear was killed. It had appeared in Marius' dream as the huge, primitive man coming up from the basement (the symbolism here is obvious).

The following day, when Marius had been placed in a deeply relaxed state, this entity began to speak through him. After a great deal of questioning and some hostile bickering, it finally gave its name as Morlac, and said that, in the remote past, it had been worshiped as a goat and a stag. "It had fed off the life and energy of those who worshiped it." For thousands of years it had been worshiped in various forms; "it detested affection and love but it prospered in an atmosphere of violence and fear." It described itself as a kind of "shimmering" in space, "a sort of vortex, completely dark, with a 'rim' of some kind." It actively disliked the feelings of concern and benevolence that Crabtree and his fellow workers were directing at Marius.

When Marius became exhausted—which happened frequently during work with the entity—they stopped until the next day. Marius retained no memory of what took place during these sessions.

Back in Toronto, the strange conversations with the entity continued; it remained contemptuous, but was no longer totally uncooperative. Then after some more sessions, the entity began to remember. "It realized it had come from some other place and had a history which preceded its earth experiences, though it could not remember that history."

The next paragraph makes it clear why Crabtree felt so embarrassed about describing this particular case.

> *Then one day the entity realized something about itself: that it was not totally dark, as it had always thought: in fact, its "rim" had a tinge of light. From that point things moved quickly. The entity recognized that it did not have to fear the "white light," that it had long ago in some other place lived in "the light." Next came the recognition that it must leave the host it was possessing. At first the entity feared starvation without a victim to feed upon, but when it realized that "the light" would nourish it, it left.*

Crabtree records that, in the eighteen months since this happened, Marius has experienced no recurrence of the problem, and his family life has returned to normal.

As usual with Crabtree's cases, there is nothing here that could not be interpreted in terms of mental illness. Having said that, it is necessary to add that psychics from Swedenborg to Rosalind Heywood would agree that there is another possible explanation: that there *are* disembodied entities, and that some of them are evil and dangerous.

Rosalind Heywood's description of an encounter with such an entity may serve as a conclusion to this chapter. It happened in 1927, in a house in Sussex that had been converted out of a group of old barns. She and her husband arrived together with their furniture, late one night, and after putting up two beds, slept heavily until morning. On waking up, both of them had the same thought: "We cannot bring the baby here." "We were simply aware of hate—that hostile invisible nonhuman entities belonged to the place and desperately wanted to drive us away."

They had signed the lease and could not afford to look for somewhere else. Her husband decided that the answer might be an exorcist. He came back later with a priest, who asked for salt and water. She went into the kitchen and was shocked:

> *It was a hell's kitchen, a raging whirlpool of hate, dismay and, strongest of all, panic. . . . However, although at the time I knew nothing of systematic investigation, the instinct to test the unusual was too strong. . . .*

She deliberately returned without the salt and asked her husband to go get it. When he returned he said, "Good gracious, that kitchen."

The ritual of exorcism apparently worked, and when she sat in the kitchen with the light turned out, "the raging hate had gone, the terror had gone, and in their place was a quiet shining peace."

With her usual fair-mindedness, Rosalind Heywood is willing to admit that this may have been simply due to suggestion. A few years later they lent the house to her sister, who found it impossible to venture into the kitchen at night without feeling something that filled her with terror. Neither Rosalind Heywood nor her husband ever again picked up the sense of the hostile nonhuman entity.

This episode, like so many others discussed in this chapter, sounds as if it belongs to the world of mediaeval superstition. In fact, it fits into a pattern of discovery that has begun to emerge in the last century and a half, and which we must now consider in its historical perspective.

Chapter Three

Invasion of the Spirit People

THE LITERARY SENSATION OF THE YEAR 1848 WAS a book entitled *The Night Side of Nature* by Catherine Crowe. She was an Edinburgh housewife, who had already achieved modest success with novels like *Susan Hopley* and *Lily Dawson. The Night Side of Nature*—subtitled "Ghosts and Ghost Seers"—made her a celebrity, and went on to become one of the most influential books of the nineteenth century.

Regrettably, Catherine Crowe did not enjoy her success for long. In 1859, she produced a treatise called "Spiritualism and the Age We Live In"—which, according to the *Dictionary of National Biography*, evinced "a morbid and despondent turn of mind," and soon after this she went insane—a fate her contemporaries must have felt she had invited by her interest in such macabre subjects. She recovered, but wrote little between then and her death in 1876. *The Night Side of Nature* remained as popular as ever, and was still on sale on railway bookstalls (price two shillings) at the turn of the century.

The author of the piece in the *Dictionary of National Biography* was clearly not a believer in ghosts and ghost seers; for while he admits that Mrs. Crowe's book is "one of the best collections of supernatural stories in our language," he attacks her for being "extremely credulous and uncritical." The reproach is unfair. The book would not have become so influential if it had been merely a collection of ghost stories. What the Victorians liked about it was its air of sturdy common sense, and its attempts to treat the phenomena with detachment. It would be more than thirty years before scientific investigators approached the supernatural in a spirit of systematic research. But Mrs. Crowe did her best, citing letters and documents and offering names of witnesses and dates.

The book that inspired *The Night Side of Nature* was another nineteenth-century bestseller called *The Seeress of Prevorst*, by Justinus Kerner. Catherine Crowe had published her own translation from the German original only three years earlier. It was the first full-length study of a clairvoyant in literary history. The seeress of Prevorst was a peasant woman called Friederike Hauffe, who had been seeing strange visions and conversing with invisible spirits since childhood. At the age of nineteen, Friederike had married a cousin and had a baby; then she went into postnatal depression, and developed symptoms of hysteria. Every evening she fell into a trance and saw spirits of the dead. Kerner, a wealthy doctor and amateur poet, was summoned to try to cure her.

Understandably, he treated her visions as delusions. He was fascinated by one claim that was undoubtedly genuine. Friederike could read with her stomach. She would lie on a bed, and an open book would be placed, face down, on her naked midriff. With her eyes closed, she would read as easily as if it was in front of her face. She also claimed to be able to see into the human body, and possessed a knowledge of the nervous system that was extraordinary for a peasant.

Kerner changed his mind about her visions after a strange experience. She told him that she was being haunted by a man with a squint, and Kerner recognized the description of a man who had died a few years earlier. The dead man, said Friederike, was suffering from a guilty conscience because he had embezzled some money and another man had been blamed. Now the embezzler wanted to clear the innocent man's name, for the sake of his widow. The proof, he said, resided in a chest of documents, which would be found in the room of a certain official. The "spirit" had shown her the official sitting in his room, with the chest open on the table. Her description was so good that Kerner recognized a judge called Heyd. The judge had to admit the accuracy of Friederike's account of his room, and both he and Kerner were staggered when the document was found exactly where she said it would be—she even knew that it had been filed in the wrong place.

From now on, Kerner took Friederike seriously, and made a note of her basic ideas. She told him that we are surrounded by invisible spirits, and to prove it, persuaded them to make rapping noises, throw gravel, and make a stool rise up into the air. A book opened itself, a candle was extinguished by invisible fingers, and something tugged off Friederike's boots as she lay on the bed. Kerner himself saw a "spirit," which he described as looking like a gray pillar of cloud surmounted by a head.

Friederike spoke a strange, unknown language, which she claimed to be the original language of the inner life—scholars later found that it resembled Coptic. She talked about various complicated cycles of human existence—sun-circles and life-circles. Most significant, she declared that man consists of four parts: body, nerve aura, soul, and spirit; the nerve aura being an ethereal body that carries on the vital processes when we are asleep or in trance. All this corresponds precisely to the views of Steiner, as described in chapter two.

These spirit manifestations did her health no good, and she died at the age of twenty-nine, in 1829, the same year that Kerner published *The Seeress of Prevorst*. It caused a sensation. Kerner was a respectable literary man, a friend of poets and philosophers, as well as an eminent physician, so it could not be dismissed as lies or fantasy. The well-known theologian David Strauss had also witnessed many of the things described in the book, and vouched for their truth. Strauss' "destructive" *Life of Jesus* would soon be causing a national scandal, but even this hardly compared with the European scandal caused by *The Seeress of Prevorst*. The nineteenth century was the age of rationalism triumphant. Scientists would come to terms with David Strauss' skepticism—but not with Friederike's invisible spirits. The doctors of Paris and Vienna had destroyed the career of Dr. Franz Mesmer by denouncing "mesmerism" and hypnosis as a fraud. They refused even to look at the evidence for telepathy or clairvoyance. It was easier to believe that *The Seeress of Prevorst* was a hoax than to ask what it all meant. The tremendous popular success of the book only deepened their conviction that it was some kind of imposture.

All this helps to explain why it took Kerner's book almost two decades to reach England. Britain, after all, was the original home of skepticism. David Hume had dismissed miracles by asking which was more likely: that witnesses should tell lies, or that the laws of nature should be violated? The English were proud of their tradition of bold thinking; they liked to point out that, unlike the French and Italians and Bavarians, they had no reason to fear being sent to the stake if they called the pope a liar. The British medical profession entirely approved of the decision of their French colleagues to denounce Mesmer as a charlatan. When a nonconformist doctor named John Elliotson declared that he took mesmerism seriously, an eminent surgeon named Sir Benjamin Brodie stated in print that it was "a debasing superstition, a miserable amalgam of faith and fear."

Catherine Crowe published her translation of *The Seeress of Prevorst* in 1845, and came to no harm—after all, she was a woman, and a novelist at that. The book excited as much attention as it had in German. It convinced her of the reality of the supernatural. She had so far been a disciple of the famous Edinburgh doctor George

Combe, Britain's most famous exponent of phrenology—the doctrine that a man's character can be read through the bumps on his skull—and Combe was a determined skeptic about ghosts and such matters. Kerner and Friederike made her a convert. It now came to her as a revelation that the "scientific spirit" had gone too far. "Because, in the 17th century, credulity outran reason and discretion, the 18th century, by a natural reaction, flung itself into an opposite extreme." The nineteenth century had carried this attitude to the point of absurdity; in fact, it had become a new kind of superstition, refusing to face facts that contradicted its dogmas.

Catherine Crowe was not particularly credulous. She set about unearthing her own facts, and found that they seemed to fit together into a logical pattern. Almost everything she wrote about would later be studied more systematically by parapsychologists and carefully documented in scientific archives: dreaming of the future, death-bed visions, premonitions of disaster, phantasms of the living and of the dead, poltergeists, spontaneous psychokinesis, even possession. She reproaches contemporary scientists for insisting that the supernatural can be explained in terms of hysteria or nervous derangement, and points out, quite fairly, that they "arrange the facts to their theory, not their theory to the facts." What is now needed, she says, is investigation. "And by *investigation* I do not mean the hasty, captious, angry notice of an unwelcome fact . . . but the slow, modest, pains-taking examination that is content to wait upon nature, and humbly follow out her disclosures, however opposed to preconceived theories or mortifying to human pride." Here she seems to be echoing a famous remark by Thomas Henry Huxley about the duty of the scientist: "Sit down before fact as a little child, be prepared to give up every preconceived notion, follow humbly wherever and to whatever abysses nature leads, or you shall learn nothing." It is interesting to discover that Huxley wrote this sentence in 1860, more than a decade after *The Night Side of Nature* was published; Huxley may, in fact, be echoing Mrs. Crowe.

Catherine Crowe's aim, she readily admits, is to see whether the evidence proves that some part of man can survive death. The first step in this direction—and it was later followed by most of her eminent successors, such as Myers and Tyrrell—was to try to show that man possesses powers that cannot be explained by science. She devotes several chapters to dreams and presentiments of the future, and includes a number of experiences gathered from friends.

Another friend lately dreamt, one Thursday night, that he saw an acquaintance of his thrown from his horse, and that he was lying on the ground with the blood streaming from his face, and was much cut. He mentioned his dream in the morning, and being an entire disbeliever in such phenomena, he was unable to account for the impression it made on his mind. This was so strong that, on Saturday, he could not forebear calling at his friend's house, who he was told was in bed, having been thrown from his horse on the previous day, and much injured about the face.

If Mrs. Crowe had lived to become a member of the Society for Psychical Research, she would have gone to the trouble of getting signed statements from her friend, the man who had the accident, and the person he told about the dream the morning after. As a pioneer in the field, she obviously felt that this was unnecessary. Otherwise, it is difficult to fault her method.

Like every writer on the paranormal, Catherine Crowe is particularly fascinated by out-of-the-body experiences, for she rightly regards these as potential proof that there is something in man that can exist outside the body. Again, she does her best to offer facts that could be checked:

The late Mr. Holloway, of the Bank of England, brother to the engraver of that name, related of himself that being one night in bed with his wife and unable to sleep, he had fixed his eyes and thoughts with uncommon intensity on a beautiful star that was shining in at the window, when he suddenly found his spirit released from his body and soaring into that bright sphere. But, instantly seized with anxiety for the anguish of his wife, if she discovered his body apparently dead beside her, he returned and re-entered it with difficulty. . . . He described that returning was returning to darkness; and that whilst the spirit was free, he was alternately in the light or in the dark, accordingly as his thoughts were with his wife or with the star. He said that he always avoided anything that could produce a repetition of this accident, the consequences of it being very distressing.

Her main problem was that, working mainly from hearsay, she had no simple way of distinguishing the authentic from the inauthentic. A typical example is a case she cites from Heinrich Jung-Stilling. Now Jung-Stilling was a serious investigator of the paranormal, a Professor of Economics at Marburg, and a follower of the doctrines of Mesmer. He ought to have been a reliable authority. The story he tells is in many ways a good case of what was later to be called a "phantasm of the living." In Philadelphia, around the year 1740, says Jung-Stilling, a clairvoyant was approached by the wife of a sea captain, who was anxious because she had not heard from her husband for a long time. The clairvoyant asked her to excuse him, and went into another room. After a while, the woman became impatient, and went and peeped through a crack in the door; the clairvoyant was lying on a sofa, apparently asleep. When he came back, he told her that her husband was alive and well, but had been unable to write to her for various reasons, which he explained. At this moment, he said, the captain was in a coffee house in London, and would soon be back home.

In due course, the captain returned, and confirmed the reasons that the clairvoyant had given for failing to write. When he was introduced to the clairvoyant, the husband recognized him as a man he had seen in a London coffee house on the eve of his departure for America. According to the captain, the man had spoken to him, asked him why he had not written to his wife, and then vanished into the crowd.

The clairvoyant's power of "projecting" himself across the Atlantic brings to mind similar stories of Swedenborg, bringing messages from the dead. His appearance in a London coffee house has dozens of parallels in *Phantasms of the Living*, compiled in the 1880s by members of the Society for Psychical Research. What rings totally false here is the information that the captain spoke to him and explained why he had failed to write to his wife. There are hundreds of recorded cases of projection, but in very few (I can recall only one[1]) does the phantasm actually talk to anybody. When we learn that these events supposedly took place in 1740—the year Jung-Stilling was born—it becomes clear that, even if basically true, the story had probably been "improved" in the telling. Mrs. Crowe had no way of knowing that the story failed to conform to the general pattern of "phantasms of the living," because in her day, there had not been enough research for the pattern to emerge.

In view of this difficulty, Mrs. Crowe did remarkably well, and her book deserved its high reputation. Most of her conjectures would do credit to a modern investigator. For example, in the chapter on "The Poltergeist of the Germans," she discusses a recent case of a French girl named Angelique Cottin who, in 1846, had been weaving silk gloves when the loom began to move violently. Angelique—who was fourteen—had apparently turned into a human magnet, and objects held close to her would fly through the air and stick to her. Oddly enough, she had no attraction for metals; but this was clearly some form of electricity, for she gave people electric shocks. It could only be prevented if she stood on a piece of thick cork. Catherine Crowe went on to make the sensible suggestion that poltergeist phenomena might be electrical in nature—a remarkably perceptive insight when most writers on the subject assumed that poltergeists were malevolent specters.

In other ways, her "credulity" was often far ahead of her time. She cites a story from another early researcher, Joseph Ennemoser:

---

1. In *Autobiography of a Yogi* by Parahansa Yogananda, the author describes how a visiting Yogi had told him that a friend was on his way. When the friend arrived, he told of how the Yogi had approached him in the street, and mentioned that Parahansa was waiting for him in his room. At the time this happened, the Yogi had

*It appears that Van Helmont, having asserted that it was possible for a man to extinguish the life of an animal by the eye alone (*oculis intentis*), Rousseau, the naturalist, repeated the experiment when in the East, and in this manner killed several toads; but on a subsequent occasion, whilst trying the same experiment at Lyons, the animal, on finding it could not escape, fixed its eyes immovably on him, so that he fell into a fainting fit, and was thought to be dead. . . .*

This is the kind of tale that makes us smile sarcastically; we know that these stories of the hypnotic power of snakes and other creatures are old wives' tales. Yet a modern investigator, Dr. Ferenc Andras Volgyesi, devoted many years to studying hypnosis in humans and animals, and arrived at some interesting conclusions. He observed—and photographed—dozens of cases in which snakes "fascinated" rabbits or rats and then ate them. He also observed many cases of "battles of wills" between the snake and its potential victims—his book contains photographs of a giant anaconda "fascinating" a rat, and a python immobilizing a hare. Another shows a battle of wills between a bird, the *cucullus senegalensis*, and a rattlesnake. He states: "The battle, which begins with a mutual fixing of the gaze, usually ends in victory for the bird." Another photograph shows a toad winning a battle of wills with a cobra. Volgyesi also describes a battle between two lizards. They confronted one another for about ten minutes, gazing intently at one another (as Mrs. Crowe says, *oculis intentis*) then one slowly ate the other, which remained immobile.[2] Van Helmont's tale about killing animals with the gaze may be an exaggeration, but it is based on an observed reality.

There is a great deal in the literature of hypnosis to support Mrs. Crowe's view that it involves the deliberate use of some mental force.

---

been with Parahansa. From the point of view of a psychical investigator, the case is dubious because we have only the author's word for it.

2. Ferenc Andras Volgyesi, *Menschen und Tierhypnose* (1963), translated as *Hypnosis of Man and Animals* (London, 1966).

In 1885, French psychologist Pierre Janet observed the experiments of a doctor named Gibert, who could induce hypnosis in a patient called Leonie by merely thinking about her, and summon her from the other side of Le Havre by the same means. In the 1890s, Dr. Paul Joire caused blindfolded and hypnotized patients to obey his mental commands, and the same kind of experiments were repeated in the 1920s by the Russian scientist L. L. Vasiliev, who described them in a book called *Experiments in Distant Influence*. These leave no possible doubt that some kind of mental force *can* be exercised at a distance.

What fascinated Catherine Crowe was the clear implication that human powers are far greater than we realize. If people can leave their bodies and witness things that are going on elsewhere, if a hypnotized subject can describe things that are happening in the street, if a girl can turn into a human magnet, if a man can dream accurately about the future—then materialistic science must be somehow fundamentally mistaken about our human limitations. She translated *The Seeress of Prevorst*, and it was perfectly clear to her that unless Kerner was an out-and-out liar, then something *very* queer was going on. This was not the secondhand reporting of spooks and specters, as in Jung-Stilling's *Pneumatology*; this was firsthand reporting by a man who had no reason to lie or deceive himself. Kerner described—and Mrs. Crowe cites in *The Night Side of Nature*—how Friederike had awakened one night crying, "Oh God!" and how a doctor who was sitting near the corpse of her father, many miles away, clearly heard the exclamation, and rushed into the room to see if the corpse had come to life. This was not a question of spirits. It was some curious power possessed by Friederike herself. While such powers seem to be beyond the control of the individual who exercises them, Mrs. Crowe could see that there is no earthly reason why this should always be so. That is why the hardheaded Victorians found her book so exciting. Their explorers were penetrating new continents, their railways were stretching to the ends of the earth, their industries were creating new wealth, their science was uncovering the secrets of the universe. If Mrs. Crowe was correct, a new science of the supernatural would demonstrate that humans were far more extraordinary creatures then ever suspected. Her book was not a morbid collection of tales to make the flesh creep, but a work of buoyant optimism about human potentialities.

Unfortunately, a Victorian lady novelist was hardly the person to persuade scientists that they were ignoring an important subject. The Victorians had fought hard for their intellectual freedom. Witches were still being executed in the 1690s; as late as the 1750s, the Church forced the great naturalist Buffon to withdraw his statement that the earth was a fragment of the sun, and that fossils were the remains of primitive ancestors of present-day creatures. By 1800, intellectuals were utterly sick of the authority the Church had been exercising for centuries. They longed to see the downfall of these ecclesiastical bullies. So every time someone dared to challenge the intellectual authority of the Church, cheers echoed throughout Europe. In 1830, two years after *The Night Side of Nature* was published, the German theologian Ludwig Feuerbach produced a book, *Thoughts on Death and Immortality*, in which he dismissed the idea of a personal God, and jeered at the desire for immortality as selfish stupidity. Feuerbach was persecuted by the police and forced to give up his post at the university. Ten years later, Feuerbach published a far more radical book, *The Essence of Christianity*, which landed like a bombshell and frightened even the freethinkers; he declared that God and immortality were dangerous delusions, and that man has to learn to live in the present instead of wasting his time dreaming about a nonexistent heaven. (The book had a deep influence on Karl Marx, who expressed its basic message in the phrase "Religion is the opium of the people.") In his novel *Green Heinrich*, the Swiss poet Gottfried Keller describes Feuerbach as "a magician in the shape of a bird who sang God out of the hearts of thousands." The same book has a portrait of a schoolteacher who lost his job because he is an atheist, but who travels around Germany exclaiming: "Isn't it a joy to be alive?" and "forever marvelling at the glory of being free from the encumbrance" of God.

This is why the scientists and philosophers were not willing to pay attention to the evidence for the supernatural. They were too delighted to see the Church getting a black eye, and had no intention of letting religion sneak in again by the back door. So when Catherine Crowe began her book by admitting that she wanted to prove the reality of man's immortal soul, most of them read no further. Whether Mrs. Crowe intended it or not, she was giving aid and comfort to the enemy.

In fact, in the year *The Night Side of Nature* was published, this particular enemy was preparing to mount a full-frontal assault.

With the wisdom of hindsight, we can see that the most interesting and significant pages of *The Night Side of Nature* are those that concern the haunting of a house owned by an industrialist named Joshua Proctor. Here Catherine Crowe presents the kind of carefully documented account that would be the aim of the later investigators of the Society for Psychical Research. This is the true stuff of psychical research. She prefaces the account with a letter from Joshua Proctor to herself, vouching for the accuracy of the details of the report that follows.

The haunted house was a millhouse built only forty years earlier in 1800. The newly-built Newcastle and Shields railway passed overhead on a viaduct. In June 1840, news reached the outside world that the Proctor family—who were Quakers—had been disturbed by knocking noises, and had seen some unpleasant things. A surgeon named Edward Drury, who practiced in Sunderland, heard about the haunting from a local farmer. Dr. Drury was skeptical about such matters. Nevertheless, he had been fascinated by the account of a famous poltergeist haunting at Epworth in the rectory of the Rev. Samuel Wesley, grandfather of the founder of Methodism. This spook, known as Old Jeffrey, had banged and groaned around the rectory for two months in 1716. There were sounds of heavy breathing, breaking glass, footsteps, and various unidentifiable noises. The

Rev. Samuel noticed that the disturbances seemed in some way connected with his nineteen-year-old daughter Hetty, who trembled in her sleep before the sounds began. The scientist Joseph Priestley had investigated the case, and decided it was a hoax. Dr. Drury was inclined to agree with him; so when he heard of the hauntings of Willington Mill, he wrote to its owner, Joshua Proctor, offering to "unravel the mystery" (that is, expose the hoaxer). Mr. Proctor replied politely, saying that he and his family were going away on a visit on the date Dr. Drury had suggested; one of his employees was going to act as caretaker while they were away. Nevertheless, if Drury wanted to come and stay overnight, he was welcome.

Dr. Drury decided take a friend along for moral support. He also took a brace of pistols, intending to allow one of them to fall on the floor, as if by accident, to deter any practical joker. When he arrived, he found that Joshua Proctor had returned alone—from his holiday. Proctor was so obviously an honest man that Drury decided the "accident" was unnecessary.

What happened to Edward Drury that night convinced him completely of the reality of the supernatural. It also gave him such a fright that he went partially deaf in one ear and suffered a temporary breakdown in health. He seems to have been too shattered to describe what he had seen immediately afterwards, but he promised to write Joshua Proctor a letter with a full account. This letter was written on July 13, 1840, ten days after his night in the haunted millhouse.

He arrived with his friend, T. Hudson, and was made welcome by Proctor, who showed him the house. At eleven o'clock, Dr. Drury and Hudson settled down on the third-story landing outside the "haunted room." (Although he says he "expected to account for any noises that he might hear in a philosophical manner," he presumably decided that discretion was the better part of valour.) About an hour later, they heard pattering noises, "as if a number of people were pattering with their bare feet." Then there was a knocking sound from the floorboards at their feet, as if someone was rapping with his knuckles. After this, they heard a "hollow cough" from the haunted room, but seem to have decided not to investigate. Then they heard a rustling noise, as if someone was coming upstairs.

At a quarter to one, feeling cold, Dr. Drury said he thought he would retire to bed; Hudson said he intended to stay up until dawn. Dr. Drury looked at his watch, and noted the time. As he looked up, he saw a closet door open, and "the figure of a female, attired in grayish garments, with the head inclining downward, and one hand pressed upon the chest, as if in pain" walking towards him. Hudson was fast asleep, but was awakened by Dr. Drury's "awful yell." Drury rushed at the figure, "but instead of grasping it, I fell upon my friend, and I recollected nothing distinctly for nearly three hours afterwards. I have since learnt that I was carried downstairs in an agony of fear and terror."

Catherine Crowe not only publishes the full correspondence between Dr. Drury and Joshua Proctor, but an account by a local historian, another by the owner of a local journal, and descriptions by four other people who had seen the ghost. In fact, there seemed to be more than one; there was also a man in a surplice who glided across a second-floor room a few feet off the floor. The local historian adds to his account the information that Proctor had recently discovered an old book that states that similar hauntings had taken place in an older house that had been built on the same spot two hundred years before. Mrs. Crowe ends her account by mentioning that Proctor has now decided to leave the house, and turn it into "small tenements" for his workpeople.

What makes this report so interesting is that the case resembles in so many respects the haunting that would occur eight years later in Hydesville, New York, and that would launch the Spiritualism movement of the nineteenth century. In Willington, as in Hydesville, there was a mixture of poltergeist phenomena and the more conventional type of haunting. If Dr. Drury had shown the same kind of courage and curiosity shown later by Mrs. Margaret Fox at Hydesville, it seems highly probable that the Spiritualist movement would have been launched ten years earlier in England.

The Hydesville affair began on March 31, 1848, in a wooden frame house inhabited by a Methodist farmer named James D. Fox, his wife Margaret, and their two daughters, Margaretta, age fourteen, and Kate, age twelve. Hydesville is a small township not far from Rochester, New York. James Fox had moved into the house in the previous December. A previous tenant, Michael Weekman, had been disturbed by various loud knocks, for which he could find no cause.

The Fox family was also kept awake by various banging noises in the last days of March 1848, but since it was a windy month, they were not unduly disturbed. On Friday, March 31, the family decided to retire early to make up for lost sleep. Mr. Fox went around the house checking the shutters and sashes. The children observed that when he shook the sashes to see how loose they were, banging noises seemed to reply like an echo.

The whole family slept in two beds in the same room. Just before the parents came to bed, the rapping noises started again. Kate said cheekily: "Mr. Splitfoot, do as I do," and began snapping her fingers. To the amazement of the girls, the raps imitated her. Margaret interrupted: "Do as I do," and began to clap. Again, the sounds imitated her. Remembering that the next day would be April the first, the children decided that someone was playing a joke. In her account of what happened, Mrs. Fox wrote:

I then thought I could put a test that no one in the place could answer. I asked the noise to rap my different children's ages, successively. Instantly, each one of my children's ages was given correctly, pausing between them sufficiently long to individualize them until the seventh [child], at which a longer pause was made, and then three more emphatic little raps were given, corresponding to the age of the little one that died. . . .

Now rather frightened—this was evidently no joke—Mrs. Fox asked if it was a human being who was making the raps; there was no reply. "Is it a spirit? If it is, make two raps." Two thunderous bangs followed, so loud that the house shook. She asked if it was an "injured spirit," and again the bangs shook the house. Further questioning revealed that the knocker was a man who died at the age of thirty-one, that he had been murdered in the house, and that he had a wife and five children. Mrs. Fox asked if the spirit had any objection to her calling in the neighbors; the raps replied, "No."

The Foxes summoned in about fourteen neighbors. One of them was a man called William Duesler, who assured his own wife that the whole thing was ridiculous, and that there could be nothing mysterious about the noises. When he got there, some of the neighbors were too nervous to go into the bedroom, but Duesler was not worried. He went and sat on the bed, and was astonished when Mrs. Fox's questions were answered with a rapping noise that made the bed vibrate. (Later writers were to insist that the two children made all the noises by cracking their joints, but it is hard to see how the cracking of joints could make the house shake and cause a bed to vibrate.)

Duesler took up the questioning of the "spirit." By a code of knocks, he established that the entity was a man who had been murdered in the house, a peddler named Charles B. Rosma, who had been attacked for the $500 he carried. The murder had taken place five years earlier, and had been committed by the man who was then the tenant of the house, a Mr. Bell. A maid named Lucretia Pulver later confirmed that a peddler had spent the night in the house, and that she had been sent home; when she returned the next day, the peddler had gone.

As news of these amazing occurrences spread throughout the community, hundreds of people came to the house. On Sunday, April 2, Duesler learned from the murdered man that his body had been buried in the cellar. This seemed to offer a method of verification, and James Fox and his neighbors took shovels to the cellar—which had an earth floor—and proceeded to dig. At a depth of three feet they encountered water, and abandoned the attempt. But in July, when the water had gone down, they dug again, and at a depth of five feet found a plank; underneath this, in quicklime, there was some human hair and a few bones.

Mr. Bell, on being told that he had been accused of murder by a ghost, indignantly denied it, and produced a testimonial to his good character from his new neighbors in Lyon, New York. The spirit had already prophesied that the murderer would never be brought to justice.

In his account of the case in *Modern Spiritualism*, the skeptical Frank Podmore comments: "No corroborative evidence of the supposed murder, or even of the existence of the man supposed to have been murdered, was ever obtained." This was written in 1902. Two years later, in November 1904, a wall in the cellar of the Fox house collapsed, revealing another wall behind it. Digging between the two walls uncovered a skeleton and a peddler's tin box. It looked as if someone had dug up the body from its original grave and interred it next to the wall, then built another wall to confuse searchers.

In those days immediately after the first manifestations, a committee was set up to collect the statements of witnesses. Not all the investigators were convinced that the sounds had a supernatural origin; but no one suggested that the Fox family could be responsible. With the family all together in the same room, it was obviously impossible that either the parents or the children could be causing the bangs.

What everyone soon noticed was that nothing happened unless the children were in the house—particularly Kate. A committee of skeptical Rochester citizens came to the house to investigate; they agreed that Margaret was certainly not responsible. A second and a third investigation produced the same result. The children were stripped and searched to see if they had some mechanical device for producing the sounds; there was nothing. They were made to stand on pillows with their ankles tied; still the raps occurred.

The children were separated; Kate was sent to stay with her elder sister Leah in Rochester, and Margaretta with her brother David in Auburn. The "spirits" followed them both. Rapping noises were heard, and people felt themselves touched by invisible hands. In Leah's house, a lodger called Calvin Brown took a mildly satirical attitude towards the spirit, and it began to persecute him, throwing things at him. Mrs. Fox's cap was pulled off and the comb pulled out of her hair. When members of the family knelt to pray, pins were jabbed into them. In brother David's boarding house, similar things were happening. It was clear that the murdered peddler was not responsible for all this—he was back in the Hydeville house, making terrifying gurgling noises and sounds like a body being dragged across the floor. Mrs. Fox's hair turned white. One spirit who communicated with Kate claimed to be a dead relative named Jacob Smith. Sister Leah Fish discovered that she could also communicate with the spirits, and began producing messages. One sixteen-year-old girl named Harriet Bebee, who visited the house in Auburn and witnessed the rapping noises, returned to her home twenty miles away and found that the noises had followed her.

The Fox family moved to Rochester, but the manifestations continued. Sometimes the bangs were so loud that they could be heard miles away. Poltergeists had apparently taken over from the original "injured spirit." One day, a visitor named Isaac Post started asking the spirit questions, and was answered by a thunderous barrage of knocks. Then, by means of an alphabetical code, the spirit spelled out a message: "Dear friends, you must proclaim this truth to the world. This is the dawning of a new era; you must not try to conceal it any longer. God will protect you and good spirits will watch over you." Then began a series of manifestations that were to become typical of "Spiritualism."[3] Tables moved and rapped with their legs; musical instruments were played by unseen fingers, objects moved round the room. The spirits intimated that they would prefer to manifest themselves in the dark—which confirmed the skeptics in their opinion. Other believers decided it was time to put the spirit's injunction into operation and "proclaim this truth to the world." On November 14, 1849, the first Spiritualist meeting took place in the Corinthian hall in Rochester.

---

3. When I speak of Spiritualism with a capital "S," I refer to the religion of that name. Spiritualism with a small "s" denotes the belief in spirits or life after death.

In his account of the haunting of Willington Mill, the local historian, M. A. Richardson, had remarked:

> *Were we to drawn an inference from the number of cases of reported visitations from the invisible world that have been made public of late, we might be led to imagine that the days of supernatural agency were about to recommence, and that ghosts and hobgoblins were about to resume their sway over the fears of mankind.*

For 1840, that was a remarkably perceptive observation. Whether it was merely due to improved communications and the increase in the number of newspapers, it *does* seem clear that there was an apparent increase in ghostly manifestations at about this period. In retrospect, it looks oddly as if the spirits had decided that the time had come to make themselves noticed. Of course, there had been such manifestations for centuries—the Elizabethan astrologer Dr. John Dee devoted a large book to an account of his communications with spirits through the agency of a "scryer" (or, as they later came to be called, a medium) called Edward Kelley. Cases like the Epworth poltergeist, the Stockwell poltergeist (described by Catherine Crowe), the Cock Lane ghost, and the phantom drummer of Tedworth[4] had aroused widespread excitement and was the subject of contemporary pamphlets. In 1847, a young American shoemaker named Andrew Jackson Davis was placed under hypnosis and wrote an extraordinary and erudite work called *The Principles of Nature,* which subsequently became a literary sensation. In this remarkable book, Davis prophesies that "the truth about spirits will 'ere long present itself in the form of a living demonstration, and the world will hail with delight the ushering in of that era when the interiors of men will be opened." Within four years of its publication, Spiritualism had spread across America and was sweeping Europe.

---

4. For accounts of these cases see my book *Poltergeist* (1981).

For whatever reason, the Fox sisters began a Spiritualist explosion. People discovered that all they had to do was to sit in a darkened room, preferably with a medium present—someone who had already established a communication with the spirits—and the manifestations would usually follow immediately. No apparatus was required, except possibly a few musical instruments. In the Rochester area, more than a hundred mediums appeared in the year 1850. In Buffalo, New York, two brothers and a sister named Davenport attended a séance at which the Fox sisters produced their manifestations, and decided to try it themselves—in fact, inexplicable raps and bangs had sounded in their home in the year 1846, two years before the Hydesville manifestations. When Ira, William, and Elizabeth Davenport sat in a darkened room, with their hands on a tabletop, the table began to move, raps were heard all over the room, and when Ira picked up a pencil his hand began to write automatically. A few nights later, with witnesses present, all three children were seen to levitate into the air. At their fifth "séance," Ira was instructed—by means of raps—to fire a pistol in the corner of the room. As it exploded, it was taken from his hand, and by the light of the flash, a figure of a man was seen holding it. He vanished a moment later, and the pistol fell to the floor. The man introduced himself—through the code of raps—as "John King"; he was one of the first examples of a "control" (or master of ceremonies), who acted as intermediary between the medium and the spirits. John King was soon taking over the brothers directly and speaking through their mouths. The Davenport brothers went on to become even more famous than the Fox sisters.

In Dover, Ohio, a well-to-do farmer named Jonathan Koons discovered his own talents as a medium by sitting in a dark room and going into a trance. The spirits who spoke through him told him that all eight of his children were gifted mediums. They instructed him to build a special house made of logs, sixteen feet by twelve, to be used exclusively for spiritualist activities. There were large numbers of musical instruments: drums, triangles, tambourines, a banjo, an accordion, a harp, a guitar, and so on. The room was dimly lit with sheets of wet paper smeared with phosphorus. When the mediums—usually Koons and his eighteen-year-old son Nahum—were seated at a small table, with the audience on benches, Koons would play the violin, and the spirits would soon join in, producing the effect of a full orchestra. Witnesses also speak of a heavenly choir joining in. The racket was impressive, and could be heard a mile away. A voice would then deliver a homily, using a speaking trumpet, which floated in the air. A spirit hand floated around the room, touching people and shaking their hands. People came from all over the county to witness these marvels, and the spirits impressed everyone by producing information about strangers that none of the audience could have known.

This was, in fact, one of the most convincing things about the spirits; they seemed to have access to all kinds of information. In Boston, the wife of a newspaper editor, Mrs. W. R. Hayden, startled the wife of the English mathematician, Augustus de Morgan, by giving her detailed messages from dead friends about whom she could not possibly have known. The result was that Mrs. de Morgan invited her to England, where she held séances under "test conditions" in the de Morgan's home. She was loudly ridiculed by the English newspapers, who were convinced that this latest American craze must be based on fraud and deception (which the British were too sensible to swallow), but she convinced most of those who actually saw her. Respectable members of the British middle classes who tried "table-turning" to while away the long evenings were amazed to discover that it actually worked. One journalist wrote a few years later: "In those days you were invited to 'Tea and Table Moving' as a new excitement, and made to revolve with the family like mad round articles of furniture." Even Queen Victoria and Prince Albert tried it at Osborne, and the table moved so convincingly that the queen had no doubt whatsoever that no trickery was involved—she decided that the answer must lie in some form of electricity or magnetism.

The French were more than prepared to adopt this new form of entertainment, for half a century of controversy about Mesmer—

who had taught that healing, clairvoyance, and other such mysteries were due to a mysterious force called "animal magnetism"—had accustomed them to strange phenomena. By 1851, table-turning had become the latest craze. The spirits soon made a highly influential convert. He was a fifty-year-old educationalist named Denizard-Hyppolyte-Leon Rivail, who was to become famous under the name Allan Kardec. Rivail had been a pupil of the celebrated educator Pestalozzi, and he had opened his own school at the age of twenty-four. He had written popular books on arithmetic, grammar, spelling, how to calculate in your head, and educational reform, and had given immensely successful courses of free lectures on astronomy, chemistry, physics, and anatomy. He was also an enthusiastic student of phrenology and animal magnetism.

It was in May 1855 that Rivail attended a hypnotic session with a certain Madame Roger, who was placed in a trance by her "magnetizer," M. Fortier, and was able to read minds and perform other puzzling feats. There Rivail met Madame Plainemaison, who told him that even stranger phenomena were taking place regularly at her house in the rue Grange-Bateliere. Rivail agreed to go, and was amazed by what he saw. The tables did more than merely "turn"; they also jumped and ran about the room. The disciple of Mesmer felt that these phenomena challenged the powers of reason to which he had devoted his life, and he determined to try to get to the bottom of it. At Madame Plainemaison's, he met a man named Baudin, who told him that his two daughters practiced automatic writing. The young ladies seem to have discovered their powers accidentally, in the course of entertaining their friends with table-turning; they were, says one commentator, "of a worldly and frivolous disposition." This did not deter the serious-minded Rivail, who proceeded to ask the table major philosophical questions. Asked if mankind would ever understand the first principles of the universe, it replied, "No. There are things that cannot be understood by man in this world." When Rivail asked if matter had always existed, the table replied (perhaps a trifle wearily), "God only knows."

It was obvious to Rivail that the entities who were communicating were genuine spirits, not the unconscious minds of the young ladies. (Even in those days, the concept of the unconscious was accepted.) In fact, the communicators identified themselves as "spirits of genii," and said that some of them (but not all) had been the spirits of those who had been alive on earth.

With excitement, Rivail realized that this material had an impressive inner-consistency, and that the total pattern revealed a philosophical scheme that embraced the whole universe. Other friends who had been collecting "automatic scripts"—including the playwright Sardou—handed over their own material to Rivail, more than fifty notebooks. Rivail was told to bring all this material together into a book, which should be called *The Spirits' Book*. The spirits even gave Rivail the pseudonym under which he should publish the work: Allan Kardec. Both of these names—according to the spirits—were names he had borne in previous incarnations. When it appeared in 1856, *The Spirits' Book* achieved instant celebrity, and swiftly became a classic of Spiritualism (or Spiritism, as Kardec preferred to call it).

The message of *The Spirits' Book* is easily summarized. Man is a fourfold being, made up of body, "vital principle" (aura), intelligent soul, and spiritual soul—the divisions we have already encountered in *The Seeress of Prevorst* and in Steiner. Spirits are intelligent beings, who constitute the "population of the universe." Man is a spirit enclosed in a physical body. The destiny of all spirits is to evolve toward perfection. There are three basic categories of spirit: the "low spirits," who are trapped in materiality, the "second degree spirits," whose moral nature has evolved to the point where they experience only a desire for good, and the "perfect spirits," who have reached the peak of their evolution. The low spirits range from evil spirits who are activated by malice to mere "boisterous spirits" who enjoy getting into mischief. These latter are also known as poltergeists. After death, a spirit spends some time in the spirit world, and is then reincarnated on earth or some other world. The purpose of earthly life is to enable the spirit to evolve. To some extent, the spirit is able to choose the trials it will undergo in its next life. (This means that it is pointless to bemoan our lot, since we have chosen it ourselves.)

In all but one respect, Kardec's "spirit teaching" agreed basically with those of most other spiritualists since Swedenborg; but that one aspect, reincarnation, was to prove a source of severe contention within the French spiritualist movement. *The Spirits' Book* had already been anticipated by a work called *Arcanes de la vie future dévoilée* or "Secrets of the Future Life Unveiled," by Alphonse Cahagnet, published in 1848 (and a second and third volume later). Cahagnet was a cabinet maker who had become fascinated by "somnambulism" (hypnotism) in his mid-thirties; he placed various subjects in a hypnotic trance, the most impressive being a woman called Adèle Maginot, and recorded what they told him of life after death. Adèle was so remarkable because her messages from the dead—and sometimes from living people who had disappeared—were so full of convincing evidence. Cahagnet started a journal called *The Spiritualist Magnetiser*, and this was later transformed into *The Spiritualist Revue*, edited by Z. Piérart. Cahagnet, who was a follower of Swedenborg, did not believe in reincarnation, and the French spiritualist movement was soon split by a bitter war of words between the followers of Cahagnet and the followers of Kardec. Kardec was critical of trance mediums—like Adèle—because they had nothing to say about reincarnation, and Cahagnet and his followers regarded automatic writing with suspicion and disdain. Kardec, who had heart problems, died in 1869, only thirteen years after *The Spirits' Book* was published, while Cahagnet lived and flourished until 1885, publishing many more influential books. So it was Kardec's version of spiritualism that gradually faded away as the movement became increasingly powerful. It was only in Brazil—a country whose witch doctors frequently called on the spirits for magical aid—that Kardec's version of Spiritism took root, and where it still flourishes today as one of the country's major religions.

It may be as well, at this point, to pause and ask the question: What does it all mean? There is something about spiritualism that is peculiarly irritating. It is one thing to accept that some people, like Rosalind Heywood, possess strange powers of clairvoyance, and quite another to swallow spirit teachings that sound like the ramblings of an uninspired Sunday school teacher. It is not that the doctrines of Swedenborg or Kardec are in themselves unacceptable. The notion that man possesses a vital body, an astral body, and an ego body seems reasonable enough; some may even learn, through self-observation, to distinguish between the promptings of the low self and the detached observations of some higher part of us that looks down ironically on our sufferings and humiliations. But when Kardec tells us that God created spirits, and then set them the task of evolving toward perfection, it sounds boringly abstract. *Why* did God bother to create spirits in the first place? Why did he not create them perfect to begin with? Surely spirits ought to have something better to do than to communicate with their living relatives through mediums and deliver anticlimactic messages about the joys of the afterlife and the trivial problems of the living? If we compare the revelations of spiritualism with those of science or philosophy, or the visions of the great mystics, they seem oddly banal.

This explains why spiritualism aroused such instant hostility among scientists and philosophers. Spiritualism was like a volcanic explosion of belief, the scientists replied with a blast of skepticism that was like cold water. The combination of boiling lava and cold water produced an enormous cloud of steam that obscured everything. It was not that most scientists disbelieved the evidence; they refused even to look at it. T. H. Huxley expressed the general feeling when he remarked: "It may all be true, for anything that I know to the contrary, but really I cannot get up interest in the subject."

Such an attitude can hardly be defended as scientific. For anyone who has an hour to spare, the evidence is seen to be overwhelming. There are hundreds—thousands—of descriptions of out-of-the-body experiences, of poltergeists, of apparitions of the dead, of accurate glimpses of the future. Any reasonable person ought to be prepared to come to terms with these, not to dismiss them with the comment, "I really cannot get up any interest in the subject."

Can we come to terms with them without making any commitment to life-after-death or the existence of spirits? Just about. Consider, for example, the haunting of Willington Mill. One interesting point that emerged was that the male apparition walked across the room several feet above the ground, at the level of the window sill. This suggests that it was walking on a floor that had now been demolished. We know that the millhouse was built on the site of an older house. It looks as if Sir Oliver Lodge's "tape recording" theory can explain this particular ghost. We also observe that the house was at the bottom of a valley, next to a stream, and therefore almost certainly damp. T. C. Lethbridge suggested that ghosts are "recordings" on the electrical field of water, and are found most frequently in damp places.

We may also note the comment of the local historian that although the mill was built around 1800, no haunting was recorded until the disturbances experienced by Mr. Proctor's family—a family of young children. Later in the nineteenth century, investigators of poltergeist phenomena observed that children are usually present, and that one of them often seems to be the "focus" of the disturbance—indeed, we may recall that the Rev. Samuel Wesley noticed that his daughter Hetty trembled in her sleep before "Old Jeffrey" began banging around. Split-brain physiology has taught us that we have two people inside our heads. Perhaps Old Jeffrey was some kind of manifestation of Hetty Wesley's unconscious mind or right brain?

In fact, this plausible theory of psychic phenomena was put forward later in the nineteenth century by a brilliant newspaper editor, Thomson Jay Hudson, in a book called *The Law of Psychic Phenomena* (1893). Hudson was fascinated by hypnotism, and by the unusual powers that people can develop under hypnosis. He became convinced that a human has two "selves," which he called the "objective mind" and the "subjective mind." The objective mind is the part of us that deals with everyday problems—the left brain. The subjective mind is turned *inward;* it controls our inner being, what goes on inside us. Normally, the subjective mind is impressed and overawed by the objective mind, so it hardly dares to express itself. But when the objective mind is put to sleep by a hypnotist, the subjective mind can reveal its hidden powers.

In the late years of the nineteenth century, a hypnotist named Carl Hansen used to go around America, and his favorite trick was to make someone so rigid that he could be placed across two chairs like a plank—his head on one chair and his heels on the other—while the heavy Hansen jumped up and down on his stomach. Such things as these, said Hudson, were the very least of the powers of the subjective mind (or, as we would say, right brain). The subjective mind can perform miracles—in fact, the miracles of Jesus were probably merely the manifestation of his subjective mind. It is the subjective mind, said Hudson, that is responsible for such mysterious phenomena as telepathy and clairvoyance.

He then turns his attention to spiritism. The phenomena, he admits, are undeniable, but they are not produced by the spirits of the dead. What produces the phenomena is "essentially a human intelligence, and neither rises above nor sinks below the ordinary intelligence of humanity." This is why spiritualism is so oddly boring and disappointing—because it is, as Nietzsche would say, "human, all too human . . . we have already seen what remarkable powers the subjective mind possesses in certain lines of intellectual activity, and with what limitations it is hedged about; and we find that the intellectual feats of mediums possess all the characteristics belonging to subjective intelligence—the same wonderful powers and the same limitations."

It is a convincing theory, and surprisingly modern; in all the years since *The Law of Psychic Phenomena* appeared, nothing more plausible or "scientific" has been advanced. But does it really cover all the facts? Hudson's solution to the problem of spirits is that "the subjective mind of the medium, being controlled by suggestion, believes itself to be the spirit of any deceased person whose name is suggested." This fails to explain cases—like Swedenborg's case of the "secret drawer" mentioned in chapter one—where the medium was able to produce information that was only known to the dead person. Also, how did Sir Alexander Ogston, (as mentioned in chapter two), know that the R. A. M. C. surgeon had died in another part of the hospital, unless his mind had, in some sense, left his body and wandered around the hospital? We might explain these cases—and many others like them—by some form of telepathy. Perhaps Ogston's mind picked up the death throes of the surgeon, perhaps Swedenborg contacted the mind of the carpenter who made the desk with the secret drawer. But the explanations are becoming absurdly complicated, and they violate the principle known in philosophy as Occam's razor, which states that, in trying to solve a problem, it is best to look for the simplest and most economical explanation. It seems, on the whole, more straightforward to accept the possibility of life after death—or the spirit's independence of the body—as a working hypothesis.

The other major objection to spiritualism—that it somehow "reduces" the spiritual to the material—was expressed by Dean Inge when he wrote: "The moment we are asked to accept scientific evidence for spiritual truth, the alleged spiritual truth becomes neither spiritual nor true. It is degraded into an event in the phenomenal world."[5] Oddly enough, Rudolf Steiner agreed with him, remarking: "The spiritualists are the greatest materialists of all." This sounds baffling, in view of the fact that Steiner not only accepted the reality of life after death, but of reincarnation as well.

The explanation is important, and accounts for the general feeling of hostility that is so often aroused by Spiritualism. One of Steiner's basic doctrines was that "the supersensible world appears to us in

---

5. *Outspoken Essays*, Vol. 1, p. 269, quoted by David Lorimer in *Survival?*, p. 160.

such a way that it resembles our perceptions of the sense world."[6] So that he says of Swedenborg:

> *He was a man who, in the time of dawning natural science, had become accustomed only to recognize the sensible, the visible. . . . Since he insisted on recognizing as true only what he could calculate and perceive with his senses . . . he drew down the supersensible world into a lower sphere under the influence of his habits of natural science.*[7]

What Steiner is saying here is something that soon dawns on most readers of accounts of near-death experiences. Some find themselves walking toward a celestial city, some find themselves in flowery meadows, some find themselves drawn toward a heavenly gateway or a whirlpool of light. It looks as if everyone is interpreting the experience in terms of their own familiar concepts. Steiner is suggesting that visionaries like Swedenborg, who have caught a glimpse of the "supersensible world," are bound to interpret it according to their ingrained mental habits, and that this explains why the revelations of spiritualism often seem slightly ludicrous.

Oddly enough, Steiner thoroughly approved of Kardec, who obtained the material for his books from automatic writing. This clearly suggests that what Steiner disliked so much about Spiritualism was its literal-mindedness—the trumpets and accordions floating through the air, the tables dancing around the room, the spirits made of ectoplasm. His attitude should be compared to that of a Christian mystic who wishes to explain that heaven is *not* full of angels sitting around on clouds and playing harps.

At the same time, there is bound to be an element of unfairness in such an attitude. Many mediums who started off by producing automatic writing later became "voice mediums" and some even "materialization mediums." It is impossible to draw a sharp line between

---

6. "The History of Spiritis," lecture delivered in Berlin, May 30, 1904.

7. Ibid.

them. Steiner is not really criticizing Spiritualism; he is criticizing spiritualists. Once we have grasped this, one of the major problems disappears—or at least, is revealed as a misunderstanding.

It was a misunderstanding that caused a great deal of trouble and bitterness in the early days of Spiritualism. It was useless for investigators like Catherine Crowe and Allan Kardec to demand a fair hearing for the supernatural; scientists and intellectuals felt they were being asked to swallow a farrago of childish nonsense. They pointed angrily at the Spiritualist churches that were springing up all over America, and asked how anybody could be serious about a religion started by two silly girls. Their skepticism seemed to be justified in April 1851, when a relative of the Fox family, Mrs. Norman Culver, announced in the *New York Herald* that Kate and Margaretta Fox had shown her how they made the rapping noises with their knees and toes. This may or may not have been true. The girls, and their mother, had become celebrities, and spent a great deal of time travelling around the East coast giving demonstrations. Fate had promoted them from the boredom of small-town life in upper New York State to the equivalent of stardom. If the spirits were occasionally uncooperative, it would have been surprising if they had not been tempted to do a little cheating. What seems perfectly clear is that the original phenomena—bangs that were strong enough to make the house vibrate—could not have been caused by cracking the joints of the knees. Neither could Kate and Margaretta have answered all the questions about the people in the room. The accusations of fraud were just one more excuse for refusing to look dispassionately at the evidence.

The real tragedy in all this was that the cloud of polemical steam obscured a great deal of serious research into the paranormal. In the 1840s, a German scientist named Baron Karl von Reichenbach had rediscovered Mesmer's recognition that human beings can be affected by magnets. Reichenbach found that sick people seemed to be more sensitive to magnetism than healthy ones, and his "sick sensitives" could see different colors streaming out of the two poles of the magnet—red from the south pole, blue from the north. They could detect the same emanations in crystals. Most importantly, they could see it streaming from the finger-ends of human beings. Reichenbach called it "odyle" or "the odic force," and the announcement of his discovery caused widespread excitement when he first made it in 1845. What Reichenbach had really discovered was the human "life field," investigated in the 1930s by Harold Burr and F. S. C. Northrop. But by 1850, the rise of spiritualism made scientists feel that any kind of "unseen force" was suspect; Reichenbach suddenly found himself as discredited and ridiculed as Mesmer.

Joseph Rodes Buchanan was a professor of medicine in Kentucky, who was intrigued when a bishop told him he could detect brass when he touched it—even in the dark—because it produced a bitter taste in his mouth. Buchanan tested his students with various chemicals wrapped in brown paper packages, and found that many of them could distinguish them by touch. He concluded that we have a "nerve aura" streaming from the ends of our fingers, and that this can "taste" things, just like the tongue. Then he discovered that some of his best subjects could hold an unopened letter in their hands, and "sense" the mood of the writer—in fact, some of them could describe the writer with remarkable accuracy.

Now all this fits in perfectly with Sir Oliver Lodge's tape recording theory about ghosts—that strong emotions can "imprint" themselves on their surroundings, and that this "recording" can be detected by people who are sensitive to such things. Buchanan's subjects were virtually human bloodhounds. Buchanan called this strange faculty "psychometry," and his book about it aroused widespread interest in 1848. It caused a professor of geology named William Denton to try similar experiments on his students, using geological specimens. The results were astounding.[8] Lumps of volcanic lava

---

8. For accounts of Reichenbach, Buchanan, and Denton, see my book *The Psychic Detectives: The Story of Psychometry* (1984).

brought visions of exploding mountains, mastodons' teeth, visions of primeval forests, and meteorites visions of the depths of space. Denton believed that he had discovered a "telescope into the past," an unknown faculty through which man can travel backwards in time. Regrettably, no one paid much attention to Denton's book *The Soul of Things*, nor to Buchanan's *Manual of Psychometry*. Such things sounded too much like Spiritualism, and any scientist who took them seriously would have condemned himself to ridicule.

To some extent, spiritualists were themselves to blame for all this hostility. They were too gullible, too prone to accept any banal nonsense as a message from "the other side." Hundreds of fake mediums took advantage of their credulity to practice barefaced impositions, and whenever one of them was caught in the act, scientists shook their heads wearily and made comparisons with the medieval witchcraft phenomenon. Most of them had become too blasé even to say "I told you so." Genuine mediums like the Davenport brothers did themselves no good by appearing in theaters and performing hair-raising feats of escape that would have done credit to Houdini. They allowed themselves to be tied so tight that the ropes cut into their flesh and caused bruises, but after a brief period in a cabinet, they would step out with the ropes around their feet. Professor Benjamin Pierce, a member of an investigating committee, sat between them in the cabinet. As soon as the door was closed, a hand shot the bolt—both brothers were trussed up like mummies—and briefly felt the professor's face before going on to untie the brothers. Professor Loomis of the Georgetown Medical College admitted that the manifestations were produced by a force with which he was unacquainted. But this kind of testimony meant nothing compared to the fact that the brothers appeared on the same bill with conjurors and acrobats.

All this explains why so little was achieved by the most remarkable medium of the nineteenth century—perhaps of all time—Daniel Dunglas Home. Home retained his powers for more than a quarter of a century, with the exception of a period of one year when, as we shall see, the spirits decided to punish him. He performed his astonishing feats in broad daylight. He caused heavy articles of furniture to float up to the ceiling; he himself floated out of one window and into another. He washed his face in blazing coals. He could make himself several inches taller at will. He was tested dozens of times by committees of skeptics, and was never once caught in anything that looked like fraud. Yet posterity remembers him chiefly as the man Dickens called "that scoundrel Home," and about whom Robert Browning wrote a scurrilous poem called "Mr. Sludge the Medium."

A typical Home séance is amusingly described by his biographer Jean Burton. It took place on an evening in January 1863, in the fashionable home of Madame Jauvin d'Attainville, and the guests included Princess Metternich and her husband, the Austrian ambassador. The guests—fifteen in all—sat at the table in the magnificent Second Empire drawing room, while Home sat in an armchair three or four yards away. When everyone was ready, he sat back in his chair, became paler, and went into a light trance. He asked, "Bryan, are you there?" (Bryan was his spirit guide.) Sharp raps came from the table, the chandeliers began to swing, and a chair moved of its own accord across the room and stopped in front of the guests. At the same moment, Princess Metternich screamed, as she felt a powerful but invisible hand grip hers. Others also felt hands lightly touching them. (All this was in a room "blazing with light.") The tapestry tablecloth now rose into the air, and underneath it, something seemed to be moving, like a hand or a small animal, toward them. This was too much for the men, most of whom were skeptics; Prince Metternich dived under the cloth and tried to grab the "creature"; there was nothing. One of the men pulled the cloth away, while others dived under the table to find the source of the raps; again, they were disappointed. As they scrambled out again, a hailstorm of raps sounded, as if in derision. The angry Prince Metternich was now convinced that they were coming from under the table, and scrambled underneath again. Raps sounded, and Metternich yelled indignantly: "No jokes, please!" The company assured him that they were not responsible.

Apparently in a trance, Home pointed to a corsage of violets on the piano and asked that it should be brought over to them. The violets glided across the piano, floated unsteadily across the room, and fell into the princess' lap. Prince Metternich bounded forward and grabbed them, then proceeded to search for the thread that he was convinced must be attached; he found nothing.

In a faint voice, Home now demanded an accordion, a popular instrument of the period. When it came, the princess was asked to stand alone in the middle of the room with the instrument held high above her head. As she stood there, her arm in the air, an expression of astonishment crossed her face. There was a tug on the accordion, and it proceeded to play, moving in and out. What impressed everyone was that it was a fine performance, the playing so soft and melodious that it brought tears to the eyes of some of the audience. After that, anything would have been an anticlimax, so the séance finished. But, typically, the men began to speculate how it had been done; no one seemed to doubt that it had been some form of conjuring trick; others spoke of electro-biology and mass hypnosis. The princess had to admit that she had no sensation of being hypnotized.

Daniel Dunglas Home (he pronounced it "Hume") was born near Edinburgh in March 1833—his mother was a Highlander and had a reputation as a seer. He was probably illegitimate—he liked to claim that his father was Lord Home. At the age of nine, he moved to America with an aunt, Mary Cook, and her husband. His mother and "father," and seven brothers and sisters, were already there. Daniel suffered from tuberculosis, and was subject to fainting fits—a typical "sick sensitive." His closest friend was a boy called Edwin, and they went for long walks in the woods of Connecticut. They made a boyish pact—that whoever died first would show himself to the other. In 1846, when Daniel was thirteen, he told his aunt and uncle that he had just seen Edwin standing at the foot of his bed, and that the figure had made three circles in the air with his hand—which Daniel took to mean that he had died three days ago. It proved to be true.

There were no more supernatural experiences for another four years. Then Home saw a vision of his mother, and knew she was dead. Soon after that, he was brushing his hair when he saw, in the glass, a chair moving across the room toward him. He was terrified and rushed out of the house. In bed, he was awakened by three loud bangs on the headboard. The next morning at breakfast, when his aunt was mildly teasing him about tiring himself out by attending too many prayer meetings (Home was a religious young man), raps sounded from all over the table, and his alarmed aunt cried: "So you've brought the devil into my house, have you?" and threw a chair at him. The Baptist minister was called in to pray the devil away but had difficulty in making himself heard above the hail of knocks. Unaware that poltergeist phenomena were usually harmless, his aunt requested him to leave her house. So, at the age of seventeen, Home had to fend for himself.

Home had such charm and gaiety that there were dozens of acquaintances who were delighted to offer him hospitality. The spirits gave him their full support. He went easily into trance, and in that state talked fluently in French and Italian—neither a language in which he had become proficient. He could not have chosen a better time to launch himself on the world, with everyone in the United States talking about spirits. An evangelist named Dr. George Bush—a professor of Asian languages—persuaded him that he ought to become a Swedenborgian and use his considerable preaching talent in the pulpit. Home agreed, then came back two days later to say that his dead mother had expressly forbidden it, telling him that he had a "more extended" mission.

Looked after by the spirits and by kindly acquaintances, Home wandered through New England, always a welcome guest in the homes of the well-off middle classes; his pale good looks brought out the protectiveness in middle-aged ladies. In Springfield, Mass., he stayed at the home of a wealthy citizen named Rufus Elmers, and agreed to be investigated by a delegation from Harvard, including the poet William Cullen Bryant. They, like many other "delegations" after them, had no doubt about the genuineness of the phenomena. The table not only rapped and floated off the floor, but stood on two legs like a circus horse while three members of the committee sat on it and tried to force it down again. The floor vibrated to shocks that were as powerful as cannon fire. All this took place in broad daylight, and members of the committee held Home's hands and feet while most of the phenomena were taking place. Their report, entitled "The Modern Wonder," concluded: *"We know that we were not imposed upon nor deceived."* Rufus Elmers was so impressed that he offered to adopt Home and make him his heir. Home declined with thanks.

In August 1852, sitting in a circle, Home floated up to the ceiling—a feat that became virtually his trademark. His other phenomena continued to be almost as astonishing. Grand pianos would float across the room, bells would ring, cymbals clash, and there would be sounds of bird songs and assorted animal noises. One day, a table with a candle on it tilted at an angle, and the candle flame went on burning at the same angle, as if it was still resting on a horizontal surface. On another occasion, at the home of the Rev. S. B. Brittan, he went into a trance, and a voice announced: "Hannah Brittan here." Home began to wring his hands, and for the next half hour, talked in a wild, distracted way about the torments of hell. The Rev. Brittan was staggered, for he was certain that no one knew that the lady—a relative—had fallen prey to religious mania, and had died insane, obsessed by visions of eternal punishment. (On a subsequent appearance, Hannah Brittan told them that her present life was calm, peaceful, and beautiful, and that the torments of hell had been a delusion of her distracted brain.)

Most women adored Home, who was attentive and thoughtful—he loved sending flowers on anniversaries. Men either liked him or loathed him. He had effeminate manners, and many suspected he was homosexual. (For some odd reason, a surprising number of mediums are.) He was undoubtedly rather vain about his good looks and silky, auburn hair. He loved expensive clothes, and was an outrageous snob, who took pleasure in being inaccessible. (He would only condescend to know people if introduced by a mutual acquaintance.) He would be mortally offended if anyone offered him money, and he resented being treated as a "performer." As far as he was concerned, he was the social equal of anyone he met, including kings. Yet he was becomingly modest about his achievement, insisting that he himself had nothing whatsoever to do with the phenomena. All he had to do was to relax and put himself in the right mood (and "right" is probably the operative word here) and things simply happened.

By 1855, Home's consumptive cough had become so bad that his admirers decided he ought to move to a healthier climate. For some unaccountable reason, he chose England. Admirers paid his passage, and with a crowd waving frantically, he sailed from Boston in March; he was just twenty-two.

As usual, the spirits were looking after Home. In London, he moved into Cox's Hotel on Jermyn Street. The owner, William Cox, was a Spiritualist, and welcomed Home "as a father would a son." So Home got free lodging and an introduction to the London society who made regular use of the hotel. In no time at all he was calling on marchionesses and baronesses. He went to visit the novelist Lord Lytton, who made literary use of many of Home's séance phenomena—a luminous form that dissolved into a globe, a disembodied hand, loud bangs, fiery sparks—in his famous story "The Haunted and the Haunters." Lytton declined to believe spirits were responsible; he thought the phenomena were due to Home's unconscious mind. He became a friend of the socialist Robert Owen, who was a convert to spiritualism, and who introduced him to his old friend Lord Henry Brougham, a Voltairean skeptic. Brougham and Sir David Brewster had a private session with Home at which the table rose into the air and a bell floated across the room. Brewster described these things in his diary and told them to friends, but later insisted that the table had only "appeared" to rise, and that Home had probably moved the bell with some hidden apparatus. The resulting controversy brought Home much publicity, and provided the spiritualists with some excellent ammunition to use against scientific dogmatism, since Brewster's diaries justify Home.

Elizabeth Barrett Browning called on Home, together with her husband Robert. Ghostly hands materialized, music sounded from the air, the table rapped loudly and invisible spirits caressed them. Elizabeth Browning was totally convinced; her husband—vigorous, sturdy, and just over five feet tall—sat there scowling, and resolutely declined to accept the evidence of his eyes. Home became an unmentionable subject in the Browning household, and after his wife's death, Browning wrote the flagrantly unfair "Mr. Sludge the Medium." He may have been prejudiced by an episode that took place at another Home séance, when a detached hand took up a garland of flowers and placed them on the poetess' brow; Browning was jealous of his wife. Home made things worse by telling people that Browning had tried to place himself in the trajectory of the wreath so it would alight on his brow.

By popular request of the English community, Home moved on to Florence. There the manifestations were stronger than ever. A grand piano floated up into the air and remained there while a countess played on it; a spirit conversed with a Polish princess in her own language; in a haunted convent, Home conversed with the spirit of a monk—also a murderer—and caused his skinny, yellow hands to materialize. When the novelist Nathaniel Hawthorne came to Florence three years later, people were still talking about Home, and Hawthorne collected dozens of well-attested accounts of the phenomena. Hawthorne made the interesting and significant observation:

> *These soberly attested incredibilities are so numerous that I forget nine tenths of them . . . they are absolutely proved to be sober facts by evidence that would satisfy us of any other alleged realities; and yet I cannot force my mind to interest itself in them.*

This is perhaps one of the most important comments ever made about Home or about spiritualism in general.

Unfortunately, Home's success began to go to his head. He was not a particularly strong character, and being treated as a messenger from the gods would have been enough to unbalance a far more independent nature. When he went to stay at the villa of a titled Englishwoman who was separated from her husband, former admirers were scandalized—English self-control produces a morbid fascination with sexual scandal and he began to sense a new atmosphere of hostility. He was attacked on his way back to his hotel and slightly wounded—a sign that the spirits were becoming inefficient or lazy—and on February 10, 1856, the spirits told him that his recent conduct was not worthy of a representative of the other world, and that his powers were about to leave him for a year. A Polish count had invited him to Naples and Rome. Home felt obliged to admit to him that his powers had deserted him, but his luck held; the count insisted that it made no difference, and Home accompanied him to Naples. In spite of the loss of his powers, he remained a social lion. They came back, as the spirits had prophesied, exactly one year to the day, on the stroke of midnight.

By now Home was in Paris, and had taken the precaution of insuring himself against the disapproval of the Church by becoming a Catholic. His father confessor—recommended by the Pope himself—was less than enthusiastic about the return of the spirits, whom he assumed to be demons—but there was little he could do about it. Neither would Home have wished it, for he was by now a favorite of the Emperor Napoleon III and the Empress Eugenie. His luck aroused widespread envy and hostility, but after the year of desertion by the spirits, he no longer allowed it to go to his head.

After a tour of northern Europe, he returned to Rome, where he met and wooed a beautiful seventeen-year-old Russian countess named Sacha; they went to St. Petersburg (together with the novelist Dumas) and her relatives organized a spectacular wedding. Home was received by the Russian royal family as cordially as by Napoleon III. Unfortunately, Sacha caught his tuberculosis, and died not long after the birth of a son. At least her death was not a separation; Home was able to keep in constant touch with her.

In 1862 his luck again seemed to desert him. The police ordered him to leave Rome, declaring that he was a sorcerer (the spirits made things worse by rapping on the desk of the police chief). For the next four years he again became a wanderer. In 1866, he met an effusive and vulgar old lady with a working-class accent, Mrs. Jane Lyon, who told him she wanted to adopt him as her son, and presented him with numerous large checks. Home changed his name to Home-Lyon, but the two were far from soul mates, and the relationship soon began to deteriorate badly—he found her boringly affectionate and she found him cold. He had a breakdown, and fled to various watering places to take a cure. When he returned to London, he found that Mrs. Lyon had transferred her allegiance to a female medium, and was brooding on how to recover her money. She wanted back about thirty thousand pounds—only about half of what she had given him. She accused him of extortion, and Home was arrested. At the trial in April 1868, she alleged that she had given him the money because he had brought her instructions to that effect from her dead husband. Home's case was that she had tried hard to seduce him after he became her "son." Mrs. Lyon was undoubtedly—as Home declared—vengeful and untruthful, and many of her lies were exposed in court. But a "spirit medium" stood no chance of getting an unprejudiced trial. The judge remarked that if everyone who gave money to a religious charity was allowed to ask for it back, the result would be chaos; however, since Spiritualism was a fraud and a cheat, he would make exception in the present case. Home was ordered to repay the money. The trial did Home immense damage, strengthening the impression already created by Browning's "Mr. Sludge" that he was a confidence trickster. The notoriety had one advantage: a reading tour of England drew enormous audiences and helped to recoup his loss.

During his "water cure" in Malvern, Home had met a young aristocrat, Lord Adare, and during the next year or two he spent much time with him. In 1870, Adare published *Experiences in Spiritualism with Mr. D. D. Home*, perhaps one of the most extraordinary and impressive books about a medium ever written. Adare was an ordinary young Englishman, more interested in hunting, shooting, and fishing than ghosts. It was Adare who saw Home float out of one upper-story window and into another. He also saw the materialization of various spirits—including Sacha and the American actress

Ada Mencken and all the other phenomena that Home had been producing for the past twenty years. He saw Home stir up the fire until the coals were blazing, then pick them up in handfuls and rub his face in them—neither his face nor his hair was burnt. He also witnessed Home standing against a wall, where his height was carefully taken (five feet ten inches), and elongate himself to six feet four.

In 1871, Home agreed to be investigated by the young scientist William (later Sir William) Crookes. The antispiritualists smiled with satisfaction; they had no doubt whatsoever that Crookes would finally demolish the conjuror's reputation. In the event, Crookes was totally convinced, and published a report to that effect—to the disgust of his fellow scientists, who decided that he had been duped. In the controversy that followed, Crookes exploded indignantly: "I didn't say it was possible—I said it was true."

In the following year, 1872, Home decided it was time to retire. A lawsuit about his wife's estate was decided in his favor, so he was a Russian landowner. He lived on for another fourteen years, to the age of fifty-three, spending his time between Russia and the French Riviera. He was wasting away from consumption; but with a beautiful second wife, a comfortable income, and hosts of admiring friends, his final years were far from unhappy.

The article on Home in *Encyclopedia Britannica* calls Home an "unsolved enigma." This is true, but not quite in the sense the writer intended. As far as Home was concerned, there was no enigma. He had simply inherited unusual psychic powers from his mother's side of the family (and he passed these on to his son Grisha), so the spirits were able to operate through him.

As we have seen, this answer failed to satisfy many people who witnessed his feats and accepted their genuineness. Lord Lytton thought that Home somehow caused the phenomena himself. Most modern researchers would probably agree with him, since most of them are unwilling to accept the spirit hypothesis. Yet one thing that becomes very clear to anyone who reads the accounts of Home's phenomena—as recorded by Lord Adare or Sir William Crookes—is that the spirits are not only the simplest explanation, but in many cases, the only explanation. A large percentage of the phenomena can only be explained if we assume the existence of disembodied intelligences. At this point, it is necessary to acknowledge that, sooner or later, most investigators of the paranormal are finally driven to the conclusion that spirits almost certainly exist. They do this with the utmost reluctance. It would be far more convenient, and far more logically satisfying, if we could explain all the phenomena in terms of the unrecognized powers of the human mind. Total honesty forces the admission that this is impossible, and this is nowhere more obvious than in the case of Daniel Dunglas Home.

Chapter Four

Psychical Research Comes of Age

LOOKING BACK OVER THE HISTORY OF SPIRITUALism, it certainly looks as if the spirits made a tremendous and concerted effort to convince the Victorians of their reality. If that is the case, it seems equally clear that they made a miscalculation. The leaders of Victorian public opinion—politicians, intellectuals, church officials—remained indifferent. Most scientists were intensely hostile. In the decade after the "Hydesville rappings," they made a determined attempt to destroy spiritualism by ridicule.

They were hardly to blame. If they had behaved in any other way, they would not have been Victorians. It was their very best qualities—their sense of excitement about the future, about the tremendous scientific and technical advances, and the possibilities of humanitarian social reforms—that made them turn their backs on the supernatural. T. H. Huxley expressed this spirit in a burst of magnificent exasperation when someone tried to persuade him to attend a séance: "If anybody could endow me with the faculty of listening to the chatter of old women and curates in the nearest cathedral town, I should decline the privilege, having better things to do."

When the less waspish investigators could be persuaded to listen to the "chatter of old women and curates," they often found it unexpectedly interesting. When he started his career as a schoolmaster, Alfred Russel Wallace was a skeptic and a disciple of Voltaire; but when he went to listen to a lecture on mesmerism, he was sufficiently intrigued to try it out on his students. One boy proved to be an unusually good subject. When placed in a trance, he seemed to "tune in" to Wallace's mind. When Wallace pricked himself with a pin, the boy cried out and put his hand on the same part of his own body. When Wallace sucked a lump of sugar, the boy also went through sucking motions. Fifteen years later, Wallace became famous as the man who had, together with Charles Darwin, discovered evolution by natural selection—and who, moreover, had allowed Darwin to take priority. In 1865, Wallace attended a séance at the house of a skeptical friend, and witnessed a heavy table moving and vibrating—in broad daylight—while raps resounded from around the room. That convinced him. A year later, he met an enormous young lady named Agnes Nichols, and watched with incredulity as the elephantine girl floated up into the air. Agnes could also produce "apports"—objects that fell from the air—and when Wallace asked if the spirits could produce a sunflower, a six-foot sunflower with a clod of earth around its roots fell on to the table. Agnes' spirits never did things by halves; on another occasion when someone requested flowers, what looked like the whole contents of a flower shop cascaded from the air. Their most spectacular feat occurred in 1871, when Agnes herself, now married to a man called Guppy, became the apport. She was seated at the dining-room table doing her accounts when she vanished as if the ground had swallowed her. Four miles away, some ardent spiritualists were seated at a table with their eyes closed, begging the spirits to vouchsafe some small manifestation. There was an almighty crash that caused screams, and when someone struck a match, the mountainous Mrs. Guppy was found lying on the table, still clutching her account book. Again, the spirits had miscalculated. The story of Mrs. Guppy floating four miles certainly caused widespread hilarity, but it didn't bring thousands flocking to the Spiritualist churches.

Wallace had no doubt that Mrs. Guppy could convince the skeptics, so he invited three of the most hostile—Professor W. B. Carpenter, Professor John Tyndall, and G. H. Lewes, the husband of novelist George Eliot. Carpenter came, sat silently through a cannonade of raps, then went away without comment; he never came back. Neither did Tyndall, whose only comment was "show us something else." Lewes simply refused to come, as did T. H. Huxley—this was the occasion when Huxley remarked that he simply could not "get up an interest in the subject."

Yet in spite of the refusal of scientists to believe their own eyes and ears, psychic phenomena remained a thorn in the flesh of Victorian intellectuals. After all, it was the business of science to explain mysteries, not ignore them. Some scientists, such as William Crookes, discoverer of the element thallium, developed a bad conscience about it, and decided to conduct their own investigations. When Crookes saw a concertina in a cage playing music of its own accord, while Daniel Dunglas Home held it up by one handle, he knew that he was dealing with unknown forces. His "credulity" caused much headshaking among his colleagues. Later, when he decided that a young lady called Florence Cook—whose guide, Katie King, materialized and walked around the room—was genuine, some of them whispered that Florence had become Crookes' mistress as the price of his cooperation.

The mathematician Charles Dodgson—who wrote *Alice in Wonderland*—was another who felt that the phenomena ought to be explained, not dismissed. He wrote to a friend in 1882:

> *That trickery will* not *do as a complete explanation of all the phenomena . . . I am more than convinced. At the same time, I see no need as yet for believing that disembodied spirits have anything to do with it. . . . All seems to point to the existence of a natural force, allied to electricity and nerve force by which brain can act on brain. I think we are close to the day when this shall be classified among the known natural forces. . . .*

That was the ideal aim: to track down this unknown force and stick a label on it. This was the truly Victorian way of banishing this revival of witchcraft. The only problem was that the spirits often converted the skeptics who were trying to disprove their existence. There was, for example, the embarrassing case of the American Congressman Robert Dale Owen, son of the great social reformer Robert Owen. The latter had been a lifelong freethinker—until he encountered the American medium Mrs. Hayden. Then, at the age of eighty-three, he declared himself a Spiritualist. His son, another freethinker and social reformer, was furious, and decided that the old man was senile. He was, at the time, American *chargé d'affaires* in Naples. In 1856, the Brazilian ambassador persuaded him to attend a séance in his apartment, and there Owen saw the table moving without human agency. It was, he decided, merely an "electropsychological phenomenon," but he wanted to know how it worked, so he spent the next two years reading books on mesmerism and animal magnetism, and attending séances. He met Home, who had lost his powers at the time, but the stories of Home's powers made him feel that he should at least consider the possibility that spirits were responsible for the phenomena. As a result, he became convinced, and wrote a book called *Footfalls on the Boundary of Another World* that achieved the same popularity as Catherine Crowe's *Night Side of Nature*. *Footfalls* deserved its popularity; it was an exhaustive, carefully argued book, full of the latest discoveries in modern science, and of some highly convincing cases of clairvoyance, precognitions, poltergeists, and "phantasms of the living." But it is doubtful that it convinced a single scientist.

What finally turned the tide in favor of spiritualism was not scientific evidence, but the deep Victorian craving for religious certainty. Nowadays the chief affliction of the intellectuals is *angst*, a kind of free-floating anxiety. In the Victorian age, it was "Doubt" with a capital "D." One of the great Victorian bestsellers was a novel called *Robert Ellesmere* by Mrs. Humphry Ward, about a clergyman who experiences Doubts and feels obliged to resign his living. We find the idea slightly comic—Evelyn Waugh poked fun at it in *Decline and Fall*—but that is because we take doubt for granted. We can scarcely imagine what it was like to be born into the blissful certainty of a respectable Victorian household—certainty about salvation, about the inspiration of the Bible, about the truth of the Thirty-Nine Articles. Victorian children were brought up to believe that Adam was created in precisely 4004 B.C., and that any kind of doubt on religious matters was as disgraceful as being a drunkard or a prostitute. So when Sir Charles Lyell's *Principles of Geology* (1830) argued that the earth was millions of years old, Victorians felt as shocked as if an active volcano had appeared in Trafalgar Square. It was from that point that they began to be undermined by Doubts.

One of these unhappy questioners was Professor Henry Sidgwick, of Trinity College, Cambridge. Doubt tormented him like a nagging tooth all his life. In 1869, at the age of thirty-one, he even felt obliged to resign his fellowship at Trinity because he could no longer subscribe to the Thirty-Nine Articles of the Church of England. His fellow dons sympathized, and the moment the religious tests were dropped, reappointed him. He went on to write a celebrated book on ethics that ended with the statement that all man's attempts to find a rational basis for human behavior are doomed to failure.

Sidgwick's pupils regarded him as a kind of Socrates. There were many brilliant young men among them, including Arthur Balfour, a future prime minister, Edmund Gurney, heir to a Quaker fortune, and Frederic Myers, the son of a clergyman. Myers, another Fellow of Trinity, also felt obliged to resign because of Doubts.

One evening in December 1869, Myers paid his old master a visit, and they went for a walk under the stars. It was the year in which Sidgwick had resigned his fellowship, and inevitably, the subject of religion came up. Although neither of them could still call themselves Christians, neither of them could accept that the universe is a great machine and that human beings have been created by pure chance. It was Myers who asked, with a certain desperation, whether, since philosophy had failed to solve the riddle of the universe, there might be just a chance that the answer lay in the evidence for ghosts and spirits. Neither of them felt much optimism, but Sidgwick went on brooding about the idea—particularly when, in the following year, Crookes announced that he intended to investigate Daniel Dunglas Home. The attacks on Crookes outraged their sense of fair play, and in 1873, they formed a loose association for the investigation of spiritualism and the paranormal. Myers became a school inspector, which left him time to attend séances. At first he found it discouraging work; he began to wonder whether there was something about him that made the spirits stay away. Then he had an experience that convinced him. He attended a séance with a medium named Charles Williams—at one of whose séances Mrs. Guppy had landed on the table—and a hand materialized in the air. Myers held it in his own, and felt it grow smaller and smaller until it faded away, leaving nothing behind. That could not be trickery. Myers now began seeking actively for more evidence. Together with Edmund Gurney, Arthur Balfour, Sidgwick, and Lord Rayleigh—the scientist who discovered the element argon—Myers became a dedicated psychical researcher. They were joined by a remarkable clergyman, Stainton Moses, who was also an automatic writing medium. His obvious genuineness reinforced Myers' conviction.

A new impetus came from an Irish professor of physics, William Barrett, who taught at the Royal College of Science in Dublin. Like Alfred Russel Wallace, Barrett had become interested in mesmerism, and when he was staying with a friend in County Westmeath, he persuaded some of the village children to subject themselves to hypnosis. Two proved to be excellent subjects. With one of them, Barrett observed what Wallace had experienced with his schoolboy two decades earlier, "community of sensation." When his friend placed his own hand over a lighted lamp, the girl snatched hers away as if afraid of burning. When he tasted sugar, she smiled; when he tasted salt, she frowned. She also proved to be able to read Barrett's mind. The skeptical Professor Carpenter had explained such phenomena by saying that people under hypnosis become abnormally sensitive, so they can recognize almost undetectable sounds or smells. But that would not explain how this girl could hold against her head a book containing a playing card, and describe the card exactly.

Barrett wrote a paper about the case, and sent it to the British Association in London. It would probably have been ignored, but it happened that Wallace was chairman of the committee that decided which papers to publish. He threw his weight behind Barrett, and although the committee eventually overruled him, Wallace made sure that Myers saw the paper.

By this time, Barrett had found another case that excited him—the family of a clergyman called Creery, who lived at Buxton in Derbyshire. Creery's daughters were unusually good at playing a favorite party trick called the "willing game," in which a person went out of the room while the others decided what he ought to do; when that person came back, everyone had to try to "will" him or her to do it. In Barrett's presence, Creery's four daughters demonstrated the willing game again and again, with hardly a single failure.

Barrett met Myers and his fellow psychical investigators in London, and suggested that they ought to form a society for investigating these mysteries. Myers and Gurney were dubious; they felt they were already doing their best. Barrett's enthusiasm prevailed, and the result was the formation of the Society for Psychical Research (SPR), which met for the first time in February 1882. Its original members were the "Cambridge group"—Myers, Gurney, Sidgwick and his wife Eleanor, Balfour, Barrett, Rayleigh, and Wallace. Soon they were joined by distinguished Victorians such as Tennyson, Gladstone, J. J.

Thomson (discoverer of the electron), Mark Twain, William James, Lewis Carroll (Charles Dodgson), John Ruskin, Sir Oliver Lodge, and the painters Frederick Leighton and G. F. Watts.

The Society had no objection whatsoever to skeptics, for its aim was to bring the methods of science to bear on the "psychic world," and try to prove or disprove it once and for all. One result was that Myers and Gurney accepted with pleasure the services of a skeptical post office employee named Frank Podmore, whose original faith in spiritualism had been badly shaken in 1876 by the trial and subsequent flight of a "slatewriting" medium named Henry Slade.[1] The three-way collaboration produced the classic *Phantasms of the Living* (1886), which took four years to compile. The Society also produced a vast Census of Hallucinations, which showed that one person in every ten had experienced some kind of hallucination.

Now, at last, it should have been possible for the spirits to win over the great majority of the British public. We have seen that mediums like Home, Mrs. Hayden, and Mrs. Guppy had no problem convincing scientists once they were given a fair chance. In fact, the Society did some very impressive work, establishing the reality of apparitions, telepathy, clairvoyance, and out-of-the-body experiences beyond all reasonable doubt. This early work culminated in Myers' masterpiece, *Human Personality and Its Survival of Bodily Death*, which will be examined more fully in the next chapter.

Astonishingly, all this did little or nothing to influence public opinion. The vast audience that had bought *The Night Side of Nature* and *Footfalls on the Boundary of Another World* could not be bothered to read huge works full of signed statements and detailed examinations of the evidence. Skeptics such as T. H. Huxley and Sir Ray

---

1. The antispiritualist Sir Ray Lankester had managed to grab the slate before the spirits had had a chance to get to work, and found a message already on it. In spite of strong evidence in his favor, Slade was found guilty on the curious grounds that writing by spirits was a violation of the laws of nature, so he *had* to be a fraud.

Lankester felt there would be no point in reading them anyway, since anyone who could believe in such nonsense must be a gullible idiot.

Regrettably, there was another factor that prevented the public taking the SPR seriously. In its first two decades, a whole series of "exposures" provided the skeptics with all the ammunition they could wish for. The result was that, by about 1902, the Society had become a kind of joke, rather like the Flat Earth Society.

One of the most damaging of the exposures had taken place in 1880, two years before the Society was formed. The medium Florence Cook, with whom William Crookes had worked, was caught cheating by Sir George Sitwell—father of Edith, Osbert, and Sacheverell. Florence was a "materialization medium." She sat in a cabinet with drawn curtains in a dimly lit room, and after a few minutes, a figure in white would emerge from the cabinet and talk to people in the audience. The "spirit" called herself "Marie," and claimed that she "materialized" herself with substances taken from the medium's body. As she passed by Sitwell's chair, he grabbed her and held her tight until someone produced a light. Then it was found that Marie was Florence Cook in her corset and petticoat; Florence's other clothes were found in the cabinet.

That looked conclusive, although spiritualists accepted Florence's explanation—that she was in a trance at the time and had no knowledge of what had happened. Sir William Crookes immediately came to her defense. He pointed out that in 1873, a man called Volckman had suddenly grabbed the "spirit" as it walked around the room—in those days, a woman who called herself Katie King. One person present claimed that "Katie's legs and feet had dissolved away and that she had escaped from Volckman's clutch with an upward movement like a seal." The audience rushed to the cabinet and found Florence still there, dressed in black, her knots and seals intact. No trace of the white gown in which Katie had been dressed was found in the cabinet.

Crookes also described how he had once been allowed to hold Katie in his arms at a séance, and found her to be quite solid, like a normal woman. Naturally suspicious, he asked her if he could see

Florence in her cabinet. Katie agreed, and Crookes entered the cabinet and found Florence in a trance. As far as Crookes was concerned, that was conclusive. As far as the skeptics were concerned, it proved one of two things: either that Florence had an accomplice—perhaps her sister Katie, also a medium—or that Crookes was a liar.

After the Sitwell exposure, an authoress named Florence Marryat sat with Florence in the cabinet, tied to her with a rope. "Marie" appeared as usual and walked out amongst the audience, but Florence's reputation had suffered badly, and she soon went into partial retirement.

Crookes *was* undoubtedly deceived by a personable general's daughter named Rosina Showers. He had no reason to suspect her, for she refused all payment for her séances, at which a figure dressed in white appeared. Crookes devised a simple test to prevent Florence Cook from cheating—he made her dip her hands in a colored dye before the séance, then examined Katie King's hands. Katie passed the test without difficulty, but Rosina's "apparition" had dyed hands. Crookes allowed himself to overlook this—after all, the spirit drew its substance from the medium, and might have borrowed the dye, too. But Rosina was unable to keep her secret to herself, and told the American medium Annie Fay that she had cheated. Mrs. Fay immediately passed this on to Crookes, who demanded a private interview with Rosina. She confessed her deception, and promised never to do it again. Crookes, in turn, promised not to expose her. This promise was to cause him some embarrassment. Rosina's mother found out about the secret meeting, and put the worst possible construction on it. Having promised Rosina to keep silent, Crookes had to endure stoically while Mrs. Showers spread scandal among her friends and accused him of being a Casanova who habitually seduced his mediums. It was already general gossip that he had slept with Florence Cook when he was "investigating" her in his own house. Crookes finally decided that psychical research was more trouble than it was worth, and gave it up.

In 1888, there was a double scandal. The four Creery girls, whose "will game" had so impressed Barrett—and caused him to found the SPR—were caught cheating. They had been constantly tested ever since Barrett discovered them, and had become thoroughly bored with it all. They admitted that they had devised various simple signals to aid their card-guessing games—an upward glance for hearts, down for diamonds, and so on. They insisted that they had only decided to cheat fairly recently, and Myers and Gurney believed them, having made quite sure that the girls could *not* cheat in their own earlier tests. No one else believed them.

Then, worst of all, the two Fox girls, whose manifestations had launched the Spiritualist movement, publicly confessed that they were cheats. By 1888, both were in their fifties, widowed, and drinking too much. People were no longer interested in spirit rappings. Sister Leah, on the other hand, was still doing rather well; she and her sisters were barely on speaking terms. It was Leah, in fact, who had launched the fashion for materializations when, at a séance with Robert Dale Owen in 1860, a veiled white figure had walked around the room. With a supporter like Owen, she could hardly fail. Her sisters, on the other hand, had been badly treated by life. Kate's children had been taken from her by the Society for the Prevention of Cruelty to Children as a result of her drunkenness. Margaretta had managed to smuggle them to England to a guardian, but had been sorely tempted to commit suicide by jumping overboard on the return journey. Her strongest desire was to get her own back on her elder sister Leah. So when she arrived back in America, she took the opportunity of an interview with a reporter to declare that all the rappings had been a cheat. On October 21, 1888, she and Kate appeared on a platform at the New York Academy of Music, and Margaretta confessed that she had made the raps by means of a double joint in her big toe. She went on to demonstrate with a series of muffled raps. They were not in the least like the thunderous knockings that had shaken the bedroom of the Hydesville house, but the audience was willing to be convinced, and Margaretta and Kate were able to share $1,500 between them. The reporter Reuben Davenport, who had organized the confession, went on to write a book called *The Death Blow to Spiritualism*. Much of the $1,500 was spent on alcohol. In due course, Margaretta wrote a recantation of the confession, which she handed to a wealthy spiritualist, who allowed her to live in an apartment he owned. Her alcoholism made her an impossible tenant and he had to evict her. She died in 1895 and was buried in a pauper's grave, followed soon afterwards by Kate. In retrospect, the most significant thing about her confession was that Kate sat silently beside her on stage. She neither confirmed the confession nor offered to demonstrate how *she* had been deceiving the public with raps for the past thirty years. The inference seems to be that she agreed to share the platform for the sake of the $750, but refused to go further than that.

Another embarrassment to organized psychical research was the remarkable Italian medium Eusapia Palladino. She was an illiterate peasant, of large proportions, who had been discovered in Naples in 1872 when she was eighteen. She was the most powerful medium since Daniel Dunglas Home. Chairs retreated or moved toward her when she frowned or beckoned them, and hung suspended in the air. She herself could float up into the air and lie there as if on a couch. She had been investigated by criminologist Cesare Lombroso, who had no doubt of her genuineness. She was a highly unstable character: violent, impulsive, and sly. When coming out of trances she would make openly sexual overtures to males who attracted her. What was worse, she cheated. The absurd thing was that her cheating was clumsy, and the least competent researcher had no difficulty in catching her at it. Eusapia herself claimed that this cheating was done by hostile spirits, which may or may not have been true (since she was often wide awake when she did it). Yet her other phenomena were so impressive that there could be no question of cheating. The French astronomer Camille Flammarion found a better explanation of her cheating when he observed her over a period. After séances at which obviously genuine phenomena had occurred—such as musical instruments floating around the room when Eusapia was tied to her chair—he observed that she was violently ill, sometimes for as much as two days, vomiting up any food she tried to eat. If genuine phenomena produced this effect, it was no wonder she tried to get away with cheating. When Eusapia came to England in 1895, she was tested by the SPR at Cambridge, with the conjuror Maskelyne present. Her English hosts were far less indulgent toward her outrageous cheating than Lombroso had been, and issued a thoroughly unfavorable report. This should have convinced skeptics that the Society had no interest in protecting impostors. It only spread the impression that most mediums were such frauds and that no sane person would waste time on them.

In 1888, the Society suffered another serious blow—the death of one of its most brilliant investigators, Edmund Gurney. In June, he went off to Brighton on some mysterious errand, and was found dead in his hotel bed the next morning with a bottle of chloroform beside him, and a sponge bag over his face. An inquest decided that he died accidentally when taking chloroform for a toothache, but there was gossip at the SPR that it was suicide. Gurney had been testing various Brighton youths for telepathy, and had been impressed. One of his "telepaths" had to leave hastily for South Africa as a result of a divorce scandal, and twenty years later, he published a confession, declaring that he had cheated consistently. It has been suggested that Gurney found out that he had been hoaxed for years, and that if he was honest about this, it would do even more damage to psychical research.[2] Whatever the truth, his death was a serious loss to the Society.

It was not the first time Gurney had been hoaxed. Just as he was putting the finishing touches to the second volume of *Phantasms of the Living* in 1886, he received a letter from a Portsmouth naval cadet named Sparks, who described how he had been hypnotizing a fellow cadet named Cleave. One day when Cleave wondered what his girl-

2. Trevor H. Hall, *The Strange Case of Edmund Gurney* (1964).

friend was doing in Wandsworth, Sparks hypnotized him and suggested that he should go to see her. When he came out of the trance, according to Sparks, Cleave said that he had gone into the room where the girl was sitting with her little brother; she had stared at him and looked pale as if she was going to faint. Two days later, Cleave received a letter from the girl asking whether anything had happened to him, because she had seen him in the room.

This case was too good to miss, so Gurney went to the trouble of getting confirmatory letters from Cleave (who was eighteen) and from the girlfriend, as well as from two other cadets who claim to have been present. He printed a full account in *Phantasms of the Living*. Ten years after his death, Myers and Podmore had to publish a note in the SPR *Proceedings* admitting that Cleave had now confessed to hoaxing Gurney. It was a lesson in not paying too much attention to "witness" statements. Yet in another sense, the case vindicated the authors of *Phantasms*. The hoaxers had all been teenagers. The majority of people quoted in *Phantasms* are respectable middle-aged citizens, many of them clergymen, and most of them had no possible motive for hoaxing the SPR.

In 1898, Myers himself was involved in a minor scandal that brought discredit on the SPR. In the late 1880s, Myers had met an attractive girl named Ada Goodrich-Freer, who claimed to come from an upper-class Highland family and to be clairvoyant. Myers had a keen eye for a pretty girl, and he and the girl were soon convinced that they were soulmates. There is some evidence that they had a love affair. Myers persuaded her to try crystal gazing, and he felt the results were impressive—she claimed to have located a lost key and a medical prescription, and obtained from the crystal an address she had accidentally destroyed. Myers wrote a paper about it, which came out in the Society's journal (he called her simply "Miss X"). The Society had no reason for doubting such a well-born and refined young lady—after all, why should she lie? What Myers did not know what that the upper-class Miss Goodrich-Freer was actually the daughter of an Uppingham vet, and her name was simply Freer. She was thirty when Myers met her, not a teenager, as she claimed. She was a pathological liar. Her motivation has never been made clear, but it was probably simply a desire for attention.

The Society sent Miss Goodrich-Freer to the Highlands to investigate the whole subject of second sight; it emerged later that she simply borrowed a manuscript from a folklore-collecting priest and printed his material as her own. Sent to investigate a haunting in Surrey, she told the owners of the house that she had seen nothing, but told the SPR that she had seen a hooded female ghost as she dressed for dinner. That should have made them suspicious, but the attractive and well-mannered Miss Goodrich-Freer seemed above suspicion.

In 1897 she heard rumors that Ballechin House, in Scotland, was haunted, and persuaded a member of the SPR to rent it for her, for "shooting and fishing." Once there, she claimed to have witnessed all kinds of unearthly phenomena—thumps, bangs, ghostly screams, phantom footsteps, and elusive presences. There was a poltergeist that tore the clothes off the bed, and a ghostly nun, who was spotted by Miss Goodrich-Freer in a nearby glen. Oddly enough, guests who came to stay with Miss Goodrich-Freer never encountered the more terrifying phenomena, but they heard ominous bangs and footsteps. Back in London, she proceeded to write her *Alleged Haunting of Ballechin House*, but was incensed when one of her guests, a certain J. Callendar Ross, beat her past the post with an article in *The Times* entitled "On the Trail of a Ghost"; its tone was skeptical, not to say satirical. A furious correspondence ensued in the columns of *The Times*, in the course of which it became clear that Miss Goodrich-Freer and the SPR had rented the house under false pretenses. Its owner was naturally displeased at the damage to his rental prospects of all this sensational publicity. Myers, who had been a visitor to Ballechin House, naturally felt obliged to support Miss Goodrich-Freer. But when the wife of the owner denounced the SPR in *The Times*, he hastened to declare that he had long ago decided against publishing his own observations. Another guest who had been at

Ballechin with him immediately contradicted him, saying that Myers had definitely expressed his intention of writing about the haunting. Miss Goodrich-Freer herself was enraged by what she felt to be Myers' unchivalrous desertion. Callendar Ross expressed the general feeling when he referred to "the suspicion and disgust that close contact with the SPR tends to excite." When Miss Goodrich-Freer published her book on Ballechin, there was still more bad feeling.

The scandal may well have brought on the illness that was to kill Myers in 1901. Miss Goodrich-Freer herself experienced a sudden coldness on the part of other SPR members, and in his review of her book on Ballechin, Frank Podmore came very close to calling her a liar. There is evidence[3] that she was caught cheating at a table-rapping séance in 1901, and she decided to leave England for Jerusalem, where she married a man who was sixteen years her junior—convincing him that she was two years younger than he was. She died in 1931 at the age of seventy-four but continued to lie to the end—her death certificate gives her age as fifty-six.

These preposterous scandals—mediums in their underwear and ghosts with double-jointed big toes—had the unfortunate effect of suggesting that the SPR was a collection of bumbling crackpots. In fact, looking back after more than a century, we can see that its achievement during those first two decades was monumentally impressive. It had set out to answer the question: Can the paranormal be taken seriously, or is it a collection of old wives' tales and delusions? What undoubtedly surprised those pioneers was the sheer mass of evidence for the paranormal. It must have seemed incredible that one person in ten had experienced a hallucination, and that so many people had seen apparitions of dying relatives or had out-of-the-body experiences. Newspaper scandals about fake mediums may

3. John L. Campbell and Trevor Hall, *Strange Things* (1968), p. 211.

have impressed the public, but what impressed the SPR was that so many mediums were obviously genuine, and that so much evidence for life after death stood up to the strictest examination. When Callendar Ross spoke about the "suspicion and disgust" excited by the SPR, he was expressing the feeling of most healthy-minded people toward a morbid subject like psychical research. Morbid or not, it refused to go away. The Society made it harder to ignore by accumulating a positive mountain of evidence. *Phantasms of the Living* may be one of the most boring books ever written, but its two thousand pages of cases finally batter the mind into the recognition that this is something that has to be faced.

Since we have devoted so much space to scandals and exposures, it is only fair to look more closely at a cross-section of the kind of evidence that finally convinced those pioneers that they were dealing with reality.

On October 21, 1893, Prince Victor Duleep Singh, a son of a maharajah, went to bed in a Berlin hotel, where he was staying together with Lord Carnarvon. Before switching off the light, he looked across the room at a framed picture that hung on the opposite wall. To his surprise, he saw the face of his father, looking at him with an intent expression. Thinking that the picture might resemble his father, he got out of bed to see; in fact, it showed a girl holding a rose and leaning on a balcony. Prince Victor described the experience to Lord Carnarvon the next morning. Later the same day, he received a telegram announcing that his father had died of a stroke the previous day. The prince had seen his father's face at the time when the maharajah was lying unconscious after the stroke, a few hours before he died.

On the night of October 16, 1902, the wife of a railway guard woke up at about 3 A. M. for a drink of water. She was alone in bed, because her husband was on night duty, and the room was dimly lit by a gas mantle. As she looked into the water, she saw a clear image of goods wagons smashing into one another, and observed which of them was the most damaged. She was worried about her husband, in case he had had an accident. At nine the next morning her husband returned home, and she told him what she had seen. He told her that there *had* been an accident on the line that night, and it had happened just as she had seen.

The odd point about this case is that her husband had passed the scene of the accident twice: once at the time his wife had seen her "vision" in the glass of water, and again four hours later, when his train was on its way back. When he passed it for the first time, it was dark and he could not see what was happening. At 7 A. M. it was light, and he had then been able to see the scene clearly—as his wife had seen it in the water. Of course, her husband may have seen far more subconsciously than he was aware of seeing. If this was telepathy, then he had managed to convey to his wife far more than he was aware of seeing.

The next case is perhaps one of the most famous ever recorded by the SPR. On July 9, 1904, the novelist Rider Haggard suffered such a bad nightmare that his wife shook him awake. In his dream, he had seen his daughter's black retriever dog, Bob, lying on its side among the undergrowth beside some water. Its head was at an unnatural angle, and it seemed to be trying to tell him that it was dying.

The next morning at breakfast Haggard told his daughter Angela about his dream. She was not worried because she had seen Bob the previous evening and he was safe and well. It was only later in the day that they learned Bob was missing. Four days later, the dog's body was found floating in the nearby river. It had been struck by a train on the night Haggard had dreamed about it. He was able to work out the precise time the accident had taken place—a few hours before he had awakened from his nightmare.

On March 19, 1917, Mrs. Dorothy Spearman was in her room in a hotel in Calcutta, feeding her infant son. Her little daughter was also in the room. She felt there was someone behind her, and looked round to see her half-brother, Eldred Bowyer-Bower, standing there; he was an officer in the Royal Flying Corps. He looked perfectly normal, and Mrs. Spearman assumed he had been posted to India and come to see her. She told him that she would put the baby down, and then they could have a long talk. But when she had finished tucking in the baby, her half-brother had vanished. Her daughter did not appear to have seen anyone. She learned later that her half-brother had been shot down over the German lines at about the time she had seen him.

On December 7, 1918, Lieutenant J. J. Larkin, an RAF officer, was writing letters in the billet when he heard someone walking up the passage outside. Then the door opened, and his friend Lieutenant David McConnel shouted "Hello boy!" Larkin turned and saw McConnel standing there, holding the doorknob in his hand. He said: "Hello, back already?" and McConnel replied, "Yes, had a good trip." He had been ferrying a plane to a nearby aerodrome. Then McConnel closed the door with a bang and clattered off.

When Larkin learned several hours later that McConnel had crashed that afternoon, he assumed that it must have been after he had seen him. In fact, McConnel had been killed at roughly the same time that Larkin saw him at the door.

The next case has also become famous, and is regarded as one of the strongest pieces of evidence for survival after death. In June 1925, James Chaffin of Davie County, North Carolina, dreamed that his father stood by his bedside, wearing an old black overcoat, and told him: "You will find the will in my overcoat pocket." The father, James L. Chaffin, had died four years earlier, leaving his farm to his third son Marshall, and nothing to his wife or other three sons. The will had not been contested, since there seemed no reason to do so.

The next morning, James Chaffin hurried to his mother and asked about his father's old black overcoat; she told him it had been given to his brother John. He found the coat at John's house and examined it carefully. Sewn into the lining of the inside pocket—which his father had indicated in the dream—he found a roll of paper stating: "Read the 27th chapter of Genesis in my daddy's old Bible."

Taking a neighbor as witness, James Chaffin went back to his mother's house, and unearthed the old Bible. In the twenty-seventh chapter of Genesis there was another will—made later than the one that left everything to Marshall—dividing the property between the wife and four sons. The first reaction of Marshall Chaffin was to contest the will, assuming it to be a forgery. But once he examined it, he had to admit that it was obviously genuine. Ten witnesses testified that it was in old Chaffin's handwriting, so the property was divided according to the wishes of the second will.

Like Marshall Chaffin, the reader's first reaction is to suspect skulduggery. But the Canadian member of the SPR who heard of the case hired a lawyer to investigate it, and the genuineness of the will was established beyond all doubt. The significance of the twenty-seventh chapter of Genesis is that it contains the story of how Jacob deceived his blind father Isaac into granting him the inheritance of his brother Esau. This thought had apparently come to old Chaffin not long before his death, and he made the new will. Instead of having it properly witnessed, he inserted it in the Bible, no doubt expecting it to be found after his death—together with its implied criticism of his son Marshall. Unfortunately, the Bible was decrepit, and it may have been that the Chaffin family was simply not religiously inclined; so after four years it seems the old farmer had to draw attention to his change of heart.

Catherine Crowe's *Night Side of Nature* has a whole chapter devoted to similar cases, in which important messages are delivered by dreams or apparitions. She tells, for example, of a butcher who dreamed that he was going to be attacked and murdered on his way to market by two men dressed in blue. He decided to go to the market with a neighbor, and when he came to the place where the attack had taken place in his dream, saw the two men in blue waiting there. But all she tells us by way of detail is that the butcher's name was Bone and that he lived in Holytown. This can hardly be regarded as "confirmatory detail." The records of the SPR contain many equally melodramatic cases, but they took the trouble to get signed statements from all concerned, and the result is far more convincing. In a typical case of 1869, a couple identified as Mr. and Mrs. P were lying in bed in a dimly lit room when Mrs. P saw a man dressed as a naval officer standing at the foot of the bed. Her husband was dozing, and she touched his shoulder and said: "Willie, who is this?" Her husband roared indignantly: "What on earth are you doing here, sir?" The naval officer said reproachfully: "Willie!" As Mr. P leapt out of bed, the officer walked across the room and disappeared into the wall. Mrs. P said he looked like a solid human being, and that as he passed a lamp on his way across the room, he cast a shadow.

Realizing that they had seen a ghost, Mrs. P began to wonder if it foreboded some disaster to her brother, who was in the navy. When she mentioned this to her husband, he said: "No, it was my father." P's father had been dead for some years.

After this visitation, Mr. P became seriously ill for several weeks. When he recovered, he told his wife that he had been in financial trouble for some time, and before seeing the apparition, he had decided to take the advice of a certain individual which, he now realized, would have ruined him and probably landed him in jail. He was convinced that the "ghost" had come to warn him not to do it.

Intrinsically, this case is no more convincing than that of Mr. Bone of Holytown, but the SPR obtained signed depositions from Mr. and Mrs. P, and from two friends to whom Mrs. P had told the story immediately after it had happened. It is still possible to dismiss it as a dream or a "collective hallucination," or simply as a downright lie, but the signed statements make this seem at least unlikely.

An interesting point about the experience is Mrs. P's comment that the figure looked quite solid and normal—most ghosts do—and that it cast a shadow. This obviously suggests that it was made of some kind of solid substance, like the materializations that appeared in the séance room.

A "warning"of a different kind seems to have been involved in a case that came to be known as the "red scratch case." It involved a commercial traveller, identified as "FG," who was in his hotel room in St. Joseph, Missouri, in 1876, when he became aware of someone sitting at the table. It was his sister Annie, who had died of cholera nine years earlier. She looked exactly as she had when alive, except that she had a bright red scratch on her right cheek. As FG sprang to his feet, his sister vanished.

He was so shaken that he took a train straight back to his parents' home in St. Louis. When he told them about the scratch, his mother fainted. When she recovered, she told them that she had accidentally made the scratch on the face of the corpse. She had covered it up with powder, and never mentioned it to anyone.

A few weeks later, the mother died, "happy in the belief that she would rejoin her favorite daughter." Her son obviously took the view that the purpose of the apparition was to prepare her mother for her own death. This is another theme that runs fairly constantly through reports of apparitions and death-bed visions collected by the SPR. Sir William Barrett was later to devote a book to them, and its opening case is typical of the kind of thoroughness the SPR brought to its investigations.

Barrett's wife was an obstetric surgeon in the Maternity Hospital at Clapton in North London. A woman she calls Mrs. B was in labor and suffering from heart failure. As Lady Barrett was holding her hands, she said: "It's getting dark." Her mother and husband were sent for. Then Mrs. B looked at another part of the room and said: "Oh lovely." "What is lovely?" asked Lady Barrett. "Lovely brightness—wonderful things." Then she exclaimed: "Why, it's father!" Her baby was brought in for her to see, and she asked: "Do you think I ought to stay for baby's sake?" She looked towards her "father" and said: "I can't stay." When her husband had arrived, she looked across the room and said: "Why, there's Vida!" Vida was her younger sister, who had died two weeks earlier. The death had been kept from Mrs. B so as not to upset her. She died soon after. Lady Barrett, the matron, and the husband and mother all vouched that she seemed to remain conscious of the dead relatives up to the time of her death. With his usual thoroughness, Barrett obtained a letter verifying all this from the mother. It is the first of a number of cases cited by Barrett in which people on the point of death have "seen" relatives whom they did not know to be dead. Barrett points out that there is no known case of a dying person "seeing" someone who is still alive.

Sir Oliver Lodge, who was twice president of the SPR, was himself to supply one of the most convincing cases of "communication with the dead." It is recorded in his book *Raymond.*

On August 8, 1915, Sir Oliver Lodge received a message from a Boston medium, Leonore Piper, containing an obscure reference to a poem by the Roman poet Horace, about a tree being struck by lightning. Lodge interpreted this as a warning of some disaster. The message purported to come from Frederic Myers, who had been dead for fourteen years. A week later, Lodge heard that his youngest son Raymond had been killed in the Ypres campaign.

After this, a number of mediums relayed messages that purported to come from "Raymond," but Lodge remained unconvinced—most of them were of the "having a lovely time" variety. In the following month, Lodge's wife was taken to a séance held by a remarkable medium, Mrs. Osborne Leonard. Neither the medium nor Lady Lodge knew one another by sight, and they were not introduced. Nevertheless, Mrs. Leonard announced that she had a message from Raymond, who stated that he had met many of his father's friends since death. When asked to name one of them, Raymond replied, "Myers."

Another message from Raymond was relayed to Lady Lodge via a male medium called Vout Peters. In it, Raymond spoke about a photograph showing himself in a group of people, and referring to a walking stick. The Lodges knew nothing about such a photograph. Two months later, the mother of one of Raymond's fellow officers wrote to say that she had a group photograph including Raymond, and offered to send a copy. Before this arrived, Lodge himself visited Mrs. Leonard, and when her "control" (Feda) announced Raymond's presence, he took the opportunity to ask about the photograph. Raymond explained that it had been taken outdoors, and mentioned that someone had wanted to lean on him. When the photograph arrived a few days later, it showed a group of officers outside a billet. Raymond, sitting in the front row, has a cane resting on his leg, and the officer sitting behind him is using Raymond's shoulder as an arm rest.

Lodge's book gives many more examples of evidence of Raymond's "survival"; but, as he points out, this one is particularly convincing because it involves two mediums, both of whom spoke of the photograph before Lodge knew of its existence—thus ruling out any possibility of telepathy.

To conclude this chapter, here is a final example of a type of phenomenon so beloved by Catherine Crowe and other early writers on the supernatural: the full-scale haunting.

In February 1932, the grandchildren of a chimneysweep named Samuel Bull refused to go to sleep, insisting that there was someone outside the door of the cottage. (They were sleeping in a downstairs room, recovering from influenza.) Their mother, Mary Edwards, looked outside the door, but there was no one there. Soon afterwards, she and the children saw the figure of Samuel Bull—who had been dead since the previous June—walk across the room, up the stairs, and through the door of the room in which he had died. (This was closed.) They all screamed. This was the first of many appearances of the dead man at his cottage in Oxford Street, Ramsbury, Wiltshire. The "ghost" was apparently aware of the presence of his family, for he twice placed his hand on the brow of his invalid wife Jane, and once spoke her name. Samuel Bull, who had died of cancer, looked quite solid, and could be seen so clearly that he children noticed the whiteness of his knuckles, which seemed to be protruding through the skin. They also noticed that the expression on his face was sad. After the first appearance, the family no longer felt alarmed—the children seemed "awed" rather than frightened. They assumed that the ghost was looking sad because of the miserable conditions they were living in—the cottage was damp and some rooms were unfit or habitation. On the last two occasions on which he appeared, Samuel Bull no longer looked sad, and Mrs. Edwards assumed that this was because the family was to be rehoused in a council house.

The family was already on the move when the two investigators from the SPR arrived, but the local vicar had already interviewed the family and recorded their accounts of what took place. The investigators were understandably upset that they had not been told about the case earlier, but their conversations with witnesses, and the evidence of the vicar, left them in no doubt that the haunting was genuine.

This ragbag of assorted visions and apparitions underlines the enormous variety of cases investigated by the SPR in the first century of its existence. None of them are, in themselves, more impressive than cases cited by Jung-Stilling or Catherine Crowe or Robert Dale Owen. But they are more convincing because honest investigators have obviously done their best to confirm that they are genuine. Anyone who is willing to spend a few hours browsing through volumes of the *Proceedings* the SPR (or its American counterpart) is bound to end with a feeling that further skepticism is a waste of time. Even if half the cases proved to be fraudulent or misreported, the other half should still be overwhelming by reason of sheer volume. It is easy to understand the irritation of Professor James Hyslop when he wrote in *Life After Death*:

> *I regard the existence of discarnate spirits as scientifically proved and I no longer refer to the skeptic as having any right to speak on the subject. Any man who does not accept the existence of discarnate spirits and the proof if it is either ignorant or a moral coward. I give him short shrift, and do not propose to argue with him on the supposition that he knows nothing about the subject.*

Where skeptics are concerned, he certainly has a point. Sir John Bland Sutton, a well-known surgeon, remarked: "Death is the end of all. My experience is that all of those who have studied the subject scientifically and deeply have come to the same conclusion." Such a statement simply lacks the ring of truth. There have been many basically skeptical investigators—Hyslop himself was notoriously "tough-minded," and much disliked by fellow members of the SPR because he seemed an incorrigible "doubting Thomas." But in every single case where a skeptic has persisted in studying the facts, he has ended up more or less convinced of the reality of life after death. I say more or less because a few investigators, such as Dr. Gardner Murphy and Louisa Rhine, feel that most of the "facts" can also be explained by what might be called "super ESP"—mind-reading clairvoyance, and so on.

Hyslop himself finally abandoned the super ESP hypothesis through an experience that has become known as the "red pyjamas case." He received a communication from a medium in Ireland to the effect that a spirit calling itself "William James" had asked him to pass on a message asking him if he remembered some red pyjamas. Now William James, who had died in 1910, had agreed with Hyslop that whichever of them died first should try to communicate with the other. But the message about red pyjamas meant nothing to Hyslop. Then suddenly he remembered. When he and James were young men, they went to Paris together, and discovered that their luggage had not yet arrived. Hyslop went out to buy some pyjamas, but could only find a bright red pair. For days James teased Hyslop about his poor taste in pyjamas. Hyslop had long forgotten the incident. As far as he could see, there was no way of explaining the red pyjamas message except on the hypothesis that it was really William James who had passed it on.

Twenty-six years after Hyslop's death, he was quoted by the psychologist Carl Jung in a letter. Jung was discussing the question of the identity of spirits who communicate through mediums:

> *I once discussed the proof of identity for a long time with a friend of William James, Professor Hyslop, in New York. He admitted that, all things considered, all these metaphysic phenomena could be explained better by the hypothesis of spirits than by the qualities and peculiarities of the unconscious. And here, on the basis of my own experience, I am bound to concede he is right. In each individual case I must of necessity be skeptical, but in the long run*

I have to admit that the spirit hypothesis yields better results in practice than any other.[4]

Yet it is significant that Jung never made this admission in any of his published work, where he continued to insist that the facts about the paranormal could be explained in terms of the powers of the unconscious mind.[5]

As far as the present investigation is concerned, we shall proceed on Jung's assumption that the spirit hypothesis fits the facts better than any other. The question of whether it is ultimately true must, for the time being, be left open.

---

4. *Collected Letter*, Vol. 1, p. 431.
5. This is discussed at length in my book on Jung, *The Lord of the Underworld* (1984).

Chapter Five

Rediscovering a Masterpiece

In the autumn of 1863, a woman named Sarah Hall had the interesting experience of seeing her own ghost. She was sitting at the dining table, with her husband and another couple, when all four of them saw another Mrs. Hall standing at the end of the sideboard. The figure was wearing a spotted dress, quite unlike the one Sarah Hall had on. Her husband said: "Why, it's Sarah!," and as they all stared at it, it disappeared.

The case is irritating because it has no sequel. Sarah Hall was still in good health when she wrote and told Gurney about the case twenty years later, so it was not some ominous portent. A few years later, Mrs. Hall apparently owned a spotted dress like the one her "ghost" was wearing, but that also seems to be neither here nor there. The only clue that makes any sense is Mrs. Hall's comment that the house they were living in used to be a church. We have seen that Christian churches were often built on pagan sites, as if the ground itself had some inherent power or force that the ancients regarded as sacred. That still takes us no nearer to the explanation of how four people saw Mrs. Hall's "double."

If the case were unique, we might dismiss it as a prevarication, but there are hundreds of reports of doubles in the literature of psychical research. No less a person than the poet Goethe recorded seeing his own double (or doppelgänger) riding toward him along a road in Alsace as he was taking leave of his sweetheart. The figure was wearing a gray and gold suit. Eight years later, on his way to visit the same girl, he passed the spot and suddenly realized that he was now wearing the gray and gold suit. Robert Dale Owen recorded in detail the case of a schoolteacher named Emilie Sagée whose double frequently appeared standing beside her in the classroom. One of her pupils noticed that the "real" Emilie looked pale and ill when her double appeared, as if the material for the double came from Emilie's own body.

Cases like this make it very clear that, while we have a few plausible theories about ghosts, apparitions, and such things, we lack any *comprehensive* theory that would explain them all. Even a belief in spirits gets us no closer to an explanation of Mrs. Hall's peculiar experience.

Frederic Myers, the man who was most responsible for creating the Society for Psychical Research, was keenly aware of this deficiency. From the age of twenty-six, when he took the famous "starlit walk" with Henry Sidgwick, until his death thirty-two years later, he never ceased trying to fit all paranormal phenomena into a single pattern. The result of these efforts appeared two years after his death in a work called *Human Personality and Its Survival of Bodily Death*. The book is a masterpiece, probably the most comprehensive work ever written on the subject of the paranormal. Unfortunately, it is almost unknown to the general reader, largely on account of its offputting title, which makes it sound as if it is full of accounts of séance rooms and messages from the dead. Nothing could be further from the truth. It is an ambitious attempt to review the strange powers of the human mind; the question of life after death is raised only toward the end.

Because the book is so little known, and because its conclusions are so important, let us consider it in some detail. Myers begins by discussing clinical cases of what we would now call "multiple personality." On September 7, 1824, a German epileptic named Sörgel murdered an old woodcutter in the forest, chopping off his head and feet with his own axe. After this, he drank the man's blood. Back in town, he talked quite openly about what he had done, explaining that drinking blood is a cure for epilepsy. Sörgel was already known as a "Jekyll and Hyde" personality who developed criminal tendencies after his fits. A week later, by the time he appeared in front of the magistrate, he had reverted back to the Jekyll personality, quiet and polite, and without the slightest memory of the murder. He was found not guilty and sent to an asylum.

Another case cited by Myers offers at least one interesting clue to this mystery of multiple personality. Louis Vivé was ten years old when he was sent to a children's home in 1873. He was of a quiet, obedient disposition. Four years later, he had a terrifying encounter with a viper, which produced a state of shock. After this, he began having epileptic fits, and developed hysterical paralysis of the legs. He was sent to an asylum at Bonneval for observation, and for the next two months worked quietly at tailoring. Then he had a fit that lasted for two days, with violent convulsions and moods of ecstasy. When he woke up, the paralysis had vanished, and he was a changed person.

He had no memory of anything that had happened since the viper attack. He was also violent, dishonest, and badly behaved. The former Louis had been a teetotaler; the new one not only drank, but stole the wine of other patients.

After serving in the Marines and spending some time in jail for theft, Vivé was sent to the Rochefort asylum, where three doctors became fascinated by his case. Vivé now suffered from paralysis of the right side of his body, and from a speech defect that made him stutter badly. In spite of the speech defect he was a nonstop talker, and was inclined to preach atheism and violent revolution.

The 1880s saw a revival of interest in the doctrines of Mesmer, including his belief that the "vital powers" can be moved around the human body by means of magnets. Vivé's doctors were interested in a variation of this doctrine—that various metals could get rid of paralysis. When they tried stroking Vivé's upper right arm with steel, it had the astonishing effect of promptly transferring the paralysis to the left side of his body. Immediately, the old, gentle Louis Vivé came back. He had no memory of the person he had become after the long epileptic attack.

We have a clue that was unknown to Vivé's doctors—that the left brain controls the right half of the body, and vice versa. So when the "criminal" Vivé's right side was paralyzed, his left brain was affected, and the personality that expressed itself was the right-brain Vivé. The left brain is the speech hemisphere—hence the stuttering. A rough outline of Vivé's problem becomes discernible. His early childhood had been difficult, with a drunken and violent mother; he became a timid and repressed personality. The "social I," as we have seen, lives in the left brain. His right-brain self—the "intuitive" Vivé—had no chance to express its aggressions or frustrations. The shock of the encounter with the viper caused the total withdrawal of the timid, left-brain self, and left the "other Vivé" free to express itself. From then on, Vivé turned into a classic case of multiple personality.

Myer's account of the case (which gives the impression that he personally interviewed Louis Vivé) ends with an interesting footnote; he mentions that when a magnet was placed on Vivé's head, he instantly became "normal" again, except that his memory stopped short of the day before the encounter with the viper. It seems quite clear that "magnetism" *did* work, and that modern science may be neglecting an interesting line of research.

Myers goes on to discuss other examples of multiple personality. There was the celebrated case of a man called Ansel Bourne, who was standing on a street corner in Providence, Rhode Island, when he lost his memory. The next thing he knew, he was waking up in a strange room in a strange bed. It was two months later, and he was in Norristown, Pennsylvania. During that time, Bourne had gone to Norristown, rented a confectionery shop, and carried on business under the name of A. J. Brown. No one even suspected that he had a case of amnesia.

Even stranger is the case of Clara Fowler, described by psychiatrist Morton Prince, who called her "Christine Beauchamp." When trying to cure Clara of severe depression, Prince placed her under hypnosis, and a completely new personality emerged: a bright, mischievous child who called herself "Sally." Sally could "take over" Clara when she felt inclined. She used to enjoy playing tricks, like going for a long walk in the country—Sally was as strong as a mule—and then "abandoning" the body and leaving the exhausted Clara to walk home. On one occasion, Sally "borrowed" Clara's body for weeks, went off to another town and got a job as a waitress, then finally abandoned it and left Clara to make her own way back to Boston. Like Louis Vivé's alter-ego, "Sally Beauchamp" stuttered badly.

The case of Clara Fowler was more complicated than this. Under hypnosis, a third personality emerged, who was more adult and balanced than either Clara or Sally. So the "double brain" explanation that seems to fit the case of Louis Vivé or Ansel Bourne no longer applies here. In his chapter on hypnosis, Myers seeks a new explanation. He describes a series of experiments carried out by Edmund Gurney, and later by Mrs. Sidgwick, which revealed that most people could be hypnotized to two different "depths" or levels, and that one subject could even be hypnotized through nine different depths. The subject would be placed under hypnosis and told some "fact"—for example, that a local hotel had just been burned down. Then he would be hypnotized more deeply, and told another fact that there had been a railway accident. Then down to a third "depth," and yet another fact—that the Emperor of Germany had been forced to cut short a state visit to Queen Victoria because a relative had died.

When subsequently rehypnotized, the subject would remember each fact as he reached the correct level, but would have no memory of any of the others. Myers inferred that this could be an explanation of multiple personality—that we all have many layers or levels, and that a shock—like Louis Vivé's viper—can produce an effect like hypnosis and plunge the patient to another level of personality. This explanation may or may not be correct, but it shows Myers' determination to try to find a key to the mysteries of the unconscious mind.

This emerges most clearly in his chapter on genius. He says: "Genius . . . should be regarded as a power of utilizing a wider range . . . of faculties *in some degree innate in all.*" (My italics.) This is what fascinates Myers; that such powers are not some kind of freak of nature, but probably exist in all of us. He goes on to cite many stories of extraordinary mental feats. A five-year-old boy, Benjamin Blyth, was out walking with his father, and asked him what time it was; his father said it was half past seven. A few minutes later the child said: "In that case, I have been alive . . ." and named the exact number of seconds since his birth. When they got home, his father took a sheet of paper and worked it out. "You made a mistake—you were wrong by 172,800 seconds." "No, I wasn't," said the child. "You forgot the two leap years, 1820 and 1824." Myers also speaks of Professor Truman Henry Safford who, at the age of ten, could perform multiplications in his head when the answer came to thirty-six figures, and the peasant boy Vito Mangiamele, who took half a minute to extract the cube root of 3,796,416.

A modern case can illustrate more clearly what is at issue: the "calendar calculating twins" John and Michael, idiot savants who spent most of their lives in a state mental hospital in America. They have been described by psychiatrist Oliver Sacks.[1] Although the twins are mentally subnormal, with an IQ of only sixty, they can name the day of the week of any date in the past or future forty thousand years. If

1. *New York Review* (February 28, 1985), p. 16.

asked, let us say, about March 6, 1877, they shout almost instantly, "Tuesday." They have no more difficulty about a date long before the Great Pyramid was built. Yet, oddly enough, the twins have the utmost difficulty with ordinary addition and subtraction, and do not appear to even understand multiplication and division. The opinion of most scientists who have studied them is that they have some simple formula. But Dr. Sacks reached a quite different conclusion. He was present one day when a box of matches fell on the floor, and both twins said immediately: "A hundred and eleven." When Sacks counted the matches, there were, indeed, a hundred and eleven. The twins also murmured, "thirty-seven," and when Sacks asked them why, they explained that three thirty-sevens make a hundred and eleven. He asked them how they knew there were a hundred and eleven. "We *saw* it." They had instantaneously counted the matches as they were falling. They gave the same answer when Sacks asked how they had worked out that thirty-seven is a third of one hundred and eleven. It was as if they had seen one hundred and eleven "splitting" into three parts.

On another occasion, Sacks walked up behind them when they were repeating numbers to one another. One would say a six-figure number, and the other would savor it, then say another six-figure number. Sacks made a note of these numbers, and when he got home, studied them carefully. He discovered that they were all prime numbers—numbers that cannot be divided exactly by any other number (for example, five, seven, and eleven).

Now there is an interesting thing about prime numbers: there is no short cut to finding out whether some huge number *is* a prime, except by painstakingly dividing every other number into it. (Sacks used a book.)

How were the twins doing it? They could not be calculating them—they had virtually no power of calculation. The next day, Sacks went to see them, carrying his book on prime numbers. They were still playing the number game and Sacks joined in, repeating an *eight*-figure prime. There was a half-minute pause while they looked at him in astonishment, then both broke into smiles, and began swapping eight-figure primes. An hour later they were swapping twenty-four-figure primes—although even a computer would take some time to work out whether such a huge figure is a prime or not.

Sacks concluded that, in some extraordinary way, the twins were seeing these huge numbers instantaneously, just as they "saw" the number of matches in the box. That is to say, they were somehow using the *right side of the brain* instead of the left, as the rest of us do for calculation. Yet the fact that they are not particularly intelligent seems to demonstrate that this is not some extraordinary form of genius. It is almost certainly a power which everyone possesses—potentially—but which the rest of us have somehow "suppressed" through the development of left-brain consciousness.

Myers knew nothing of the right and left hemispheres; he only knew that such powers spring from the unconscious mind—or, as he preferred to call it, the "subliminal mind." This is not the modern "Unconscious" derived from Freud and Jung. Myers' subliminal mind is not some kind of dustbin that contains repressions, neuroses, and incestuous guilt feelings. It is the source of the flashes of intuition that we call genius. It could, therefore, be regarded as a kind of combination of the Unconscious mind of Freudian psychology and the "high self" of the Kahunas, as described by Max Freedom Long. This view is concisely expressed by Aldous Huxley in a foreword he wrote for an American edition of Myers' book: "Is the house of the soul a mere bungalow with a cellar? Or does it have an upstairs above the ground floor of consciousness as well as a garbage-littered basement beneath?" Myers, he goes on to say, takes the view that the human soul has an attic above ordinary consciousness as well as a basement below it, and that *Human Personality and Its Survival of Bodily Death* is "an immense store of information about the strange and often wonderful goings-on in the upper stories of man's soul-house." This is, in fact, precisely what makes Myers' book so remarkable.

What it all proves, according to Myers, is that our powers are far greater than we realize. If this argument sounds familiar, it is because we have already encountered it in Catherine Crowe's *Night Side of Nature*. The difference is that while Mrs. Crowe states her facts, and leaves the reader to take them or leave them, Myers wants to make the reader concede that they are facts. Mrs. Crowe cites some vague experiment about a hypnotist engaging in a "battle of will" with an animal. Myers actually took the trouble to make the journey to Le Havre, and witness experiments in which a certain Dr. Gibert hypnotized a patient called Leonie from half a mile away, merely by willing her to fall into a trance. In fact, Leonie resisted; she told the psychologist Pierre Janet: "I know very well that Mr. Gibert tried to put me to sleep, but when I felt him I looked for some water and put my hands in cold water. I don't want people to put me to sleep that way . . . it makes me look silly." He then goes on to cite a successful experiment, in which—after Gibert had tried to put her to sleep at a distance—they all went and hid near Leonie's house, and watched her walk out of the garden gate with her eyes closed, and walk towards Gibert's house.

In her little book *Spiritualism and the Age We Live In*, published in 1859 (just before her mental breakdown), Mrs. Crowe remarked:

> *there is a department of knowledge which, as far as we know, is not reducible to experimental science . . . I allude to the knowledge or science of* ourselves. *Of our bodies . . . we have, within a comparatively short space of time, learnt a great deal; but of ourselves as composite beings we know absolutely nothing. We have added nothing to the knowledge of the anicents; perhaps we have rather lost what they knew or suspected. Metaphysics gives us words without any distinct ideas, and Psychology is a name without science. . . .*

A mere twenty years later, this was no longer true; psychology was quickly becoming a real science, and it was revealing some of those secrets about "ourselves" that Catherine Crowe regarded as the most important of all kinds of knowledge. This explains the undercurrent of excitement and optimism that runs through Myers' book. He was quite convinced—he says as much at the end—that man was at some crucial turning point in his history, and that this new "science of ourselves" would transform human existence as completely as the science of Galileo and Newton had transformed it since the seventeenth century.

What abnormal psychology teaches us, he argued, was that our minds are richer and stranger than we could imagine. Even Aldous Huxley's image of a house with an upper story fails to do justice to Myers' vision of human personality. It is more like a skyscraper, with dozens of stories above ground, *and* another dozen or so below. His experiments with different "layers" of consciousness seemed to reveal that man has a whole series of "basements" below his everyday self. That in turn suggests that he also has a series of upper stories above his everyday consciousness. Moreover, if we think of a case like that of Louis Vivé, we can see that his criminal alter-ego was a more primitive, violent person than the polite, well-behaved Louis, and therefore, a step in the direction of the caveman. This also suggests that his undeveloped higher levels are a step in the opposite direction—toward the god.

For Myers, cases like the ones we discussed at the beginning of this chapter—the lady who saw her own double standing by the sideboard and the schoolteacher who was continually standing beside herself—were not psychological freaks or anomalies; they are evidence of some peculiar power we do not understand. He cites a typical case of a phantasm of the living taken from the Society for Psychical Research's "Census of Hallucinations." On a Sunday afternoon in August 1889, a girl identified as "Miss K E" changed her mind about going to church, and instead spent the afternoon in her uncle's library, studying his genealogical chart. Her two sisters, who went to church, saw her walking up the aisle with a roll of paper (evidently the genealogical chart) under her arm. All three sisters wrote an account of this odd occurrence.

The case is not as unusual as it sounds; there are well over a hundred like it in the "Census of Hallucinations" and *Phantasms of the Living*. In most of them, it seems clear that the person who projected the doppelgänger was thinking about the place where the double was seen. In his autobiography, *Legends*, the dramatist Strindberg describes how, when he was dangerously ill in Paris, he experienced a powerful longing to be back in Germany with his wife's family. For a moment, he felt he was inside the house, and could see his mother-in-law playing the piano. Shortly afterwards, he received a letter from his mother-in-law asking if he was alright. She wrote: "When I was playing the piano the other day I looked up and saw you standing there." It is important to note that Strindberg was seriously ill at the time, which suggests that the mechanism involved is much the same as in cases where people on the point of death have been seen by close relatives.

In fact, there is evidence that "psychic projection" can be performed at will. Although Edmund Gurney was undoubtedly hoaxed by the exuberant teenagers who claimed that one of them had "visited" his girlfriend under hypnosis,[2] other "experimental" cases are well authenticated. In 1881, a student named S. H. Beard decided to try "projecting" himself three miles to the house of his fiancée, Miss L. S. Verity. He made the attempt after going to bed on a Sunday evening. On the following Thursday, he went to see Miss Verity, and she told him that she had been terrified to find him standing by her bedside the previous Sunday. As the apparition moved toward her, she screamed, and woke up her eleven-year-old sister, who also saw it. In his own statement, Beard said:

> *Besides exercising the power of volition very strongly, I put forth an effort which I cannot find words to describe. I was conscious of a mysterious influence of some sort permeating my body, and had a distinct impression that I was exercising some force with which I had been hitherto unacquainted, but which I can now at certain times set in motion at will.*

---

2. See pp. 121–122.

After his studies in hypnosis, Myers found it easy enough to believe in such a force. If Dr. Gibert could hypnotize Leonie from half a mile away, then he was, in some sense, projecting himself to her. Under different circumstances, he might have made her "see" him. Myers, like Thomson Jay Hudson, was fascinated by the extraordinary powers of the subliminal mind. One hypnotist told a patient to make a cross at exactly 20,180 minutes after being awakened from the trance, and the patient did it. Yet the patient was not particularly good at arithmetic. "Something" inside her had carefully counted more than twenty thousand minutes (about fourteen days) and then obeyed the order to make a cross. This is a variation on a power most of us possess—to decide that we must wake up at a certain time, and to wake up at that precise moment as if by an alarm. If the subliminal mind has an alarm clock that can operate during sleep or count the minutes in fourteen days, then the power of projecting an image of oneself to some other place seems altogether less extraordinary. Now in our own time, when television transmitters can send images to the moon, it is a great deal easier to accept than in Myers' day.

Professor C. D. Broad, discussing the case of Sarah Hall[3]—who saw her own double by the sideboard—suggests that what she saw might have been her astral body, but that seems highly unlikely. To begin with, most accounts of the astral body state that it cannot be seen by other people. Secondly, many cases of doppelgängers include objects—like the genealogical chart held by Miss K E in church (there is no reason why a roll of paper should have an astral body). In another case cited by Myers, the doppelgänger included a horse and carriage, as well as two people. The Rev. W. Mountford of Boston described how he was standing by the window in the house of a friend, when he saw a horse and carriage arriving. He remarked to his host: "Here is your brother coming," and his host also saw the

3. *Lectures on Psychical Research*, p. 173.

carriage. It turned around the corner of the house, to the front door, but no visitors arrived. Instead, the host's niece, Mary, came into the room, looking worried. She had just walked from her parents' home, leaving them sitting by the fire; but as she was on her way, their carriage passed by her. They were looking straight ahead, ignoring her.

Ten minutes later, Mountford heard the sound of a carriage, and said: "Look, they're coming down the road again." This time, the carriage proved to be real. Its occupants were baffled when told that they had arrived a quarter of an hour earlier, and that they had passed their daughter on the road.

The question Mountford should have asked was whether one of them had fallen into a daydream while sitting in front of the fire, and imagined driving to the brother's house. The answer would almost certainly have been yes.

The implication seems to be that the subliminal mind possesses a kind of television transmitter, as well as a receiver. Mountford and his host and the niece all saw the carriage. Both of Miss K E's sisters saw her walk into church clutching a roll of paper. In both cases, the image looked perfectly real and normal.

Another interesting point about the Beard case is that, after his first successful attempt, he felt he had learned the "trick" and could then do it at will. Gurney asked Beard to let him know next time he tried the experiment. Beard did this on March 22, 1884. Miss Verity signed a statement to the effect that, at about midnight, Beard had appeared in her room and stroked her hair. She passed on this information to her little sister, who also verified it.

An American heart specialist, Dr. Michael Sabom, became interested in near-death experiences of heart-attack patients and wrote a book, *Recollections of Death*, in 1982. He noted that patients who had experienced out-of-the-body projections were often able to repeat them at will. One nineteen-year-old girl described how she had been knocked down by a car at a pedestrian crossing, and how suddenly she was "above the whole scene, viewing the accident." She watched as the paramedics arrived, and was critical of the way they lifted her on to the stretcher, After this, she woke up in the hospital. When Sabom interviewed her thirteen years later, she told him: "I knew I had left my body because this became something I could do almost at will. I realized I had *learned* to do that at the time I had probably come close to dying." She went on to describe how, lying alone in her trailer at night (her husband worked nights), she would leave her body and check that everything was safe in the trailer. One night, she noticed that the rear door of the trailer had been left open. After "returning" to her body, she got up and closed it.

The inference would seem to be that we all possess these powers potentially, but simply never learn to make use of them. If Myers is correct, there is nothing mystical or metaphysical about this assertion; it is a plain statement of fact, based on scientific evidence.

We have now arrived at a crucial, in fact, *the* crucial point in Myers' argument and, before we continue, it may be as well to look back over the steps that have brought us here.

The basic objection to personal survival is that personality is a kind of artifact. It is "built-up" little by little from our experiences. There is no more reason why my personality should survive my death than why my house should survive after it has been knocked down.

Myers' reply is to point to the mystery of multiple personality. Louis Vivé and Clara Fowler were, to all appearances, more than one person. Yet there was obviously some permanent substratum underneath these "personalities," a being for whom the personalities were various masks. In his autobiography, Alfred Russel Wallace describes his experiments in hypnotism with his pupils. He says of one of these:

> *More curious still was the taking away of the memory so completely that he could not tell his own name, and would adopt any name that was suggested to him, and perhaps remark how stupid he was to have forgotten it; and this might be repeated several times with different names, all of which he would implicitly accept. Then, on saying to him, "Now you remember your own*

> *name again; what is it?" an inimitable look of relief would pass over his countenance, and he would say, "Why, P—of course," in a way that carried complete conviction.*

The "real P—" was there all the time, in spite of having forgotten his own name.

The point is reinforced by some more recent cases of multiple personality. In *Sybil*, Flora Rheta Schreiber describes a patient with fourteen different personalities, some of them male. The rapist Billy Milligan proved to have twenty-three subpersonalities, some of them far more talented and brilliant than Billy himself.[4] Christine Sizemore, the subject of the famous *Three Faces of Eve*, reached an unbelievable total of forty alter-egos. The *Eve* case also suggests that the personality may, in some ways, be independent of the body. Christine Sizemore was allergic to nylon, but the moment her alter-ego took over, the nylon rash disappeared. She was nearsighted; her alter-ego could see perfectly without glasses. On one occasion when she was under anaesthetic, her alter-ego took over and was totally unaffected by the anaesthetic. If all this is true, then our usual assumption that personality is somehow dependent on the body may be a misunderstanding. The body may be an instrument that responds to the demands of the personality—in the same way that a car responds to its driver, but to a far greater extent. This in turn suggests that physical illness may depend on the personality, not on the body—that when a person is bent and decrepit and feeble, it is the personality that is bent and decrepit. If another personality could take it over—as the mischievous Sally took over the body of Clara Fowler—it might be instantly transformed.

All this is implicit in Myers' argument. He has also suggested that we may possess powers that would once have been termed "magical"—for example, the power to transmit our thoughts to someone

---

4. Daniel Keyes, *The Minds of Billy Milligan.*

on the other side of the world, and even to transmit a physical image of ourselves to the minds of other people. The scientific answer to that claim is that all our "powers" have been developed in the course of millions of years of evolution, as a *response* to the challenges of evolution. So why *should* we possess these powers suggested by Myers?

His answer would be to point to the powers of people of genius: a Mozart able to play a whole concerto accurately, after having heard it only once; or a five-year-old Benjamin Blyth able to calculate how many seconds he had been alive. We have certainly never had need for any of *these* powers in the course of our evolution. Myers also points out that in the case of some calculating prodigies, like Professor Safford and Archbishop Whately, their unusual powers vanished at about the age of puberty, and they then became "like the rest of us." If Whately and Safford could become like the rest of us, it clearly implies that the rest of us could, if we made the effort, become calculating prodigies like Whately and Safford, or could learn to leave our bodies at will, like Michael Sabom's patient, to check that we have closed all the doors and windows. (It is easy to see that such a faculty would have been extremely useful to a caveman, who could go and investigate a snuffling noise outside his cave without running the risk of being eaten.)

In fact, the evolutionary argument can be used to support either side. There is much evidence that primitive people are more psychic than we are. Some Australian aborigines are able to detect underground water without even the aid of a dowsing rod. Other examples are cited by Professor Hornell Hart.[5] A Scottish sportsman, David Leslie, was curious about what had happened to his eight Kaffirs, who were on a hunting expedition two hundred miles away; a Zulu witch doctor was able to tell him exactly what was happening to them, and his information later proved to be "correct in every partic-

5. *The Enigma of Survival*, p. 15.

ular." Commander R. Jukes Hughes, serving in the Transkei, received a running commentary from local natives on a battle that was now taking place three hundred miles away—a commentary that again proved to be accurate.

In any case, it seems obvious that, over millions of years of evolution, different powers and capacities are developed and then submerged again, as they cease to be necessary. Although they may be submerged, they remain encoded in the genes. When Darwin arrived on the Galapagos Islands, he discovered many types of finch that had been blown from the mainland of South America, and which had probably been there for centuries. In the early 1940s, some of these birds were brought back to California, and instantly reacted with alarm to hawks, vultures, and ravens—predators that do not exist on the Galapagos, and which no Galapagos finch had seen for hundreds of generations. Like a careful housewife, evolution never throws away anything that might one day be useful. For the past three thousand years, humans have adapted to civilization. But in the vast depths of their being, there must be thousands of characteristics that humans developed in the great droughts and ice ages of the past three million years, and which we have packed away in the storage cupboard of the genes in case they should come in useful.

So, says Myers, we seem to have demonstrated that there is some "substratum" in man which is far more durable than his everyday personality, and that this deeper "self" seems to possess some unusual powers that would startle the everyday self. Allow this much, and we come to the really interesting part of the argument: that there is evidence that this substratum survives death, and that it is able to exercise some of these powers at will.

Myers begins by citing one of the most interesting and frequently quoted cases of near-death experiences, that of Dr. A. S. Wiltse, an American doctor who "died" in Skiddy, Kansas, in the summer of

1889, and revived a few hours later. Wiltse's own account was published in the *St. Louis Medical and Surgical Journal* for February 1890.

Wiltse "died" of typhoid fever, after taking leave of his family and friends. After losing consciousness, he woke up, apparently still "inside" his body, but feeling quite unconnected with it. He was able to lie there and observe the way his bodily organs interacted with himself—his "soul." He said: "I learned that the epidermis [outer layer of skin] was the outside boundary of the ultimate tissues, so to speak, of the soul." Then he felt himself being gently rocked back and forth as he separated from his body. There was a feeling of "the innumerable snapping of small cords," and he felt as if "he" was retreating from his body, starting at the feet, toward his head. Then he found himself "peeping out" from his skull, and feeling as if he had the shape and color of a jellyfish.

> *As I emerged from the head I floated up and down . . . like a soap bubble . . . until I at last broke loose from the body and fell lightly to the floor, where I slowly rose and expanded into the full stature of a man.*

There were two ladies in the room and he was embarrassed about being naked, but by the time he reached the door, he found himself clothed. He turned around and his elbow came into contact with another man in the room; to his surprise, his elbow passed through the man.

He began to see the humorous side of the situation—with his dead body lying on the bed—and bowed playfully. Then he laughed aloud; no one heard him. He walked out of the door, and noticed a thin cord, "like a spider's web," running from his shoulders back to his body lying on the bed.

He walked along the road—which, he says, he could see perfectly clearly—and again lost consciousness. When he woke up, he seemed to be propelled forward by a pair of invisible hands. Ahead of him he saw three "prodigious rocks," while overhead a dark cloud gathered. A voice speaking directly into his head told him that if he passed beyond the rocks he would enter the "eternal world," but that if he chose to, he could return to his body. He was strongly tempted to pass through a low archway between the rocks, but as he tried to peer over the "boundary line," he saw a small black cloud and "knew I was to be stopped." He suddenly woke up, lying on the bed, and insisted on telling everyone present what had happened, although they urged him to conserve his strength.

It is, as Myers points out, easy to dismiss this experience as some kind of dream. The point to note is that Wiltse had ceased to breathe, and been pronounced dead by the doctor. It is, of course, possible that he lost consciousness for four hours, and then woke up again; but it seems strange that he should have such a precise and detailed "dream" about dying when his pulse had stopped.

Where survival is concerned, the most interesting cases are obviously those that cannot be dismissed as dreams or hallucinations. Myers cites the "red scratch" case (mentioned in the previous chapter), and follows it up with another equally convincing case that was investigated by the Society for Psychical Research. A farmer named Michael Conley, of Ionia, Chicasaw County, was found dead in an outhouse of an old people's home, and his body was sent to the morgue in Dubuque, Iowa. Since the work clothes he was wearing were filthy, they were tossed outside the door of the morgue. When the farmer's daughter was told that her father was dead, she fainted. When she woke up, she insisted that her father had appeared to her, and told her that he had sewed a roll of dollar bills in the lining of his gray shirt. She described precisely the clothes he was wearing—including slippers—and said that the money was wrapped in a piece of an old red dress that had belonged to herself.

No one took her dream seriously, assuming she was upset by her father's death, but the doctor advised them that it might set her mind at rest if they fetched the clothes. No one in the family had any idea of the clothes the farmer was wearing at the time of his death, but the coroner confirmed that they were precisely as the daughter had described. In the lining of the gray shirt, which still lay outside in the yard, they found a roll of money wrapped in a piece of red cloth and sewed into the bosom.

Myers himself investigated many such cases, taking signed statements from all the witnesses, and it was obviously this close involvement that finally convinced him of the reality of survival. It seems significant that everyone in that highly skeptical "Cambridge group" who studied the evidence for life after death ended by being convinced. Myers himself started from the same assumption as Thomson Jay Hudson—that all paranormal phenomena may be due to the extraordinary powers of the subjective mind (or subliminal mind, as Myers preferred to call it). Hudson used the evidence of hypnosis—like the patient who made a cross at the end of twenty thousand minutes—to argue that the unconscious mind has unlimited powers of observation and memory, as well as powers of telepathy and clairvoyance. According to Hudson, "spirits of the dead" are actually the unconscious mind playing games. In most cases, this explanation can be stretched to fit the facts. For example, in the "red scratch" case, Hudson would say that although the mother had covered up the red scratch with makeup, the brother of the dead girl noticed it subconsciously as she lay in her coffin. His own unconscious knowledge that his mother was close to death led his subliminal mind to conjure up the vision of his sister's ghost, complete with red scratch, in order to provide his mother with comfort in the face of death. (This kind of "unconscious observation" theory is sometimes known as "cryptomnesia," meaning buried memory.) It is altogether more difficult to stretch the "unconscious observation" theory to fit cases like that of Michael Conley. The farmer was far away from his family when he died, and they had no idea what he was wearing. The only explanation that fits the subliminal theory is that the daughter used a form of clairvoyance or second sight to find out what clothes her father was wearing and about the money sewed into his shirt. As an explanation, this one is no more "scientific,"and it is slightly more far-fetched, than the assumption that Michael Conley's spirit appeared to his daughter in a dream.

Two close friends played a major part in convincing Myers that human beings survive the death of the body: the Rev. Stainton Moses and William James. Oddly enough, both of them were originally even more skeptical than Myers.

William Stainton Moses was in many ways a typical "sick sensitive"; his health was always poor and he was to die at fifty-three. He had to resign a number of livings because of breakdowns in his health. His original reaction to spiritualism was one of hostility, and he declared that Lord Adare's book on Daniel Dunglas Home was "the dreariest twaddle he ever came across." Robert Dale Owen's second book on the paranormal, *The Debateable Land*, impressed him more. A doctor named Speers finally persuaded him to attend a séance in 1872, and he was impressed when he received an accurate description of a friend who had died in the north of England. He began attending séances by Daniel Dunglas Home, and was finally convinced by Home's incredible phenomena. Soon after this, he realized that he himself was a medium. Odd things began to happen. Raps resounded from around the room. The toilet articles in his bedroom floated on to the bed and formed a cross.

Apports—like perfume and pincushions—fell from the air. Then, to his alarm, Moses was himself lifted up into the air. The third time this happened he was thrown on to a table, then on to the sofa. He began holding séances, at which the table floated up into the air, musical instruments played, and all kinds of scents wafted through the room. His honesty and integrity were so obvious that he did more to convince Myers of the reality of mediumship than anyone else.

Since table rapping took so long, Moses decided to try automatic writing. He would write his question at the top of a page, then sit with a pencil in his hand until it began to write. The handwriting was small and neat, quite unlike Moses' own. Finally, Moses accumulated twenty-four volumes of these automatic scripts. After his death, they were passed on to Myers, who made selections from them for a volume called *Spirit Teachings*. Together with Allen Kardec's *The Spirits'*

Book, it forms the most interesting body of automatic writing in spiritualist literature.

Like Myers, Stainton Moses was inclined to believe that all this writing came from his own unconscious mind. On one occasion, he asked the "spirit"—who seemed to be literate and intelligent—to quote the first line of Virgil's *Aeneid.* The spirit wrote the answer correctly. Moses was struck by the thought that, although he himself did not know the line consciously, he might well have recollected it from his schooldays. So he asked the spirit if it would go to the bookcase, select the last book but one on the second shelf, and read the last paragraph on page 94. The spirit apparently did this without removing the book from the shelf. Moses himself had no idea what the book was, but the spirit quoted the paragraph word for word.

This could, of course, be explained by the "cryptomnesia" theory—that Moses had read the paragraph at some time, and that his subliminal mind could recall it word for word. So by way of convincing him, the spirit decided to select its own book. It dictated a paragraph about the poet Pope, and then told Moses that he would find it on the same shelf, in a book called *Poetry, Romance and Rhetoric.* When Moses took this off the shelf, it opened at the right page.

Spirit Teachings is a fascinating book because it contradicts Stainton Moses' own creed in many respects. For a Christian clergyman who had been brought up to believe that Christ is God, it must have been disconcerting to be told that Jesus was simply a great teacher, like many others, and that he himself would have disowned most of the absurd fictions that men have foisted on him. On the day after this startling communication, Moses argued long and bitterly, attacking, the "spirit teachings," and calling them "silly and frivolous, if not mischievous." But the "teachers" (there were apparently forty-nine of them) refused to budge an inch, and explained to Moses that all human history is a "progressive revelation of one and the same God"—in other words, that the idea of Jesus as the unique son of God is a purely human notion.

Like Kardec's *Spirits' Book*, Moses' *Spirit Teachings* also insists that there are a great many mischievous spirits around, most of them the "earth bound" spirits of human beings who are either unaware they are dead or have no wish to move "elsewhere." He makes the interesting observation that execution is a silly way to deal with criminals, since it lets loose a vengeful and murderous spirit that will do its best to exert a harmful influence on the living; like Kardec, the *Spirit Teachings* states that spirits can enter into our minds, and that we are often influenced by them without knowing it.

Perhaps the most impressive thing about *Spirit Teachings* is that Moses himself felt so ambivalent about them. He published extracts in *Light*, the journal of the College of Psychic Science, but deliberately left out some of the harsher exchanges—in fact, there is evidence that he destroyed one of the notebooks because the spirits were so uncomplimentary about him. Moreover, he went to considerable trouble to conceal the identities of the forty-nine communicators, obviously feeling that to reveal them—they included half a dozen Old Testament prophets, not to mention Plato and Aristotle—would simply lead most people to assume he was mad or that the spirits were leg-pullers. The names of the communicators were finally revealed more than half a century after Moses' death by a researcher called A. W. Trethewy.

William James, the other major influence on Frederic Myers, was the son of a follower of Swedenborg. In spite of this—or perhaps because of it—his attitude toward Spiritualism was originally one of bored indifference. Like Alfred Russel Wallace and Charles Darwin, James began his career as a naturalist, and went on an expedition to explore the upper Amazon. Ill health drove him back to Boston. He studied medicine in Germany and became a doctor. As a thinker, he had little patience with involved metaphysics, and he developed the doctrine called "pragmatism," a kind of predecessor of modern

Logical Positivism. Stated very crudely, this says: "It doesn't matter what you believe so long as it works." (James expressed it: "We have the right to believe at our own risk any hypothesis that is live enough to tempt our will"—a doctrine that victims of Nazism might feel to be a little simplistic.) As a psychologist his *Principles of Psychology* brought him fame—he believed that our emotions are basically merely physical sensations (a doctrine known as the James-Lange theory of emotions).

It can well be imagined that a pragmatist like James—he invented the expression "tough-minded"—would have little patience with the doctrines of Spiritualism. Reviewing a book called *Planchette* when he was a medical student, James complained that "we fail to discover among all the facts [about psychical phenomena] a single one possessing either aesthetic beauty, intellectual originality or material usefulness."

When he came to England in 1882, James met Myers, Gurney, and Podmore, and was impressed by their integrity and sincerity. But where the paranormal was concerned, he remained a skeptic. Then, in 1885, his mother-in-law, Eliza Gibbens, heard about a remarkable young medium called Leonore Piper, and went to see her. Mrs. Piper went into a trance, and then proceeded to tell Mrs. Gibbens all kinds of facts about members of the family, identifying most of them by their Christian names. When Mrs. Gibbens recounted all this to her daughter and son-in-law, James was naturally intrigued. His innate skepticism suggested that Mrs. Piper had managed to make vague general statements that sounded true. The alternative was that she had somehow read Mrs. Gibben's mind. The next day, James' sister-in-law went to see Mrs. Piper, taking with her a letter in Italian. Mrs. Piper held the letter to her forehead, and described the writer in detail. James was now sufficiently interested to go to see Mrs. Piper himself.

Mrs. Piper had discovered her own psychic powers when she went to consult a Boston healer named J. R. Cocke, and fell into a trance. On the next occasion she went to see Cocke, other people were present, including a certain Judge Frost. As soon as Cocke put his hand on her forehead, Mrs. Piper went into a trance, then went to the table and wrote a message on a sheet of paper, which she handed to the judge. It was, apparently, a message from his dead son, and he declared it "the most remarkable he had ever received." Mrs. Piper suddenly became a local celebrity.

James went to see her in a highly critical frame of mind, together with his wife Alice. The Jameses took care that Mrs. Piper should not know their identity, or that they were connected with the previous "sitters." Mrs. Piper went into her trance, and was then taken over by her "control," a Frenchman called "Phinuit." To James' surprise, Phinuit mentioned several members of the family he had already described to Mrs. Gibbens, spoke of Alice's father as "Giblin," and spoke of a child the Jameses had lost the previous year. The child had been called Herman; Phinuit called him "Herrin"—a fairly accurate approximation.

James went away badly puzzled; either Mrs. Piper knew his wife's family by sight, and had learned "by some lucky coincidence" all kinds of intimate details about them, or she possessed some kind of supernormal powers. He continued to visit Mrs. Piper, and after observing her for a long time, decided that she was undoubtedly genuine. But were the spirits genuine? James felt that "it is hard to reconcile" the theory of spirit control with "the extreme triviality of most of the communications." Besides, Phinuit—who claimed to be a Frenchman—had only the most rudimentary knowledge of French. The likeliest theory, James decided, was that Phinuit was some aspect of Mrs. Piper's own personality—in other words, that Mrs. Piper was a "split personality," like Louis Vivé. Even that failed to explain how Phinuit could get hold of so much accurate information. James kept sending his friends to her—all under pseudonyms—and Mrs. Piper continued to produce accurate information about dead relatives.

James allowed himself to be convinced. He said later: "If you wish to upset the law that all crows are black, you must not seek to show that no crows are; it is enough if you can prove one single crow to be white." It was one of the most sensible remarks ever made about spiritualism; the "crow" James had in mind was Leonore Piper.

In 1885, an American branch of the Society for Psychical Research had been founded in Philadelphia by Professor William Barrett. The London Society sent over one of its most promising young investigators, Richard Hodgson, a thoroughly tough-minded individual, who had been to India to investigate Madame Blavatsky and decided she was a fraud. Hodgson immediately called on Mrs. Piper, and was staggered when she spoke to him about a girl called Jessie, to whom he had been engaged in Australia. Jessie had died while Hodgson was abroad. What convinced Hodgson even more than Phinuit's accurate description of Jessie, was his report of a conversation that no one but Hodgson knew about. Hodgson, who had so far been a skeptic about psychical phenomena, had no doubt that Mrs. Piper was genuine. He signed her up to devote her services to the Society for Psychical Research—for £200 a year ($800)—and in 1889 she came to England. Hodgson even went to the length of having her shadowed by private detectives to see whether she had some private information network. Myers, Lodge, and the Sidgwicks tested her extensively, and decided that, whatever the nature of her powers, they were undoubtedly genuine. But then, they could have been based on telepathy.

What finally convinced Hodgson was a case involving a young man named George Pellew, who had been killed in a fall in 1892. Hodgson, who had known Pellew, took another old friend of Pellew's along to a sitting with Mrs. Piper. Phinuit immediately recognized Pellew's friend—or, rather, Pellew's "spirit" recognized him, and called him by his correct name. The friend removed a stud he was wearing and handed it to Phinuit. George Pellew immediately said (through Phinuit): "That's mine. Mother gave you that." The friend denied this, but he later turned out to be wrong. Pellew's stepmother *had* removed the studs from the body, and when the friend asked for some memento, it was she who suggested sending them to him. Here was a fact that Mrs. Piper could not have learned by telepathy.

Phinuit went on to talk about a couple named James and Mary Howard, with whom Pellew had lived for a time in New York. The friend only knew the Howards slightly, and Hodgson did not know them at all; but Pellew went on to speak of their daughter Katherine, and sent her a message: "Tell her, she'll know. I will solve the problems, Katherine." This meant nothing to Hodgson or the friend. But when James Howard was told about it the next day, he had no doubt that the message came from Pellew, who used to have long discussions about time, space, and eternity with Katherine Howard, and had used the phrase "I will solve the problems, Katherine" while he was alive.

Myers and Hodgson were finally convinced by Mrs. Piper that the messages really came from spirits, but James continued to feel that Myers' subliminal mind theory was as good as any. It was another fourteen years before he was willing to concede that the subliminal mind could not explain *all* the phenomena. In December 1905, Hodgson was playing handball at a club in Boston when he collapsed and died. That night, Mrs. Piper dreamed she was trying to enter a dark tunnel, and that a bearded man like Hodgson was trying to prevent her; the next morning, she learned of his death. Eight days later, she was holding a pencil when her hand suddenly wrote the word "Hodgson." From then on, Hodgson began to communicate through Mrs. Piper. William James and his son attended a séance, and James had to admit that this was the authentic Hodgson personality. Yet although he was willing to admit that much, he was still not prepared to concede that Hodgson's spirit had somehow survived his death. He suggested that he was confronting some kind of "after-image" of Hodgson, like a film or gramophone record. What James did not explain is how a film or gramophone record could answer questions about Hodgson's life, and convince a number of people that it was Hodgson speaking. James himself would die in 1910, and—as we have seen in the last chapter—would convince Professor James Hyslop of his survival of death by sending the cryptic message about red pyjamas via a medium who had never heard of either James or Hyslop.

Human Personality and Its Survival of Bodily Death concludes with the long account of Mrs. Piper; she was, apparently, Myers' "white crow" as well as James'. Myers never lived to see his masterpiece in print; his health had begun to fail soon after the embarrassing business of Ada Goodrich-Freer. (Miss Goodrich-Freer commented balefully that people who crossed her often came to a bad end.) William James wrote a long review of the book when it finally came out, two years after Myers' death, and the tone of the review was far from total enthusiasm: "The work, whatever weaknesses it may have, strikes me as at least a masterpiece of coordination and unification. The voluminous arsenal of 'cases' . . . might make the most erudite naturalist or historian envy him. . . ." In retrospect, James seems less than generous. It is true that the book has certain weaknesses which Myers would have undoubtedly removed if he had known about them; for example, he cites Ada Goodrich-Freer's experiments in crystal gazing, and we know enough about that lady to feel that most of her claims must be viewed with suspicion. Neither did Myers know that his secretary of many years, George Albert Smith—the hypnotist who demonstrated the nine different levels of trance memory—would one day be accused of cheating in some of his earliest experiments in Brighton with a young man named Douglas Blackburn. (It is true that there was no earthly reason why Smith should have continued to cheat when he began to work for Myers, and his severest critics concede that he was a genuine hypnotist. But again, the least breath of this kind of suspicion makes evidence valueless for scientific purposes.) Having said that, it is necessary to concede that *Human Personality* towers above all other books on psychical research like a mountain above foothills.

Where the "white crow," Leonore Piper, is concerned, one intriguing question remains. If Phinuit was not a genuine Frenchman, who was he? Eleanor Sidgwick studied the problem for twenty-three years before—in 1915—she announced her own conclusion: that Phinuit was a fragment of Mrs. Piper's personality—a multiple personality, like Clara Fowler's alter-ego Sally. Later studies conducted with other mediums—like Mrs. Osborne Leonard and Eileen Garrett—make this practically a certainty. In 1935, the researcher Whately Carington gave Mrs. Leonard a word association test—saying a word and waiting for Mrs. Leonard to reply with a word she associated with it. He made the interesting discovery that Mrs. Leonard and her control, Feda, were like mirror images as far as words were concerned. When Mrs. Leonard reacted slowly to a word, Feda reacted quickly, and vice versa. The same was found of Mrs. Garrett and her control, Uvani. This could not be coincidence. Ever since the earliest studies of multiple personality, researchers had noticed that the patient and his alter-ego had diametrically opposite qualities. In 1811, a girl called Mary Reynolds, who lived in Pennsylvania, fell into a deep sleep for twenty hours, and when she woke up, had become another person. The original Mary was a dull girl, hyper-cautious and subject to fits of depression; the new "Mary" was merry, irresponsible, and flighty. For twenty years or so the Marys alternated, then they slowly blended, creating an altogether more satisfactory personality. It was almost as if Mary's personality was made out of a child's construction kit, and Mary 1 used up one set of attributes, while Mary 2 used the rest. Janet's patient Leonie—the one who could be summoned from half a mile away by the hypnotist—had the same kind of mirror-image alter-ego. This alter-ego flatly denied that she was Leonie, declaring that Leonie was a stupid idiot. Lady Una Troubridge, who published a study of Mrs. Leonard in 1922, noticed that Feda seemed to feel contemptuous of the medium.

If Phinuit, Feda, Uvani, and the rest are simply personality fragments of the medium, how is it possible to take them seriously? The clue may lie in the case of Louis Vivé, whose alter-ego was also clearly his right-brain self. We have seen that the right brain is basically what Thomson Jay Hudson meant by the subjective mind, and what Myers meant by the subliminal mind. If they are correct, the right brain is the source of psychic powers, or at least a kind of receiver and amplifier. Under hypnosis, the left brain is put to sleep, and the right is able to exercise these powers without the unnerving critical scrutiny of the left. Wallace and Barrett became interested in the paranormal because they observed hypnotized subjects who could share their own sensations—that is, whose right brains could telepathically "pick up" their feelings. If this theory is correct, then Feda and the rest were pure right-brain entities who may have been able to pick up messages from spirits.

This could also explain their failures. After Phinuit, Mrs. Piper was controlled by a whole group of spirits who claimed to be the same ones who had dictated to Stainton Moses. But when asked about their names—which they had secretly communicated to Stainton Moses—they gave the wrong answers. One psychologist—Stanley Hall—invented a niece called Bessie Beals and asked Mrs. Leonard's "control" to get in touch with her. The control obliged, and the fictitious Bessie Beals passed on all kinds of messages. The right brain—or subjective mind—is enormously suggestible; it can conjure up a spirit as easily as a hypnotized person can conjure up an illusion that someone is sitting in an empty chair. The fact that Phinuit was able to give so much accurate information about George Pellew, including facts unknown to the "sitters," argues strongly that he was a real spirit, making use of Mrs. Piper's right brain as a telephone line.

We have not yet finished with Myers. In fact, we might say that the part played by Myers after his death—or by someone who called himself Myers—was more important than the part he played during his life.

Myers had often remarked that one of the few ways for communicators to prove beyond all doubt that they were spirits of the dead would be to give separate bits of a message to several mediums, so they only made sense when fitted together. *That* would completely rule out telepathy, cryptomnesia, or right-brain leg-pulling. If we are to believe the evidence of the celebrated series of communications known as the Cross Correspondences, this is precisely what happened.

Myers died on January 17, 1901. A few years before his death, he had handed Oliver Lodge a message in a sealed envelope; it was to be kept sealed until some spirit purporting to be Myers should claim to repeat the message.

Two of Myers' closest friends at Cambridge were Dr. Arthur Verrall, a classical scholar, and his wife Margaret, a lecturer in classics at Newnham College. After Myers' death, Margaret Verrall decided to try automatic writing, to see if she could establish contact with Myers. She was a rationalist and a skeptic, but she thought it worth a try. Her hand was soon scribbling its way across the page, but the messages seemed muddled and fragmentary. Then one day there came a message in rather poor Latin, signed "Myers." From then on, the messages flowed more freely. One of them contained the statement: "Myers' sealed envelope left with Lodge . . . It has in it the words from the *Symposium* about love bridging the chasm." The message was hastily conveyed to Lodge, who opened the envelope. To his disappointment, it contained nothing about Plato. It said: "If I can revisit any earthly scene, I should choose the Valley in the grounds of Hallsteads, Cumberland." Then someone recalled that Myers *had* referred to the *Symposium*—Plato's dialogue about love—in a privately printed book called *Fragments of an Inner Life*. It had been written as a memorial to Annie Marshall, wife of Myers' cousin Walter, with whom Myers had been in love. Annie had committed suicide by drowning herself in Ullswater, and had lived in Hallsteads, Cumberland. So there was a connection between the sealed message and Plato's *Symposium*.

Soon after this, Richard Hodgson was holding a séance with Mrs. Piper in Boston, and he suggested that Mrs. Piper's control—now a spirit called "Rector"—should try to appear to Margaret Verrall's daughter Helen, holding a spear. (Helen Verrall was also a gifted psychic.) Rector misheard and asked: "Why a sphere?" Hodgson corrected him, and Rector agreed to try the experiment for the next week. Three days later, Margaret Verrall received a message that included the Greek word *sphairos* ("sphere") and the Latin *volatile ferrum* ("flying iron"), Virgil's description of a spear. Next time Hodgson sat with Mrs. Piper, Rector said he had carried out the suggestion, and showed Mrs. Verrall a "sphear."

Before we go any further, it must be admitted that most of the "evidence" of the Cross Correspondences is just as infuriatingly vague and ambiguous as this. It has never been published complete, and if it was, it would occupy several large volumes. It is undoubtedly the most convincing evidence of survival ever obtained by mediums, and also the most boring. A skeptic might well ask why, if Myers wanted to prove he was still alive, he could not have told Mrs. Verrall that his sealed message referred to Hallsteads in Cumberland, instead of talking misleadingly about Plato's *Symposium*, and why, if he wanted to establish a connection between Mrs. Piper and Margaret Varrall, he did not write in English: "Hodgson asked me to show you a spear." One possible answer may lie in a statement made by Myers in one of the scripts.

> *The nearest simile I can find to express the difficulties of sending a message—is that I appear to be standing behind a sheet of frosted glass which blurs sight and deadens sounds—dictating feebly to a reluctant and somewhat obtuse secretary.*

Stainton Moses had also been told that the spirits who wrote out messages were a kind of secretary or amanuensis:

> *The intelligences who are able to [practice] . . . direct writing . . . are few. Most frequently the actual writing is done by one who is accustomed to manifes in that way, and who acts . . . as the amanuesis of the spirits who wish to communicate. In many cases several spirits are concerned. . . .*

In a moment of exasperation, William James suggested another explanation for the vagaries of the spirits:

> *I confess that at times I have been tempted to believe that the Creator has eternally intended this department of nature to remain baffling, to prompt our curiosities and hopes and suspicions all in*

> *equal measure, so that, although ghosts and clairvoyances and raps and messages from spirits . . . can never be fully explained away, they can also never be susceptible of full corroboration.*

To put it another way, it looks as if the spirits have been ordered to provide just enough evidence to convince those who are willing to be convinced, but never enough to win over the skeptics. This notion—which we might call James' Law—must have crossed the mind of everybody who has taken an interest in the paranormal. The evidence is abundant and plentiful, but it *always* leaves room for doubt.

Having said that, it must be admitted that some of the evidence of the Cross Correspondences is very convincing indeed. At an early stage, Mrs. Verrall received a sentence: "Record the bits, and when fitted together they will make the whole." Soon after this, Rudyard Kipling's sister, Alice Fleming (who lived in India), decided to try automatic writing, and quickly received a message which read: "My Dear Mrs. Verrall [it sounds as though Myers had got his 'secretaries' mixed up], I am very anxious to speak to some of the old friends—Miss J—and to A W." This referred to Alice Johnson, Secretary of the Society for Psychical Research, and to Arthur W. Verrall, Mrs. Verrall's husband. The message then went on to give a description of Arthur Verrall, and ended the message: "Send this to Mrs. Verrall's, 5, Selwyn Gardens, Cambridge." This was Mrs. Verrall's correct address, but Alice Fleming had no way of knowing this. She knew Mrs. Verrall's name—having read Myers' *Human Personality*—but nothing else; she had never been in Cambridge. Mrs. Fleming duly contacted Margaret Verrall at 5 Selwyn Gardens, and became another in the group of mediums who took down the Cross Correspondences. (She called herself Mrs. Holland, because her family disapproved of psychical research.) Most of Alice Fleming's early messages were signed "F"—a signature Myers frequently used.

On another occasion, Alice Fleming received a detailed description of a room. It was later recognized as a very exact description of Margaret Verrall's sitting room. There was only one inaccuracy; the description said there was a bust in the corner. When Mrs. Verrall mentioned this to a friend, the friend said: "But surely you *have* got a bust in the corner of your room?" Mrs. Verrall had some kind of filter, which looked—in the dark corner—very much like a bust on a pedestal.

Later, other communicators joined in the game, and claimed to be Henry Sidgwick and Edmund Gurney, but the conundrums remained incredibly complicated. One of Mrs. Piper's "sitters" asked Myers if he would indicate attempts to transmit Cross Correspondences by drawing a triangle enclosed in a circle. A week later, Margaret Verrall received a message which ended with a triangle inside a circle, as well as a triangle in a semicircle. Two months later, Myers spoke through Mrs. Piper and stated that he had given Mrs. Verrall a circle and tried to draw a triangle, but "it did not appear." Here we seem to have the typical muddle caused by sheets of frosted glass and obtuse secretaries.

Even this simple case has more complications. Just after the suggestion that Myers should use a triangle in a circle, Mrs. Verrall produced a script that began: "an anagram would be better. Tell him that—rats, star, tars and so on . . . or again tears, stare." Five days later, Mrs. Verrall's script began with an anagram: Aster (Latin for "star") and teras (Greek for "wonder"). It also talked about hope, and quoted Browning. Two weeks later, Mrs. Piper's script said: "I referred also to Browning again. I referred to Hope and Browning . . . I also said star." A week after this, Helen Verrall (the daughter) received a script that began with a drawing of a star, and included a reference to Browning's Pied Piper of Hamelin. But most readers might be forgiven for feeling that such complicated puzzles defeat their own purpose.

In 1908, another amateur medium joined the group. She was Winifred Coombe-Tennant, who was related to Myers by marriage (Myers' wife was the sister of Mrs. Coombe-Tennant's husband). She began receiving messages signed by Myers and Gurney. Then, in 1909, the script explained that Myers and Gurney were trying a new experiment—to make the words enter Mrs. Coombe-Tennant's mind spontaneously. Soon she was not only "picking up" words that floated into her mind, but receiving clear impressions of the personalities who were sending them; she could sense whether it was Myers or Gurney immediately. The conversations were telepathic. On the first occasion, Myers' voice—inside her head—asked, "Can you hear what I am saying?" She replied mentally, "Yes." The written scripts continued, and often included words that she had "heard." Later, Myers asked her to bring Sir Oliver Lodge along to her automatic writing sessions. Mrs. Coombe-Tennant disliked the idea, but finally gave way. Then Gurney asked if G. W. Balfour could also come along—he had been a friend of Gurney's, and knew a great deal about philosophy. The result was often tiresome for Mrs. Coombe-Tennant. She had to sit there, acting as "secretary" in philosophical discussions that she did not understand. After Balfour had given a lecture at Cambridge, "Sidgwick" started a discussion with him about the mind-body relationship, epiphenomenalism, and interactionism. Although Mrs. Coombe-Tennant (or, as she preferred to be known, Mrs. Willett) was intelligent, she had no idea of what they were talking about, and at one point, as Sidgwick tried to put words into her mind, she lost her temper and exploded: "I can't think why people talk about such stupid things!" Her irritation is far more convincing than any amount of corroboration.

Taken as a whole, the Cross Correspondences and the Willett scripts are among the most convincing evidence that at present exists for life after death. For anyone who is prepared to devote weeks to studying them, they prove beyond all reasonable doubt that Myers, Gurney, and Sidgwick went on communicating after death. The problem remains: why did they not adopt some straightforward suggestion—like the idea of using a triangle in a circle—that would make them far more simple—and therefore more convincing to skeptics? The answer—if we can accept James' Law—is that they were not out to make wholesale conversions. Of course, this is just the kind of answer that will make the skeptics shrug contemptuously.

"Myers" was nothing if not persistent. In November 1924, an Irish medium, Geraldine Cummins, was invited to tea with a retired captain and his wife. Her friend Miss E. B. Gibbes was also invited along. Geraldine Cummins, daughter of Professor Ashley Cummins, had tried automatic writing for the first time a year before, and found that she was a natural medium. The captain and his wife were hoping to contact friends through the ouija board[6], a glass on a smooth surface, surrounded by the letters of the alphabet; when fingers of the sitters are laid lightly on top of the glass, it may move from letter to letter, spelling out words. On this occasion, the board quickly spelled out the name "Frederic Myers" and asked: "Do you know my friends?" Asked which friends, he replied Barrett and Balfour. He then explained that he wanted to establish a "cross correspondence." The captain and his wife were rather disappointed to have Myers communicating instead of their own friends, so the session came to an end. But Myers continued to communicate, and a week later announced his presence at another of Miss Cummins' automatic writing sessions. Asked about the problems of communication, he explained that their method was to "impress" the "inner mind" of the medium with the message, and that the inner mind would then send it on to the brain. "The brain is a mere mechanism. The inner mind is like soft wax, it receives our thoughts . . . but it must produce the words that clothe it. That is what makes cross-correspondence so very difficult." This certainly seems to explain why the Cross Correspondences often sound so muddled.

Myers soon announced an interesting project—to try to communicate through Mrs. Leonard's control, Feda, immediately after communicating through Geraldine Cummins. He suggested that the subject of the message should be telepathy and the views of his friend Lord Balfour. Miss Gibbes pointed out that this was not a good idea, because she had recently been at a public meeting at which Balfour

---

6. So called from the French *oui* and the German *ja*.

had spoken about telepathy, and it had been reported in the press. So it could be objected that the medium was already thinking about the subject. Myers agreed, and said that in that case, he would talk about the book he had intended to write before his death, a book expressing his conviction that life after death had been proved beyond all doubt.

The next day, Miss Gibbes hurried along to see Mrs. Osborne Leonard, making quite sure she dropped no hint about her purpose in coming. Feda said that there were several spirits hanging around waiting to communicate. Miss Gibbes said she had somebody special in mind—an important man. At this, Feda announced that an elderly man was present. Trying to pick up his name, she could only get the impression of a capital M. The man, she said, was showing her poetry, which was one of his main interests: "He seems to have been rather clever in understanding old poets—Virgil particularly." She then added the important comment: "He is keeping an appointment with you." Soon after this, she announced the man's Christian name: "Fred—I keep getting Fred." (Myers was known to his friends as Fred.) She added that Miss Gibbes had been in touch with Fred on the previous day.

The next time Myers appeared at a session with Geraldine Cummins, he apologized for not coming over very clearly, and explained that he had had problems with Feda, who was too "lively" (he obviously meant scatterbrained) and that there were too many other thoughts buzzing around the room at the time. When Miss Gibbes said she thought he had "come over" very well, Myers" replied; "Good, you surprise me." All the same, he said, he felt the session had been a failure. What he had wanted to get across was that he had intended to write a book declaring his total belief in life after death. But Feda had simply not picked up what he was trying to say. Miss Gibbes' feeling was that in spite of this, the attempt to communicate through two mediums on two different days had been extremely successful. It is difficult not to agree with her. These sessions are also important because they give us a clear idea of the infuriating problems apparently faced by spirits in trying to make contact with the living—rather like someone trying to make himself heard over a very bad telephone line, with continual interruptions from "crossed lines."

The books that grew out of these communications—*The Road to Immortality* and *Beyond Human Personality*—will strike some readers as fascinating, and some as utterly tiresome rubbish. The following is a typical sentence:

> *The purpose of existence may be summed up in a phrase—the evolution of mind in matter that varies in degree and kind—so that the mind develops through manifestation, and in an everexpanding universe ever increases in power and gains thereby the true conception of reality.*

It sounds like the kind of meaningless waffle churned out by fake messiahs. On closer examination, it not only makes sense, but very good sense. This notion that mind is attempting to "insert" itself into matter is common to all forms of evolutionary vitalism, from Hegel to Shaw. It goes on to state that matter varies in degrees and kind—implying that it may be either solid or beyond the range of our senses. (Elsewhere, Myers states that it is all a question of rates of vibration—a view that has been made commonplace by modern physics.) The mind develops through this process of inserting itself into matter, and slowly develops power and a deeper sense of reality. When we look at it again, we can see that the original impression of vagueness is due to the lack of punctuation, which gives it an air of ambiguity. According to Myers, the spirit who communicates has to use the medium's own intellectual apparatus (and, presumably, her vocabulary). This, presumably, is why so much spirit communication gives an impression of feeble-mindedness. (Myers is the first to admit that many spirits *are* feeble-minded.)

This question of *what* is communicated must be left until later. For the moment, the question is whether it can be seriously accepted as a communication from the dead. All things considered, the answer to this must be in the affirmative. If Geraldine Cummins and E. B. Gibbes are telling the truth about the circumstances in which the communications were received, then it is certainly a reasonable assumption that the same spirit tried to speak through Miss Cummins and Mrs. Leonard.

The sense of genuineness is even stronger in a later book of the "scripts" of Geraldine Cummins, *Swan on a Black Sea*, which purports to be a series of communications from "Mrs. Willett"—Winifred Coombe-Tennant, the automatic writer who learned to "hear" Myers and Gurney directly. She died in 1956, at the age of eighty-one, keeping her "Willett" identity secret to the end. A year later, William Salter, president of the Society for Psychical Research, asked Geraldine Cummins if she would try to "contact" the mother of Major Henry Coombe-Tennant. Geraldine Cummins knew nothing whatsoever about Mrs. Coombe-Tennant. On August 28, 1957, "Astor," Geraldine Cummin's "control," protested irritably about the difficult task she had been set—contacting the mother of someone she had never heard of. But from Salter's letter she picked up a feeling of "writing and secrets to be kept." Then she declared she had been approached by a fragile old lady in her eighties. Asked for the old lady's name, Astor said: "Win or Wyn." From that point onward, Winifred Coombe-Tennant took over, and produced an incredible body of personal reminiscences, full of accurate statements about Mrs. Coombe-Tennant's life. It is also one of the most direct and personal documents ever dictated by a so-called spirit. Even if Geraldine Cummins had been a fraud, it would have been impossible for her to have found out so much intimate detail about the life of a woman she had never met. The only other reasonable hypothesis is that Geraldine Cummins and Mrs. Coombe-Tennant's children collaborated to concoct the scripts, which seems unlikely.

Once again we encounter the central paradox of the survival problem. *Swan on a Black Sea* is perhaps the most convincing proof of the reality of life after death ever set down on paper. Yet it does not actually *say* anything in the least important. For a message from the "other side," the mysterious realm of the all-knowing dead, it seems curiously banal, like a conversation overheard at a jumble sale in the church hall. It will convert no skeptic to the doctrines of Spiritualism because no skeptic would take the trouble to read it. So once again we encounter James' Law: that perplexing mandate that seems to assert that the evidence for life after death shall always be strong enough to reassure the converted, but never conclusive enough to have the slightest influence on the unbelievers.

Chapter Six

Dr. Steiner and the Problem of Reincarnation

ON THE EVENING OF AUGUST 22, 1900, A SLIM, mild-looking man presented himself at the library of the Theosophical Society in the Kaiser Friedrich Strasse, Berlin, and introduced himself as Dr. Rudolf Steiner. The Countess Brockdorff, who was secretary of the Lodge, looked at him without any great curiosity. Rudolf Steiner was almost forty years old, and his accent had a touch of the lower-Austrian peasant. The pince-nez glasses, attached by a cord, gave him the look of an absent-minded schoolmaster. His smile was friendly but shy. The countess knew that he had written books about Goethe, and lectured about history and politics to the Workers' Educational Association. He was to lecture that evening on Nietzsche—not entirely a suitable subject for Theosophists, who believed that most of the world's deepest wisdom came from ancient India, for Nietzsche, after all, was an atheist and an archrebel.

When Dr. Steiner began to lecture, the countess' doubts seemed justified. His voice was a little monotonous, and his sentences were sometimes abstract and involved. His own attitude to Nietzsche seemed rather odd. Dr. Steiner obviously believed in a spiritual reality underlying the universe, and Nietzsche undoubtedly did not. So what on earth was Dr. Steiner doing lecturing about him? Yet when one grew used to the rather dull manner, there was something endearing about Dr. Steiner. His eyes twinkled with friendliness, and as he talked, he seemed to take the audience into his confidence. After the lecture, in answer to a question, Steiner described his visit to Nietzsche in Weimar. The philosopher was already insane—he would die only three days after Steiner's lecture—and Steiner told of his beautiful forehead and calm eyes, which gazed blankly into space. Suddenly, said Steiner, he had a deep inner-perception of the real Nietzsche, as if he could see his soul hovering over his head.

As she was saying goodnight, the countess asked Steiner whether he meant he had literally seen Nietzsche's soul hovering over his head. To her surprise, Steiner answered: "What I saw with the eyes of the spirit was Nietzsche's astral body pressing against his physical body." "You *saw* it?" she asked. He smiled at her: "Yes, but not with the physical eyes." Then he said goodnight. He was certainly an intriguing man. By general request, the countess asked him to come back again the following week to talk to them about his own mystical interpretation of Goethe's puzzling story called *Fairy Tale*. This time he spoke with such quiet authority that no one had any doubt that he was speaking from inner experience. Steiner was asked if he would consent to give a series of lectures to the Theosophical Society, and when he suggested a series on the great mystics, they accepted with enthusiasm.

That winter, Steiner became the darling of the Berlin Theosophical Society. It was true that a few members had their reservations; what he was saying often seemed to contradict the ideas of its founder, Madame Blavatsky, and its present leader, Annie Besant. When someone pointed this out to Steiner, he only smiled mildly and said: "Is that so?" Yet it was obvious that he was not out to challenge or shock. He was speaking from direct personal experience. His erudition was formidable; he seemed to have read every important writer of the past three centuries. One rather beautiful young lady, Marie von Sivers—an actress who had been studying in Paris—made no secret of her total adoration, and Dr. Steiner was obviously charmed and overwhelmed by her attitude of discipleship; he seemed to blossom and become more confident. Some members shook their heads, knowing that he was married. The countess had never met his wife, but had been told that she was a peasant woman—at any rate, definitely not a "lady"—and that she was many years Steiner's senior.

Then—it seemed to happen overnight—Dr. Steiner had become head of the Berlin Lodge of the Theosophical Society, and was being accepted by an increasing number of people as a kind of messiah. Its membership increased remarkably. Mrs. Besant had met Steiner, and been impressed. She had seemed a little concerned about the strange, mystical Christianity preached by Steiner—but then, Madame Blavatsky had taught that all religions are roads to the same truth, so that was no cause for alarm. Steiner certainly seemed to accept Madame Blavatsky's basic teaching that the present human race is the fifth "root race" (the fourth were the inhabitants of Atlantis), and that we all go through many reincarnations. He also professed to be able to read the "Akasic records"—those invisible records of history that have been stored up on the cosmic ether—and talked with staggering authority about the childhood of Christ and the various spiritual movements in Western history.

Within ten years, Steiner had become one of the most famous men in Europe, and his following was enormous. In due course, he broke with the Theosophical Society—when Mrs. Besant tried to introduce a new "messiah" called Jiddu Krishnamurti, a mere boy—

but the German Theosophists regarded him with such reverence that almost all of them preferred to follow him into his own new organization, which he called the Anthroposophical Society. By the year 1912, many of Steiner's followers believed that he was an avatar—an incarnation of the God-principle, like Buddha and Christ, sent to earth to bring enlightenment—and that Anthroposophy would one day become the new world religion, replacing all those that had gone before. Steiner himself spoke of building a new mystical center, a magnificent temple, perhaps in Munich.

The hopes of a great new religious revival all came to nothing. Just as it seemed to be coming about, the Great War burst like a storm, and for the next four years, Europe had other things to think about besides Anthroposophy. There were even unpleasant rumors that Steiner had paved the way for Germany's defeat by giving bad advice to General von Moltke, whose wife was a Steiner disciple. Steiner built his "temple" at Dornach, in Switzerland—but it never became more than a cult-center. When the war ended, Steiner probably knew that it had cost him his chance of becoming the founder of a new religion. He went on lecturing indefatigably, but a kind of weariness set in, and he died in March 1925, not yet in his mid-sixties. His name remained well known largely because it was associated with a new type of school, and with "natural" agricultural methods.

Yet, in his way, Rudolf Steiner, the man who became a messiah between his fortieth and fiftieth years, was one of the most remarkable spiritual teachers of the twentieth century, the man who blended the Christianity of earlier epochs with the new "spiritualism" that was trying to replace it.

To understand why, we must first say a word about Madame Blavatsky. Born Helena Hahn in 1831—thirty years before Steiner's birth—the future founder of Theosophy was the daughter of a female Russian novelist. She was a plump but highly strung little girl. Sitting one day gazing into space, with a pencil in her hand, she was astonished when her hand began to write. The "communicator" announced herself as Tekla Lebendorff, an aunt of an officer in the regiment of Helena's father. Helena's father became so fascinated by all the information that Aunt Tekla gave about herself that he used his position to check on her in the government archives. To his amazement, everything she said about herself proved to be true. It seemed that the dead could communicate. Then came a shock. One day, Helena met Aunt Tekla's officer nephew, and learned that Aunt Tekla was still alive and well. Yet the information dictated by her was accurate. How could that be?

Oddly enough, this curious anomaly might be regarded as one of the more convincing proofs that humans can survive death. One of the major objections to survival is that sleep seems to contradict it. After all, our astral body is supposed to separate from the physical body in sleep, just as in death. So why do we not feel ourselves floating out of the physical body when we fall asleep, just as we are supposed to do in death? The answer of Spiritualism is that the astral body *does* wander off during sleep, but we experience total amnesia about its activities. A medium—or spirit-control—is said to be able to attract the spirit of a sleeping person just as easily as that of a dead one. This sounds highly unlikely, but that is what seems to have happened in the case of Helena Blavatsky. It also happened in a well-authenticated case of the twentieth century, when a spirit called "Gordon Davis" communicated through a medium with Dr. S. G. Soal. Davis gave an abundance of precise information about where his widow was living, and described the house on a sea front in considerable detail. When Soal finally located the house—in Southend-on-Sea—it was all as Davis had described it. But Davis was alive and well and sitting in front of the fire. Here, then, as in the case of Tekla Lebendorff, we seem to have some kind of proof that the astral body does separate from the physical body in sleep, just as it is supposed to in death.

Helena Hahn made an unhappy marriage to a man called Blavatsky, declined to surrender her virginity, and ran away from home at the age of eighteen, in 1849, the year after the strange rappings began in the home of the Fox sisters. When she arrived in New

York in 1873, she herself had developed into a formidable medium who could make raps resound from all over the room. A newspaper reporter, Henry Steel Olcott, sent to interview her became a disciple, and supported her while her hand scribbled—at an incredible pace—a book called *Isis Unveiled*. It was to make her a celebrity. Having achieved fame, Helena decided that her spiritual home was in India, and took her newly founded Theosophical Society to Bombay. Disaster came in 1884, when the Society for Psychical Research sent Richard Hodgson to investigate her claims, and a housekeeper with a grudge managed to convince him that Madame Blavatsky's spirit communications were all a fraud. Her reputation never recovered from his denunciation in the *Proceedings* of the Society for Psychical Research. She died of heart disease at the age of sixty in 1891, but her new doctrine of "Theosophy"—a combination of Hinduism, Buddhism, and Spiritualism—continued to have a worldwide influence. We may say that Madame Blavatsky's form of spiritualism achieved a far greater success than the version promulgated by the Fox sisters in Rochester in 1850, which never became more than a minority cult.

Rudolf Steiner was the son of working-class Austrians; his father was a telegraph operator on the Austrian railway. In the material sense, his childhood was "deprived"; they were very poor. But he was brought up amid beautiful scenery—mountains and forests—and, being a naturally bright boy, he made the most of the books that were available.

He was sitting in the station waiting room one day when a strange woman came in, a woman whose looks resembled those of the rest of the family. She went to the middle of the room, made some curious gestures, and said: "Try to help me if you can—now and later on." Then she walked to the big old stove and vanished into it. The child had enough self-possession to decide not to tell his parents what he had seen; they were good Catholics, and would have scolded him for superstition. He noticed that his father became sad and thoughtful in the following days. Later, he learned that a female relative he had never met had committed suicide at the time he had seen the woman in the waiting room. Since she had asked for help, it followed that she was, in some sense, still alive.

Telling this story later in one of his lectures, Steiner said:

> *From that time onward a soul life began to develop in the boy which made him conscious of worlds from which not only external trees or external mountains speak to the human soul, but also the Beings that live behind them. From that time onward, the boy lived together with the Spirits of Nature that can be specially observed in such a region; he lived with the creative beings that are behind the objects. . . .*

It seems, then, that like Wordsworth, Steiner was able to sense "unknown modes of being" in the nature around him. He was obviously—like Helena Hahn—a natural medium. He differed from all the mediums of the late-nineteenth century in one important respect: he possessed an enormous intellectual curiosity. A volume on geometry, lent to him by a schoolmaster, filled him with almost ecstatic delight. This was because he could "work out forms which are seen purely inwardly, independent of the outer senses. . . . To be able to grasp something purely spiritual brought me an inner joy. I know that through geometry I first experienced happiness."

To speak of geometry as "purely spiritual" pulls us up sharp. Spiritual? Yet this notion is the very essence of Steiner's thought, and it gives him an importance that far transcends that of any other "spiritualist" of the nineteenth, or indeed the twentieth, century. What Steiner was learning, from nature as well as geometry, was to *withdraw into himself.* The Danish philosopher Kierkegaard said: "Truth is subjectivity", meaning that the *experience* of truth—as distinguished from merely "knowing" that something is true—is a kind of *access to inner worlds.* As Chesterton points out, if I say "The earth is round," it is true, but I don't mean it. In order to mean it, I would need to be an astronaut hovering up in space. The same applies to most of our "truths." But when I relax into a warm bath and experience a deep sense of pleasure and relief, I again experience a form of "truth." The astronaut might experience this same inner certainty when he looks down for the first time and says: "My God, the earth is round!"

According to Steiner, this sense of "inwardness" is the starting point of spiritual life. What we must learn to do is to *anchor* ourselves down there, and not allow the world to drag us into a region of doubt and compromise. This, in a sense, is what Shakespeare means by "To thine own self be true." But it is more than that. It means learning to listen to inner voices, and *learning their language.* Listening to an inner voice is not merely a question of deciding either to do or not to do something, according to its advice. It is like studying some ancient wisdom written in an unknown language. It could become the study of a lifetime.

Now most of us can understand that to "retreat into oneself" can lead us to deeper appreciation of everything. To appreciate music, you close your eyes, or at least, concentrate wholly and completely on the music. When we are "in tune" with nature, it is because we are in that state of inwardness, and the paradox is that the more inward we are, the more deeply we appreciate what is "outside."

Steiner goes a step beyond this. He insists that when we are in this inward state, we also become aware of the world of the supernatural—both in the sense of spiritual and in the sense of paranormal. This seems to have been Steiner's own experience. He claims that after the vision of his father's cousin in the station waiting room, he became aware of Spirits of Nature—presumably he means the same kind of "elementals" that Rosalind Heywood claims to have encountered on Dartmoor—and of the spirits of the dead. (We may also recall Rosalind Heywood's comment, describing her telepathic encounter with her dead friend Vivian: "I quickly became aware that I could not hold the *absorbed* state which contact with 'Vivian' demanded. . . ." [my italics], suggesting that contact with the "dead" demands a certain inner-absorption.)

In his autobiography, Steiner claims two contacts with dead men, neither of whom he knew. These were not mediumistic experiences, but involved some kind of inner communion. In Vienna in his early twenties, Steiner was introduced to a cultured, middle-class family. He says: "One could sense the presence in this family of someone unknown to us. It was the father. We [Steiner and other friends] never met him, yet one felt his presence." The father was an unusual man who avoided social contact and lived like a hermit. From things his family said about him, and from the man's books, Steiner gradually came to feel that he knew him. Finally, the man died, and Steiner was asked to deliver his funeral address. He spoke of the father with such apparently intimate knowledge that the family told him that it sounded as if he knew him well.

It sounds as though Steiner means that he learned to "know" the father through hints dropped by the family. But later in his autobiography, it becomes quite clear that he means far more than this. Ten years later, he had moved to Weimar to work in the Goethe archives, editing Goethe's scientific writings. He was introduced to a widow named Anna Eunicke, who was later to become his wife. Living in her house as a lodger, he once again became intensely aware of the personality of her dead husband. In the autobiography he states: "The powers of spiritual sight which I then possessed enabled me to enter into a close relationship with these two souls after their earthly death." What Steiner claims, in effect, is that he was able to "follow" the progress of both dead men in the "spirit world."

Now it should begin to be clear why Steiner had so little patience with Spiritualism, and why he declared on one occasion: "The Spiritualists are the greatest materialists of all." A medium going into a trance, or using a pencil to trace out the words of a spirit, knows nothing of the real nature of the dead, of their inner reality. Rosalind Heywood's description of her encounter with her friend Vivian Usborne after his death comes altogether closer to it. She says that she "ran slap into 'Vivian' himself, most joyfully and most vividly alive." Vivian "conveyed in some fashion so intimate that the best word seems to be communion" what he had to tell her. Mrs. Willett also spoke about "sensing" Myers and Gurney in the same direct fashion. This is what Steiner means by contact with the dead, and he feels that Spiritualism has substituted a far more superficial and materialistic contact, without the inwardness.

According to Steiner, men in the remote past had a direct sense of contact with the dead. There is, in fact, one interesting piece of archaeological evidence for this claim. Modern human beings belong to a breed known as Cro-Magnon man, who appeared on earth about fifty thousand years ago, and who is believed to have exterminated his predecessor, Neanderthal man. Neanderthal man was small, squat, and ape-like, and his method of communication was probably confined to grunts. Yet his graves contain mysterious spherical stones, which are probably images of the sun, and other ritual objects that suggest that, like the ancient Egyptians, he possessed some kind of belief in life after death. It is hard to believe that creatures who were hardly superior to the ape should have evolved the idea of an afterlife. But if Steiner—like the modern psychologist Stan Gooch—is correct in believing that Neanderthal man was far more psychic than modern man, then his belief in a life after death was not a matter of philosophy so much as of direct experience.

And so, says Steiner:

> *If we look back with spiritual vision even but a few centuries to earlier times, we come upon something which must greatly surprise anyone ignorant of these things. We find that the intercourse between the living and the dead is becoming increasingly difficult, and that a comparatively short time ago there was a much more active intercourse between them.*[1]

According to Steiner, the dead need intercourse with the living to nourish their being. In former times there was a direct link between the living and the dead, so that the living could follow the progress of dead relatives in the afterlife. This clairvoyant faculty was gradually

---

1. "Descriptive Sketches of the Spiritual World," lectures given at Bergen on October 10 and 11, 1913.

lost, but even then, there was a kind of semiconscious feeling of the presence of the dead. Now, he says, this has virtually disappeared. Insofar as men learn to gain "access to inner worlds" through "spiritual science," they will regain the ability to communicate with the dead.

What happens to man after death is described by Steiner in one of his most important early works, *Theosophy* (although it is necessary to add immediately that even as early as 1904, Steiner's concept of Theosophy had evolved a long way beyond Madame Blavatsky's). Like all occultists, Steiner accepts that man consists of four "bodies"—physical body, etheric body (or aura), astral body, and ego. After death, the astral body and ego leave behind the physical body. The etheric body takes about three days to dissolve. During this time, the "soul" (astral body plus ego) sees the whole of its past life unfolding in review. Then it enters a realm called "kamaloca," which corresponds roughly to the purgatory of Christian doctrine. The past life is relived and examined. Since the astral body is still capable of feeling, it will suffer from its unsatisfied desires and lusts. When purified by suffering, it can finally dissolve. In kamaloca, the astral body also experiences all the sufferings it has inflicted upon others from their own point of view.

After this, the purified ego rises to the spirit world, in which it can choose its own next life. It will choose the form in which it intends to be born, and the circumstances. (Steiner emphasizes that no one should bemoan his lot, because he has chosen it himself.) These are carefully chosen to afford opportunities for evolution (which explains why we do not all choose to be fabulously successful). In due course, the soul will return to earth to live another life. One of Steiner's most fascinating books is an eight-volume work called *Karmic Relationships*, consisting of lectures delivered not long before his death, in which he claims to have used his power of "spirit vision" to trace the past incarnations of many famous men. Even for those who regard it as pure fantasy, it offers an interesting vision of Steiner's sense of the way reincarnation operates.

One eminent member of the Society for Psychical Research, Whately Carington,[2] produced in 1920 a brilliantly suggestive work called *A Theory of the Mechanism of Survival* in which he offers a criticism of Theosophy:

> *In Theosophical literature . . . we are confronted with a scheme of things built up of such terms as "Astral plane," "Etheric Double," "Causal Body," "Karma" and so forth. With all due deference to my Theosophical friends I submit that this is not scientific explanation and cannot be so unless its exponents are prepared to tell us what is and cannot be so unless its exponents are prepared to tell us what is the relation between the astral plane and the physical world, between the etheric double and the body as know to physiologists.*

It is a valid point, but it applies less to Steiner than to Madame Blavatsky. Moreover, Steiner's explanations have much in common with the theory Carington puts forward in his book. Carington begins from the concept of the fourth dimension, as discussed in the work of mathematicians such as Riemann and Lobatchevsky, and goes on to argue that much of the evidence for survival suggests that the dead exist in a world that has one more dimension than ours has. (This receives support from the near-death experience of Sir Auckland Geddes, described in chapter 2, in which Geddes said that he was "now free in a time dimension of space, where in 'now' was in some way equivalent to 'here' in ordinary three dimensional space.") In a lecture delivered in 1918 under the title "The Dead Are With Us," Steiner explains that:

> *In the spiritual sense, what is "past" has not really vanished, but is still there. In physical life men have this conception in regard to space only. If you stand in front of a tree, then go away and look back . . . the tree has not disappeared. . . . In the spiritual world*

---

2. Under the name Whately Smith.

> *the same is true in regard to* time. *If you experience something at one moment, it has passed away the next as far as physical consciousness is concerned; spiritually conceived, it has not passed away. You can look back on it just as you can look back at the tree. Richard Wagner showed that he possessed knowledge of this with the remarkable words: "Time here has become space."*

In modern physics, time is regarded as the fourth dimension; what Steiner seems to be saying is that the spirit world has, in effect, yet another dimension, which means that time is, in some sense, "static." (A modern investigator, T. C. Lethbridge, came to much the same conclusion on the basis of some curious experiments in dowsing, using a pendulum.[3])

While many people will feel inclined to dismiss Steiner's account of life after death as completely unverifiable, it cannot be denied that there is an impressive consistency about his views, and that this makes a strong appeal to the intelligence. He writes:

> *It must . . . be emphasized that this [spirit] world is woven out of the material of which human thought consists. But thought, as it lives in man, is only a shadow picture, a phantom of its true being. As the shadow of an object on the wall is related to the real object which throws this shadow, so is the thought that springs up in man related to the being in spiritland which corresponds to this thought.*

This notion that the world of the mind *is* the spirit world is somehow far more convincing—certainly more thought-provoking—than accounts of life after death that make the spirit world sound like a cross between fairyland and a holiday camp.

According to Steiner (in the lecture "The Dead Are With Us"):

> *We encounter the Dead at the moment of going to sleep, and again at the moment of waking. . . .*

---

3. See my *Mysteries*, part 1, chapter 1.

> *These moments of waking and going to sleep are of the utmost significance for intercourse with the so-called Dead—and with other spiritual beings of the higher worlds.*
>
> *The moment of going to sleep is especially favourable for us to turn to the Dead. Suppose we want to ask the Dead something. We can carry it in our soul, holding it until the moment of going to sleep, for that is the time to bring our questions to the Dead. . . . On the other hand, the moment of waking is the most favourable for the Dead to communicate to us.*

For, says Steiner, there is no one who does not bring with him "countless tidings of the dead" on waking up. There is, he explains, one rather odd problem. When we speak to the dead, the relationship is somehow reversed, and when we put a question to the dead, the question comes *from* him: "He inspires our soul with what we ask him." "And when he answers us, this comes out of our own soul." "In order to establish intercourse with those who have died, we must adapt ourselves to hear from them what we ourselves say, and to receive from our own soul what they answer."

It is interesting that in his book on Swedenborg, Dr. Wilson van Dusen (whom we encountered in the opening chapter) suggests that Swedenborg's visions of the spirit world were obtained in what he calls a "controlled hypnogogic state"—the hypnogogic state being that curious borderland between sleeping and waking. Thomson Jay Hudson, in *The Law of Psychic Phenomena*, describes how he attempted to use the miraculous powers of the subjective mind to cure a relative who had become a hopeless invalid because of rheumatism. His method was to concentrate on healing his relative—who lived in another city—just as he was on the point of sleep. He began the treatment in the middle of May 1890. A few months later, a friend who knew about the proposed treatment met his relative, and found him so much improved that he was working again, noting that the improvement had started in mid-May. According to Hudson, the subjective mind works best on the point of sleep because it is then free of its usual domination by the objective mind.

We would say, of course, that on the point of sleep, the right cerebral hemisphere is freed from its usual domination by the left-brain self.

According to Steiner: "We should not seek for the Dead through externalities, but become conscious that they are always present. Among the practical tasks of Anthroposophy will be that of gradually building the bridge between the living and the dead by means of spiritual science." He is also convinced that "a vast transformation will take place in human life when the ideas of reincarnation and karma are no longer theories held by a few people."

We have seen that, in fact, the argument about reincarnation was to split the Spiritualist movement at a very early stage, and that Kardec's Spiritism—which taught reincarnation—was virtually driven underground by the Spiritualist teaching that originated in America. Nowadays, the doctrines of reincarnation are not widely accepted by Spiritualists, although some accept it as a possibility. When I was writing *The Occult* in the early 1970s, I asked a Spiritualist friend, Professor Wilson Knight, if, next time he attended a séance, he could ask the spirits for a straightforward yes or no on this issue. In due course, he told me that the answer was neither yes nor no. Reincarnation, according to Professor Knight's "communicators," happens occasionally, but should not be regarded as a general rule.

Myers, in his communications with Geraldine Cummins (published as *The Road to Immortality*), offers an unusual interpretation of the idea of reincarnation. He speaks of the concept of the "group soul": "a number of souls all bound together by one spirit, depending for their nourishment on that spirit." He himself, he says, belonged to such a group soul while on earth. If we sometimes appear to be paying for the sins of a previous existence, this is because "a soul belonging to the group of which I am a part lived that previous life which built up for me the framework of my earthly life, lived it before I passed through the gates of birth."

The real Frederic Myers—the author of *Human Personality and Its Survival of Bodily Death*—was fascinated by one of the most striking cases of reincarnation ever collected by the Society for Psychical

Research, the case of Lurancy Vennum, and he cites it at length in his chapter on "Disintegrations of Personality."

On July 11, 1877, a thirteen-year-old girl, Mary Lurancy Vennum, living in Watseka, Illinois, had a fit and was unconscious for five hours. The next day it happened again, but then it became clear she was in a trance, for she declared she could see heaven and the angels, as well as a brother and sister who had died. For the next six months, these trances recurred, and Lurancy Vennum was apparently possessed by a number of disagreeable personalities, including an old woman called "Katrina Hogan." Relatives advised her parents to send her to an insane asylum, but some neighbors called the Roffs—whose deceased daughter Mary had also been subject to fits of "insanity"—persuaded the Vennums to see a doctor, W. W. Stevens of Janesville, Wisconsin.

When Stevens first saw Mary Lurancy Vennum, on February 1, 1878, the girl was possessed by Katrina Hogan, and sat hunched up in a chair staring sullenly into space. When Stevens tried to move closer, she told him sharply to keep his distance. Then she seemed to soften towards him, and talked about herself and her parents. (She called her father "Old Black Dick.") Soon the personality changed; the newcomer described himself as a young man called "Willie Canning." He talked disconnectedly, and then had a fit. Stevens tried hypnosis, and it worked; Lurancy Vennum reappeared, and explained that she had been possessed by evil spirits. She was still in a state of trance, and told them that she was surrounded by spirits, one of whom was called "Mary Roff."

Mrs. Roff, who was in the room, said: "That is my daughter." She advised Lurancy to accept Mary as her "control." After some discussion with the spirits, Lurancy announced that she would allow Mary Roff to possess her. Soon after, she woke up.

The next morning, Lurancy Vennum's father called at the office of Asa Roff, and told him that Lurancy Vennum was now claiming to be Mary Roff, and that Mary was asking to go home.

Mary's case history resembled, in many ways, that of Lurancy Vennum—and even more that of the Seeress of Prevorst, Friederike Hauffe. Mary had also started to suffer from fits, and in one of these she cut her arm with a knife deliberately—and fainted. For the next five days, she was delirious; yet she could read through a blindfold. After another period of fits, she died in July 1865, twelve years before Lurancy Vennum's possession. Her clairvoyant powers had been attested to by many prominent citizens in Watseka.

Before Lurancy Vennum—or rather, Mary—could be taken to the Roffs' home, Mrs. Roff and her daughter Minerva came to call at the Vennum's. Mary was looking out of the window as they came along the street, and said: "Why, there comes ma and my sister Nervie!" When they came in, she flung her arms round their necks and burst into tears of joy.

The Vennums were understandably reluctant to let their daughter go, but Mary became so homesick they finally agreed. On February 11, 1878, she was taken to the Roffs' home. On the way there, they passed the house in which the Roffs had lived at the time Mary was alive. Mary insisted this was her home, and had to be persuaded that her family no longer lived there. When they arrived at the new home, Mary said: "Why, there's our old piano, and the same old piano cover." She greeted the crowd of relatives who were waiting there with plain signs of recognition. A Mrs. Wagner, who (under the name of Mary Lord) had been Mary Roff's Sunday school teacher, was greeted with the words, "Oh Mary Lord, you've changed the least of anyone." She told them that "the angels" would allow her to stay until some time in May—three months ahead.

Her family was naturally anxious to test her, and asked her all kinds of questions. Mary soon convinced them; she was able to describe hundreds of incidents in the life of the former Mary Roff. She described in detail her stay at a water-cure place in Peoria. Asked if she remembered an incident when the stove pipe fell and burned Frank, she was able to point out the exact place on the arm where Frank was burned. Asked about an old dog, she showed them the spot where it had died. When she talked about slashing her arm with the knife, she started to roll up her sleeve to show Dr. Stevens the scar, then recollected that this was not the same body: "It's not this arm—it's the one in the ground." After her death, her parents had tried to communicate with her by means of a medium; Mary was able to tell them the message she wrote out for them through the medium's hand, giving the exact time and place.

One of the most convincing incidents occurred when Mrs. Roff found an old velvet headdress that their daughter had worn. Mr. Roff father suggested leaving it out on the hall stand. Mary came in from outside and immediately said: "Why, there's my old headdress that I wore when my hair was short." This reminded her of a box of letters, and when her mother brought this, she found one of her collars. "Look, here's that old collar I tatted."

Mary told her family that she could stay with them until May 21. On that morning, her mother wrote: "Mary is to leave the body of Rancy today, about eleven o'clock." Mary went around saying goodbye to neighbors, hugged and kissed her parents, and set out for Lurancy Vennum's home. On the way, Mary vanished and Lurancy Vennum returned.

Four years later, Mary Lurancy Vennum married a farmer, George Binning. Her parents discouraged her from using her mediumship in case it brought back the fits, but Mary Roff often "dropped in" when her own parents were there, and seemed quite unchanged from her previous visit. When Lurancy Vennum had her first baby, Mary even put her into a trance so she would not suffer the pains of childbirth.

Richard Hodgson, the skeptical young Australian who "exposed" Madame Blavatsky in 1885, and who went to America to investigate Mrs. Piper the following year, heard about the case, and instantly saw that, if genuine, it was a practically watertight proof of life after death. He interviewed all the principal characters except Lurancy Vennum herself, who had moved west with her husband. In spite of this disappointment, Hodgson ended totally convinced of the truth of the incidents as narrated by Dr. Stevens and various family members and friends. He agreed that this could be a case of multiple personality, but felt, on the whole, that all the evidence pointed to a genuine case of possession of Lurancy Vennum by the deceased Mary Roff. Myers placed the case in his chapter on multiple personality, but added that "at a later stage, and when some other wonders have become . . . more familiar . . . we may perhaps consider once more what further lessons this singular narrative may have to teach us." He died before these "further lessons" could be discussed, but it is clear that he also regarded the Vennum case as proof of the survival of personality after death.

If Hodgson and Myers are correct, then it would support the picture that began to emerge in the opening chapter through the work of Adam Crabtree and Wilson Van Dusen. We are inclined to think of death either as a dead end or as a launching into a totally new kind of existence; some strange mystical state in which all the secrets of the universe will be known. All the evidence we have considered indicates that this is a misconception. Life on the "next plane" is apparently not fundamentally dissimilar from life on earth, although many of its conditions seem to be different. According to various communicators, there *are* other planes that are inconceivable to us, but under the circumstances, these are no concern of ours. But unless the evidence of psychical research is an enormous confidence trick, devised by the collective unconscious to satisfy our craving for survival, the individual survives death in a form not unlike his present mode of being.

There are many ways in which the evidence of reincarnation is more convincing than the evidence of life after death that comes through mediums. The Cross Correspondences finally convinced the investigators that Myers and Gurney had survived their deaths; but Mary Roff's parents must have been quite certain she was still alive within hours of her moving back into their house.

Another of the early classic cases—unfortunately never investigated by a trained researcher like Hodgson—has become known as the Alexandrina case.

On March 15, 1910, a five-year-old girl named Alexandrina Samona died in Palermo, Sicily. Her mother, Adela, wife of Dr. Carmelo Samona, was distraught with grief. Three days after the death, she had a dream in which Alexandrina told her not to mourn, because she was going to return. She showed her mother an embryo. Adela Samona dismissed the dream, knowing that an ovarian operation had made it almost impossible for her to have more children.

A few days later, when Adela was sadly recalling the child to her husband, three loud knocks were heard. The parents began to attend séances, and two "spirits" spoke through the medium—one claiming to be the child, the other an aunt who had died long ago. "Alexandrina" told her mother that she would be reborn before Christmas, as one of two twins. In fact, twin girls were born to Adela Samona on November 22, 1910, just over nine months after Alexandrina's death. The two girls were of totally different personalities, but one of them had two small birth marks in the same place as the dead child; she was also, like Alexandrina, left-handed. The parents named her after the dead child. In personality, this second Alexandrina was very much like the first: introverted, tidy, and disposed to spend much of her time folding clothes and linens.

What finally convinced the parents that the child was a reincarnation of Alexandrina was an incident that happened when the twins were ten. They were told that they were going on an outing to the town of Monreale—neither of them had been there. But Alexandrina insisted that she had been there with her mother, in the company of a "lady with horns." She also described the statue on the roof of the church, and described some "red priests" they had seen there. In fact, Adela Samona *had* taken her first daughter Alexandrina to Monreale not long before her death, in the company of a woman who had some unsightly cysts on her forehead. They had been to the church and seen some priests from Greece, who wore red robes. Dr. Samona was so struck by this evidence of reincarnation that he went to some trouble to put the case on record, together with the depositions of various witnesses, and published it in the periodical *Filosofia della Scienza*.

From the point of view of the investigator, the problem here is that the mother's wishful thinking may have been responsible for the whole episode. The death of Alexandrina produced suicidal depression; her unconscious may have reacted by sending her a dream in which the child promised to return. By the time she had this dream, she may have already conceived the twins, and her unconscious mind may also have known this. So the second Alexandrina had the identity of her dead sister foisted on her. Perhaps her mother described the trip to Monreale to her, then forgot it. Or perhaps she overheard her mother speaking about it to her father.

This, of course, is always the problem with a case that took place long before anyone thought of subjecting it to scientific investigation. But this objection does not apply to a very similar case that took place in England. It is discussed by Ian Wilson in a book called *Mind Out of Time?*, which takes a skeptical view of reincarnation, dismissing most cases as a matter of "cryptomnesia"—unconscious memory.

In May 1957, two sisters, Joanna and Jacqueline Pollock, aged eleven and six, were walking along a road in Hexham, Northumberland, when a car mounted the pavement and killed them both; a nine-year-old boy was also killed. The driver was a woman who had taken an overdose of drugs and gone out with the intention of committing suicide. Their father, John Pollock, was a Catholic, but he also believed in reincarnation—a belief condemned by the Church; he felt that the death of the girls was a judgment on him for his interest in these unorthodox matters. In spite of this, he became obsessed by the idea that the girls were going to be reborn to his wife. When, a year later, his wife Florence announced she was pregnant, he told her unhesitatingly that she would have twin daughters, and this was God's way of returning Joanna and Jacqueline. When a gynecologist told her that she was definitely pregnant with only one child, she decided that her husband's obsession was getting the better of him. But in fact, twin daughters were born on October 4, 1958. Jennifer, the twin who was born second, had a thin white line across her forehead exactly where her dead sister Jacqueline had a scar—the result of falling off her bicycle. She also had a birthmark on her left hip, identical to one that Jacqueline had. There was no similar mark on the elder sister, Gillian—which seemed odd, since the twins were monozygotic (formed from the same egg).

When the twins were four months old, the family moved to Whitley Bay. One day three years later, John Pollock took them on a day trip to Hexham. They behaved as if they were quite familiar with the place. One suddenly said to the other: "The school's round the corner." "That's were we used to play in the playground." "The swings and slides are over there." "We used to live in that house." This last comment was made as they passed their old house.

The toys of the dead sisters had been packed in a box which was stored in the loft; when the twins were four, the parents decided to let them play with them. Jennifer said immediately: "There's Mary. And this is my Suzanne"—correctly naming the two dolls. "And there's your wringer." Florence Pollock, who witnessed this scene, can hardly be accused of wishful thinking, for (as a good Catholic) she thoroughly disapproved of her husband's obsession with reincarnation. She refused to let him say anything about it to the children, or even to tell them anything about their dead sisters other than that they were "in heaven."

When she heard the twins screaming one day, Florence Pollock rushed outside to find them clinging to one another and shouting, "The car! It's coming at us." A car had just started up further along the lane. On another occasion, she found them playing a curious game in which Gillian cradled Jennifer's head, saying: "The blood's coming out of your eyes. That's where the car hit you." Florence Pollock became increasingly disturbed by these incidents, and she was relieved when, at about the age of five, the twins seemed to lose all memory of their dead sisters, and became perfectly normal children.

Ian Wilson points out that the father's belief in reincarnation weakens much of the evidence. Yet it is still impossible to see how John Pollock can have faked this evidence, unless he secretly coached the children in their roles when their mother was not present. The twins themselves have denied that anything of the sort took place.

Wilson himself admits that the case of the Pollock twins is one of the few in his book where *prima facie* evidence seems to support the idea of reincarnation.

One of the most widely publicized modern cases of alleged reincarnation took place in India in the early 1930s, and was later studied by Professor Hemendra Bannerjee, director of the Department of Parapsychology at Rajasthan University (who, together with Professor Ian Stevenson, was the world's leading scientific investigator of such cases). On October 12, 1926, a girl named Kumari Shanti Devi was born in Delhi, India. When she was four years old, she began to talk about a previous life she had lived in the town of Muttra, a hundred miles from Delhi. She said she had been of the Choban caste, had lived in a yellow house, and that her husband had been a cloth merchant named Kedar Nath Chaubey. A retired school principal heard about the girl, and asked to meet her. The child told him the address she had lived at in Muttra, and the principal wrote a letter there. To his surprise, he received a letter back from Shanti Devi's "husband," Kedar Nath. He confirmed various details about his life with his former wife, and requested that a relative of his in Delhi should be allowed to talk to the child. When the man arrived, Shanti Devi recognized him as her "husband's" cousin, Kanji Mal, and soon had him convinced of her genuineness. When he reported back to Kedar Nath, Shanti Devi's "husband" no longer hesitated. He rushed to Delhi, and the child flung herself into his arms. She was able to give convincing answers to all his questions about her previous existence as his wife, and mentioned a box containing a hundred rupees that she had buried in one of the rooms of their house.

On November 24, 1935, the nine-year-old girl was finally taken to Muttra by her parents; they were accompanied by three respectable citizens—a newspaperman, a politician, and a lawyer—who went along to act as witnesses (and who later wrote an account of the case). As the train approached the platform in Muttra, Shanti Devi recognized the elder brother of Kedar Nath, who was waiting there. They then took a carriage, and Shanti Devi was told to direct it anywhere she wanted. As they drove along, she pointed out buildings that had not been there during her own life in Muttra. She directed them to the first house in which she and her husband had formerly lived, now rented to strangers. Asked by a local man where the *jai-zarur* was situated—a word used in Muttra for a privy—she pointed to the outdoor lavatory. Then they went on to the house in which she had died. There she recognized various relatives, and showed that she was intimately acquainted with the house. Finally, she led them to the room in which she had buried the money. Digging uncovered an empty tin. Kedar Nath later admitted he had removed the money. As they left the house, Shanti Devi recognized in the crowd outside her "former" father and mother.

No such case can, of course, be regarded as watertight, simply because the authors of the pamphlet failed to take the same precautions that had become commonplace in all Society for Psychical Research investigations—depositions of witnesses, double-checking on the possibilities of cryptomnesia, and so on. Three decades later, another investigator applied these precautions to his own investigations of cases of alleged reincarnation.

The striking thing about so many of Ian Stevenson's *Twenty Cases Suggestive of Reincarnation*,[4] and the subsequent three volumes of *Cases of the Reincarnation Type*,[5] is how much so many of them echo the case of Shanti Devi. Swarnlata, the daughter of a civil servant, was born in 1948, began to tell her brothers and sisters about a "previous life" in the city of Katni, where she had been called Biya, and married to a man called Sri Chintamini Pandey. At the age of three and a half, her father took her with him on a school inspection trip, and as they passed through Katni—about a hundred miles from their home—she asked the driver to turn down a road to "my house." Her father now learned that she had been telling her family

4. American Society for Psychical Research (1966).
5. University of Virginia Press (1975-80).

about her "previous life" for some time. She performed for her parents songs and dances that she claimed she had learned in her previous life, and which she had certainly had no opportunity to learn in the present one.

When she was ten, her family moved to Chhatarpur, and she there met a lady named Srimati Agnihotri, whom she claimed to recognize as someone she had known in her previous life. Her father was impressed when this lady confirmed many of his daughter's statements about Katni and her life there—for the first time he began to take her claims seriously. He began writing down her statements. Professor Hemendra Bannerjee went to meet Swarnlata in 1959, then went straight on to Katni to see how her statements compared with those of her "previous" family in Katni. He had made a list of nine points about the family house. All proved to be accurate; so did Swarnlata's descriptions of her life as Biya, the deceased wife. Soon after this, Swarnlata and her family went to Katni. What followed was very similar to what had happened to Shanti Devi. On Professor Bannerjee's instructions, Swarnlata's family not only took care to offer her no clues, but even tried to mislead her on various points—such as telling her that the family cow herd was dead, and then bringing him into her presence; she immediately recognized him. Stevenson's table of all the places, people, and events described by Swarnlata goes on for eight pages, and makes impressive reading. The result of all this was that the Katni family accepted Swarnlata as the dead Biya, and she spent much time with them and built up close ties with her previous "brothers" and "children." Stevenson himself investigated this case in 1961, with the advantage of all the documentation already made by Professor Bannerjee. So as a proof of reincarnation, the Swarnlata case seems to be as watertight as it could be.

Another of Stevenson's cases recalls that of Lurancy Vennum and Mary Roff. In 1954, a three-year-old boy named Jasbir Lal Jat died of smallpox. Before he could be buried the next day, the corpse stirred and revived. It was some weeks before the child could speak, but when he did, his parents were astonished that his personality had changed completely. Jasbir had been a rather dull, quiet little boy; he had suddenly become more lively. He announced that he was the son of a Brahmin family (a higher caste than his present family) who lived in the village of Vehedi, and he refused to eat food unless it was cooked by a Brahmin. He said he had been poisoned by doctored sweets, and had fallen off a cart and smashed his skull, as a result of which he died. Jasbir's family were understandably skeptical, assuming that his illness had affected his mind. But they began to reconsider in 1957, when a Brahmin lady from Vehedi came to Jasbir's village, and he instantly recognized her as his aunt. Jasbir was taken back to Vehedi, and, like Shanti Devi and Swarnlata, he showed a detailed knowledge of his former residence, escorting a party on a tour. His name in the previous existence had been Sobha Ram, and his detailed knowledge of his life convinced everyone that Jasbir and Sobha Ram were the same person. The accusation about the poisoned sweets was never satisfactorily cleared up—Sobha Ram was said to have died of smallpox.

The most fascinating point about this case, of course, is that Jasbir was already three when he "died" and was "taken over" by Sobha Ram, *who died at the same time.* The implication is that Sobha Ram was able to slip into the body before brain death had occurred and fight his way back to life.

Without the kind of detailed investigation undertaken by Stevenson and Bannerjee, no case of reincarnation can be regarded as proven; a case that looks superficially convincing may collapse the moment it is probed. In fact, there is evidence that Stevenson himself was deceived in such a case. Edward Ryall, who lived in Benfleet, Essex, was to claim that he was haunted by memories of a "previous existence" ever since childhood; in these memories, he was a Somerset farmer named John Fletcher, who had been killed in 1685 when he was guiding the troops of the Duke of Monmouth to attack the royalist forces at Sedgemoor. Slowly, these memories had become more and more detailed until he could remember large sections of his "earlier life." During the invasion of Italy in 1945, Ryall claimed to have heard a woman's voice in his ear telling him to take care; studying the ground ahead he saw he was about to walk into a booby trap.

In 1970, Ryall wrote a letter to the *Daily Express* about these experiences, and it aroused widespread interest. Ian Stevenson met Ryall, and decided he was genuine. It was Stevenson who persuaded Ryall to write a book about his previous existence, and *Second Time Round* appeared in 1974, two years before Ryall's death. The woman who had warned Ryall not to walk into the trip wire was, according to this book, John Fletcher's wife in Weston Zoyland.

In a BBC program soon after publication, Ryall accompanied the interviewer to the church in which he claimed to have been married, and to various other sites in the life of John Fletcher. The interviewer admitted to being totally convinced by Ryall's story, and by his obvious involvement in his past incarnation.

The parish records of the church were still in existence, and when Ian Wilson consulted these, he found no evidence whatsoever for the existence of John Fletcher or his family. Ryall claimed that Fletcher's father had been killed by a bull in 1660, and was buried by the Rev. Thomas Holt, the vicar of Weston Zoyland; Thomas Holt was the vicar, but there was no record of the burial of Fletcher's father. There is no record of Fletcher's marriage, or of the baptisms of his two sons, although he claimed they were baptized by a subsequent vicar, who kept a meticulous record of all baptisms (which is still in the County Records Office). Finally, Ryall showed himself to be extremely cautious and unhelpful in his correspondence with a local historian who wanted to help him trace John Fletcher's farm—although Ryall had claimed to know precisely where it was situated. Under Ian Wilson's analysis, a highly convincing story begins to look like a historical fantasy.

Wilson's own explanation of most of these strange cases is basically the same as that of Thomson Jay Hudson in *The Law of Psychic Phenomena*: the extraordinary powers of the subjective mind. Hudson cites a particularly fascinating case from Coleridge's *Biographia*

Literaria about an illiterate peasant girl who fell into "a nervous fever" and began talking in Latin, Greek, and Hebrew. It looked like some kind of possession, but a persistent young doctor managed to trace the girl's surviving uncle, and learned that her parents had died when she was a child, and that she had been taken into the house of an old pastor. More research revealed that the old man had a habit of walking up and down a passage, reading aloud from books in Greek, Hebrew, and Latin. Consciously, the girl could not remember a word of these languages, but her subjective mind had recorded them, and they emerged when she was in a nervous fever.

In 1933, a neurologist named Wilder Penfield, who was engaged in work with epileptic patients, was performing an operation on a female patient's brain when his electric probe touched a point in the temporal cortex. The patient (who was wide awake—the brain has no feeling, so anaesthetic is unnecessary) told Penfield that as he touched her, she was suddenly in the kitchen listening to her little boy, who was playing outside in the yard. She was completely "there"—aware, for example, of the sounds of passing cars. Another patient on whom he performed the experiment found himself at a baseball game in a small town watching a boy crawl under the fence; another was in a concert hall, hearing every instrument of the orchestra clearly. Other patients "played back" scenes from childhood in the most minute detail. It was as if Penfield had accidentally switched on some kind of video recorder that had literally captured every waking (and probably sleeping) moment of the patient's life.[6]

The conclusion was obvious. We all possess a library that contains everything that we have done or thought. Then why is it not accessible to us? Because we are too "busy." Life is difficult and complicated; we do not have the time to browse in the library. So, like those calculating prodigies who lost the ability at the age of fourteen, we have simply abandoned this capability as an evolutionary luxury. Yet Penfield's

6. Widler Penfield, *Mysteries, of the Mind* (1975), chapter 6.

experiments show that we could recover it if we really wanted to. It is not even necessary to use an electric probe. Psychiatrists who have developed a technique known as "abreaction therapy" have discovered that ordinary suggestion can make a patient relive a traumatic experience in total physical detail. There is no reason why the same techniques should not be used to make us relive some of our most delightful experiences.

But Penfield's discovery certainly provides grounds for skepticism about cases like that of Edward Ryall. Ian Wilson justifies his own skepticism by describing a remarkable case investigated by the Society for Psychical Research in 1906. Under hypnosis, a woman, called Miss C, began to recall details from the life of a woman named "Blanche Poynings," who had lived in the time of Richard II, and been a close friend of Maud, the Countess of Salisbury. Her knowledge of the countess' life certainly seemed remarkably accurate. As far as she knew, Miss C had never read any historical novel that might have provided such detail. One day, when the SPR investigator was having tea with Miss C, they began talking about the planchette, an automatic-writing device, and Miss C agreed to try to communicate with Blanche Poynings with a planchette. "Blanche" and Miss C were soon holding an animated conversation, with Blanche reproaching her for not communicating for so long. When they asked her how they could check on her story, she replied: "Ask E. Holt." E. Holt turned out to be Emily Holt, author of a novel called *Countess Maud*. Miss C had read it as a child, and long ago forgotten it. Countess Maud proved to contain every detail about the Countess of Salisbury that Miss C had given under hypnosis.

That certainly sounds like game, set, and match to the skeptics about reincarnation. But a case of the 1950s illustrates the dangers of being carried away by the passion for incredulity.

Morey Bernstein, a businessman of Pueblo, Colorado, discovered he was naturally proficient in hypnosis, and persuaded the wife of an insurance salesman, Virginia Tighe, to allow him to try hypnotic regression on her. Virginia proved to be a deep hypnotic subject, and when Bernstein regressed her beyond her birth, she began to speak with an Irish brogue, and identified herself as Bridey Murphy, who had been born near Cork, Ireland, in 1798. In six tape-recorded sessions, she gave a detailed account of her life as Bridey, the wife of a barrister who taught at Queen's University, Belfast. Bridey had died after a fall in 1864.

Bernstein wrote a book about the case, *The Search for Bridey Murphy*, which was serialized in the *Chicago Daily News*, to the chagrin of its Hearst rival, the *Chicago American*. A *Chicago Daily News* reporter went to Belfast to try to track down Bridey Murphy, but found himself hampered by the fact that records of births and deaths began in Ireland two years after Bridey's death. He did find a number of other confirmatory factors. Two Belfast grocers mentioned by Mrs. Tighe were found listed in the Belfast Directory for 1865. A twopence coin mentioned by Bridey as being in use during her lifetime had been minted shortly before her birth, and ceased to be used twelve years before her death. Bridey had said that she was born in "The Meadows," near Belfast, and a map of Belfast dated 1801 showed an area called Mardike Meadows. Other details given by Bridey—such as a Dooley Road, Belfast, and a St. Theresa's Church—failed to check. This did not deter the enthusiasm of the American public, and *The Search for Bridey Murphy* became the major bestseller of 1956.

At this point, the rival newspaper printed the results of its own investigations. It had uncovered Virginia Tighe's identity (Bernstein had used a pseudonym) and discovered that she had lived in Chicago. According to the *Chicago American*, Mrs. Tighe had an aunt who was "as Irish as the lakes of Killarney," and who had told her tales about Ireland in her childhood; she was called Mary Burns. Moreover, during her childhood, Virginia had lived opposite an Irishwoman named Bridey Corkell, whose unmarried name was Murphy. Her Irish background, according to the *Chicago American*, had fascinated the little girl. Virginia also had had a "crush" on Mrs. Corkell's son John.

The *Bridey Murphy* furor collapsed as suddenly as it had begun, and the book dropped from bestseller lists. But a Denver feature writer who investigated this "exposé" discovered that most of it was simply untrue. Mrs. Mary Burns—the aunt who was "as Irish as the lakes of Killarney"—had been born in New York, and had not met Virginia until the girl was eighteen; both she and Virginia emphatically denied that there had been any Irish stories. Mrs. Corkell proved to be strangely elusive, declining to be interviewed, so the reporter was unable to find out whether her unmarried name was Murphy. What he *did* discover was that her son John—on whom Virginia was supposed to have had a crush—was the editor of the Sunday edition of the *Chicago American*, the newspaper that had failed to secure serial rights on Bernstein's book. Virginia insisted that she had never even spoken to Mrs. Corkell, and had no interest in her son John, who was eight years her senior and married.

All this fails to prove that Virginia Tighe's Bridey incarnation was any more real than Miss C's Blanche Poynings. But it does prove that it is easier to demolish a claim than to subject it to serious investigation. Most writers on the case (for example, Martin Gardner in *Fads and Fallacies in the Name of Science*) are content to quote the exposé without mentioning the *Denver Post*'s exposé of the exposé. The "passion for incredulity" can produce as much self-deception as the uncritical will to believe.

The Bridey Murphy case had the effect of interesting other hypnotists in the subject of regression. An English doctor, Arnall Bloxham, who lived near Cardiff, regressed a girl named Ann Ockendon, who recalled her life as a man in a land where people went naked and wore animals' teeth—Bloxham concluded she was speaking of prehistoric times. Obviously, there was no way of checking on this particular incarnation. Later cases proved more fruitful. A television producer, Jeffrey Iverson, became so fascinated by a program he made on Bloxham that he set out to investigate some of the cases, and published his results in a book called *More Lives Than One?* A swimming instructor named Graham Huxtable had "become" an eighteenth-century sailor on a ship called *HMS Aggie*; he enacted a battle scene with a French ship with total conviction, and finally screamed horribly as he was wounded in the leg. Earl Mountbatten commissioned a modern historian, Oliver Warner, to try to investigate the tape recording made by Huxtable, and although he did not succeed in tracing the ship or the battle, Warner ended by being totally convinced of its authenticity—Huxtable's sailor seemed to know far more about the ships of the period than could be picked up from historical novels.

Iverson's most convincing case is of a woman who prefers to be known as Jane Evans, and who recalled seven past lives: a Roman housewife living in Britain, a Jewess murdered in a pogrom in York, a French courtesan, a maidservant to a French merchant, a sewing girl in the time of Queen Anne, a lady-in-waiting to the Spanish Infanta, and an American nun from Des Moines, Iowa. The Roman wife, "Livonia," showed a remarkable knowledge of the period, suggesting an expert on British and Roman history. Mrs. Evans insisted that her only knowledge of history came from the usual elementary course at school. Iverson went to the Loire valley to investigate her incarnation as "Alison," maidservant of Jacques Coeur, adviser to King Charles VII of France. Jane Evans had never been to the Loire valley and knew nothing about French history; but Iverson's investigations among French historians showed him just how much Alison knew about medieval France.

The most impressive "incarnation" was as a Jewess, "Rebecca," in twelfth-century York. Shortly before Richard the Lion Heart rode off to the Third Crusade, in 1189, there were anti-Jewish riots in London. The English had worked themselves up into a frenzy about "infidels," and the Jews seemed to qualify as much as the Muslims. In 1190, there were riots in York; Jews took refuge in the castle, and most of them killed their families, then themselves, to avoid the vengeance of the mob. Rebecca and her family escaped the massacre, and took refuge in the crypt of a Christian church, "just outside the big gates." But the mob found them and killed them.

Iverson decided to consult an expert on the massacre, Professor Barrie Dobson, of the University of York. Dobson was impressed by her reconstruction of the massacre—particularly since Jane Evans professed to be totally ignorant of any such thing. He decided that the church that answered her description was St. Mary's, Castlegate. There was only one problem this had no crypt. But six months later, workmen renovating the church discovered the remains of "something that seems to have been a crypt"—a room with round stone arches and vaults, under the chancel.

Ian Wilson, while admitting that this regression is impressive, has a number of criticisms. There were, he points out, forty churches in York; how can Professor Dobson be sure that St. Mary's is the right one? Rebecca described the murder of an old Jew in "Coney Street." But in twelfth-century York, Coney Street was still called Cuninga (King) Street. Rebecca refers to the "big copper gate of York," when, in fact, the Coppergate was a street. These objections lose much of their force when we discover that Professor Dobson had already raised them—and answered them. The street where the old Jew was murdered may have been Cuninga Street, but it is probable that it was actually pronounced Coney Street. The English have a habit of changing foreign pronunciations. (In my home town, Leicester, Belvoir Street is pronounced Beaver Street.) The street called Coppergate existed in York in 1190, and at the end of it was one of the gates leading to the castle. No doubt most of the residents of York believed that "Coppergate" referred to this gate.

All this also answers the third objection: how Professor Dobson could identify the church when there were thirty-nine others. Rebecca describes it specifically as being "just outside the big gates." This makes sense, since she says they had just escaped from the castle.

Ian Wilson's criticisms make it clear that the case against reincarnation is fundamentally the same as the case against spirit communication via mediums. Anything that can be explained in terms of cryptomnesia, telepathy, or possible fraud must be regarded as unproven. If we are to prove spirit communication, then we have to demonstrate that the spirit has communicated something that could not have been known to the medium or to anyone else present. A number of cases—such as the Cross Correspondences—have satisfied this criterion. If we are to "prove" reincarnation, the same thing applies. It has to be demonstrated that the "reincarnated" person knows things that could only have been learned in a previous existence. So in the case of Graham Huxtable, it makes no difference that a naval historian finds his account wholly convincing. We need to know beyond all possible doubt that Huxtable never saw a film or read a book that might have provided the material for the battle scene.

In the case of Jane Evans, it is almost impossible to see how this type of explanation could apply. If it is true that she is no great reader, and that her only knowledge of history comes from elementary school, then there is apparently no way in which she would have learned about the life of a Roman matron in Colchester or a Jewess in York. At the same time, her "incarnations" lack one important element: proof that Livonia and Rebecca and the rest actually existed. Without such proof, we can never be quite certain that they were not another amazing creation of the subjective mind.

Another English hypnotist, Joe Keeton, who lives in the Wirral, a suburb of Liverpool, has also specialized in regressions, and has formed a group whose aim is to try to find documentary evidence for past lives. Ironically, Keeton himself does not believe that he is dealing with cases of reincarnation. He prefers to believe that he may be dealing with some purely mental faculty, with some unknown form of access to the memory of the human race, something similar to Jung's collective unconscious.

I met Joe Keeton for the first time in 1978, when he came to Westward Television in Plymouth. He had been "regressing" a pretty nurse named Pauline McKay, who also came from the Wirral, and Pauline had "become" a West Country servant girl called "Kitty Jay," who said she had committed suicide near Chagford in the late eighteenth century. Joe had written to the head librarian in Exeter to ask whether he knew of a Kitty Jay, and was surprised to learn that "Jay's

Grave" lies on the edge of Dartmoor, and that she had hanged herself in Canna Farm. As a suicide, she had not been allowed burial in a graveyard.

In the television studio, Keeton hypnotized Pauline McKay, then took her back to her own past life, then finally to her life as Kitty Jay. Kitty described how she had gone to work at Ford Farm, Manaton, as a maid, and had allowed herself to be seduced by a man named Rob, who worked at nearby Canna Farm. Although Pauline had never been to the West Country, she seemed to know the area, and correctly named a bridge where she and Rob stood on their walks. She told of how Rob had deserted her, then described her suicide—at this point she became obviously distressed, and gasped for breath. It was an impressive performance. Yet it was obviously open to the interpretation of cryptomnesia. Pauline may have read the story of Kitty Jay in some volume on ghosts, such as Peter Underwood's *Gazetteer of British Ghosts*.

Since that meeting in 1978, Joe Keeton has kept me abreast of his latest cases, and some of these have been very impressive. Yet until 1983, none of them could be regarded as watertight cases of reincarnation—or racial memory. Then, finally, two of his investigators—Andrew and Marguerite Selby—were able to produce documentary evidence for the existence of a past incarnation.

The subject of the regression was a journalist, Ray Bryant, who works as a features writer for the Reading *Evening Post*. In 1980, he was asked to write a series on hypnotic regression. As a result of this series, he became interested in the subject, but found his own attempts at regression disappointing. However, he had become a member of a group, which met in London, and so he persevered. During the twelfth hypnotic session, he heard himself describing an occasion when "he" had fallen ill on a railway station. (Ray Bryant describes his sensations during these sessions as being like watching a television program and simultaneously taking part in it.) It slowly emerged that "he" was a farm laborer named Robert Sawyer, who had lived at Ongar, Essex, at the turn of the twentieth century. (Ray was born in 1938.) For the next three sessions he described his life as a farm worker, questioned by all the other members of the group. Then Joe Keeton decided it was time to go back farther. Ray Bryant was taken beyond Robert Sawyer's birth. This time he became a soldier called Reuben. When asked his second name, he could only get out the first letters: "St. . . ." But it was clear that Reuben's life had been rather more eventful than that of Robert Sawyer. He had been a sergeant in the 47th Lancashire Regiment of Foot, had been wounded in the Crimean war—where he saw Florence Nightingale—and eventually died in London, probably a suicide, in 1879, at the age of fifty-seven.

Other details emerged. He had been wounded at the "Battle of the Quarries"—of which no one in the group had heard. But a check with a reference book showed that this had actually taken place, in June 1855. (Even so, it is one of the more obscure battles of the war, which took place during the siege of Sevastopol—my own search through half a dozen books in my library has failed to find a reference to it.) He had left the army after twenty-one years' service, in 1865, and had returned for a time to live in his hometown, Ormskirk, Lancashire. His wife Mary—whom he had married when he was a corporal—had died, and he decided to follow his son, also called Reuben, to London. There he had worked as a boatman at Millwall Docks, but had been lonely and unhappy. His army career had been exceptionally happy; he loved being a soldier. Ending his life in a strange city, living alone in lodgings, depressed him. Ray Bryant said that the change that came over his personality when he changed from soldier to Thames boatman was pathetic. He died in 1865.

The chances of learning anything about an ex-sergeant in the Crimean war seemed remote, but Andrew and Marguerite Selby, who lived in South Harrow, offered to undertake the task. Andrew Selby is a civil engineer who became interested in regression when he heard Joe Keeton broadcasting on LBC, asking for subjects who would agree to be hypnotized. But where did one begin? A good starting point seemed to be the Guildhall Library, in the city of

London, and there they had an unbelievable stroke of luck. There was a book containing the casualty roll of the Crimean war, and looking under "St"—the only letters of the surname Reuben had been able to pronounce—they found a Sergeant Reuben Stafford who had been wounded in the hand at the Battle of the Quarries. He had won medals, and had been promoted; the record gave the dates. Now they had the means to find out whether Reuben "St" *was* Sergeant Reuben Stafford (later colour-sergeant). At this next regression, they asked Ray Bryant to go back to these dates and asked him what had happened. He was right every time.

This was not the end of the research. The Selbys checked the Public Record Office in Kew and the General Register of Births, Deaths and Marriages in what used to be Somerset House (now St. Catherine's House). They found Reuben's death certificate that showed that he died by drowning, and gave an address in Gravesend. Reuben had been very poor when he died, and they discovered that his grave was a "communal" one in the cemetery at East Ham. Ray Bryant has recorded how deeply moved he felt as he stood on the spot where the records showed Reuben's grave had been. Reuben's bones had vanished long ago—in these communal burial plots, room was made for someone else after twenty years or so.

In a case like this, the cryptomnesia theory is no longer tenable. Reuben "checked out" both ways: the dates he gave proved to be accurate; the dates in the records produced the correct response from Reuben. It could be argued that Ray Bryant, under hypnosis, read the minds of his questioners and gave them the answers they knew to be correct; but that fails to explain Ray Bryant's accurate knowledge about a Reuben "St" who was wounded in the hand at the Battle of the Quarries before Sevastopol. (When Reuben was regressed to dates *after* this wound, he held his paralyzed hand in a stiff and awkward manner; as soon as he was regressed further back, the paralysis disappeared.) There seems to be no way of explaining this case except to accept that Ray Bryant was Sergeant Reuben Stafford of Ormskirk in a previous existence, or that he was in some way in touch with the mind of Reuben Stafford. Andrew Selby is inclined to the "collective unconscious" hypothesis; Ray Bryant, on the whole, prefers the simpler explanation of reincarnation.

If he is correct, the implications are interesting. To begin with, we must also assume that after dying in the Thames in 1865, Reuben was reincarnated as a farm labourer named Robert Sawyer a few years later, and that he died before Ray Bryant was born in 1938. If we can accept that Robert Sawyer and Reuben Stafford were real people, then it seems highly likely that four other earlier "incarnations" who have appeared under hypnosis are also real: Wilfred Anderton, a coachman of the eighteenth century; a girl called Winifred, who died quite young; a housemaid named Elizabeth who rose to become a governess in the late seventeenth century; and an unnamed character who does not appear to understand English, and who lived about a century earlier.

This also raises in a new form the basic question of what, if anything, survives death. Clearly, not sexual differentiation, since Ray Bryant was both male and female in past incarnations. Then what is the basic "substratum" of personality that was common to all seven people. When I fired this question at him, Ray Bryant admitted that he had no idea. But he felt that all the previous six incarnations had contributed something to what he is now. In Preston, where the 47th had its barracks (and where Ray Bryant was able to examine the regimental records), he had a strong feeling of déjà-vu. His knowledge of Reuben seemed to him to explain his recurrent nightmare of falling out of a boat, and the sense of peace he has always experienced in or beside water—whether river, sea, stream, or pond. It seems, then, that something can be carried over from one "lifetime" to another—and this, of course, seems to strengthen the possibility that something of the personality survives death. It also implies that *what* survives death—Myers, Gurney, and so on—is not in itself permanent, but that it will in turn evolve to something else. This seems, in fact, to be one of the most consistent factors in all spirit teachings, from Kardec and Stainton Moses to Geraldine Cummins.

Among Hindus and Buddhists, reincarnation is an article of religious faith. The ancient Celts believed in it; so did the Greeks. Various fathers of the Church, like St. Jerome and Origen, regarded the doctrine with sympathy. But it was condemned outright by the Second Council of Constantinople—convened by the Emperor Justinian—and from then on became a Christian heresy. In a pamphlet on reincarnation published by the Catholic Truth Society, Father J. H. Crehan, SJ, sums up: "For a Catholic, it should be clear that our faith has no room for theories of reincarnation." (It may or may not be significant that Ian Wilson is a Catholic convert.)

It would probably be fair to say that the main reason reincarnation has made so little headway in the West in our own time is that most people feel it to be a license for fantasy. The force of the objection can be seen in a case I have discussed at length elsewhere: that of Dr. Arthur Guirdham.[7] Dr. Guirdham, who was senior consultant in psychiatry for the Bath medical area, had always been fascinated by the thirteenth-century heretical sect called the Cathars—"pure ones." They believed that God is not all-powerful, that evil is an independent force, perhaps as strong as good, and that the realm of matter belongs to the devil. The Church persecuted them, and, in 1244, most of them were massacred at Montségur, near Toulouse. In Toulouse and other places in the area, Guirdham had powerful feelings of déjà vu. He had also suffered most of his adult life from a nightmare in which he was lying down when he was approached by a tall man; he often woke up screaming.

In 1962, Guirdham saw a patient whom he calls Mrs. Smith, who had often had a similar nightmare. Both their nightmares ceased after she became his patient. What she did not tell him immediately was that she had recognized him as a person who had recurred in her dreams for many years. These dreams about her existence as a girl in thirteenth-century France had started after a series of peculiar

---

7. In *Strange Powers* (1973).

attacks of unconsciousness. In her dreams, she saw a young Cathar priest called Roger de Grisolles, who had come to her parents' cottage one night during a snowstorm, and with whom she had a love affair. When her parents threw her out, she went to live with Roger in his house. Her dream-memories of this house became increasingly detailed. The idyll came to an end with a murder. She was not sure who was murdered, but she knew that someone called Pierre de Mazerolles was involved. Roger died in prison, and she herself was later burned alive at Montsegur. She recognized Guirdham as "Roger."

It took Mrs. Smith a year to work up the courage to tell Guirdham about her dreams. He was thunderstruck. Mrs. Smith knew absolutely nothing about Catharism. He knew that the persecution and massacre of the Cathars had started after a man called Pierre de Mazerolles had organized the murder of inquisitors sent to Toulouse by the pope. Guirdham began to investigate the details Mrs. Smith remembered about the Cathars. Some of the details sounded unlikely: for example, that Cathar priests wore green or blue. She made a note of this in 1944; in 1965 the French scholar Jean Duvernoy discovered that some Cathar priests did dress in green or blue. She had dreamed of sugar sawed from a loaf and used as a medicinal remedy; in 1969, the scholar Rene Nelli discovered that sugar *was* imported from the Arab countries in "loaves" and was regarded as a universal remedy. Mrs. Smith's detailed description of Cathar rituals and beliefs were again confirmed by the scholars.

So far, the story sounds plausible enough to anyone who has an open mind about reincarnation. Mrs. Smith's discovery that Dr. Guirdham had been her lover in a previous existence sounds like a typical example of Freud's "transference phenomenon" (when the patient falls in love with the doctor), and the coincidence of the two coming together again in the twentieth century is a little hard to swallow. But the confirmation of the details about Catharism by scholars seems to clinch the story. If Hudson's subjective mind was really responsible for all these phenomena, then its powers must be even wider than Hudson thought.

I wrote about Guirdham in my book *The Occult*, and went to stay with him at his home near Bath. This certainly dissipated my suspicion that he might have invented Mrs. Smith, for although I did not meet her, it was quite plain that Guirdham is a perfectly normal, honest, well-balanced individual, not a crank, and his wife Mary, who confirmed the details of his book, seemed the epitome of common sense. He showed me his correspondence with various scholars, and it became clear that he had left an enormous amount of evidence out of his book, simply for fear of confusing the reader.

What worried me, even at that stage, were the later developments of his Cathar involvement. He showed me the manuscript of a book called *We Are One Another*, which begins with his meeting with a woman he calls Clare Mills, an attractive, bustling open-air girl, who asked him one day if the words "Raymond" and "Albigensian" meant anything to him—they kept repeating in her head. Albigenses was another name for Cathars, and Raymond was the name of the counts of Toulouse. All this was before he had written his book about Mrs. Smith, *The Cathars and Reincarnation*, so she had no way of knowing about his interest in the subject. Clare Mills also had dreams of being burned, and the names involved made it clear that she was also dreaming about the Cathar persecution. She dreamed of being made to walk half-naked towards a huge bonfire, and of being struck on the back by a burning torch—she had a strange birthmark there which looked like a series of hard blisters. Guirdham concluded that she was another Cathar with whom he had been acquainted in a previous existence. This was not all. The mother of a dead girl showed Guirdham a notebook her daughter had kept at the age of seven; it was full of Cathar names and sketches. Guirdham came to believe that the mother and daughter had both been Cathars. Other acquaintances became involved in the strange story, so that there was no alternative to the belief that Guirdham was studying a case of "group reincarnation" (a doctrine preached by "Myers" to Geraldine Cummins, we may recall).

More was to come. In *The Lake and the Castle*, Guirdham explains how he became convinced that this same group of people had been involved together in an earlier epoch, as members of the reincarnationist Celtic church; they had also suffered martyrdom. As if feeling that a reader who can swallow a gnat can swallow a camel, Guirdham goes on to tell how this same group had also been involved together in Roman Britain in the fourth century and in the Napoleonic era.

I have been a friend of Arthur Guirdham ever since those days in the early 1970s, and have often stayed in his home. He is also the godfather of my daughter, so I believe I know him fairly well. I have taken Clare Mills out to dinner (with the Guirdhams) and she confirmed everything he said. I have no reason to believe he is a Svengali who can persuade his patients to cooperate in his fantasies about previous lives, or that his books are inventions written to gain notoriety. Clearly, he believes every word in them. Moreover, he is far too intelligent to allow his fantasy to run away with him. Ian Wilson points out that if Guirdham had stopped after recounting the Mrs. Smith case, and perhaps written a psychiatric study of Mrs. Smith, his claims would probably have met with serious attention. He knows as well as anyone that this group reincarnation, and all the previous lives as Celts and Romans (not to mention Guirdham's own life as an ancient Greek of the thirteenth century B. C., described in *The Island*), make his story totally unacceptable to most readers. Presumably he would protest, like Sir William Crookes: "I didn't say it was possible—I said it was true."

Father Crehan's view of the case is that Guirdham, Mrs. Smith, Clare Mills, and the rest were telepathic, and that they somehow "pooled" their fantasies and the results of their reading. Guirdham's account of his relation with Mrs. Smith makes this quite impossible—she had been making detailed notes about the Cathars eighteen years before she met him. So we are left with only two possible solutions: either that Guirdham is a self-deceiver on a heroic scale, or that the concept of group reincarnation is basically true.

Fortunately, it is of no immediate consequence to this argument whether it is true or not. The picture that emerges from case histories of reincarnation seems quite clear and consistent, and it fits the general pattern of arguments for survival without contradiction. We have noted, for example, that Mary Roff knew about her parents' attempt to communicate with her through a medium, and was able to quote the words she had written at the séance. Mediumship actually seems to be a form of temporary "possession." Mary and Lurancy Vennum apparently came to an agreement about the possession of Lurancy Vennum's body for a few months. After it was all over, Mary still "dropped in" periodically.

The picture that emerges is of "disembodied" entities who can, under the right circumstances, enter or leave a human body exactly as a driver can enter or leave a car. In the case of Jasbir Lal Jat, it looks as if Sobha Ram found the abandoned car while the engine was still warm, and slipped into the driving seat. The idea seems an affront to common sense, but the evidence is there to support it.

On the whole, the "facts," as they emerge from various cases, seem to support Steiner's view of reincarnation as an evolutionary experience, as set forth in the eight volumes of *Karmic Relationships.* There is only one major point of contradiction. Steiner seemed to feel that the process of reincarnation takes anything from a hundred to a thousand years. But Steiner's own views evolved over the years. There are some major differences between *Theosophy* (1904) and *An Outline of Occult Science* six years later. Steiner never claimed to be infallible; like all mystics, he tried to describe his "glimpses" as he received them.

Steiner's importance lies in the impressive consistency of his teachings, and on his insistence that it is a mistake to try to take spiritualism too literally: "The Spiritualists are the greatest materialists of all." He never ceased to emphasize that "the spirit world is woven out of the substance of which human thought consists." What he seems to be saying is that man is somehow quite mistaken to assume that he is "imprisoned" in a material world, and in allowing this to induce a certain basic passivity toward his own life. He loves to emphasize the immense latent creative powers of the human mind. So although his attitude toward Spiritualism often seems hostile, he is fundamentally reaffirming what Myers says in *Human Personality*—and what Catherine Crowe had said before him: that human beings possess enormous hidden powers they never even suspect. The point is underlined by a passage that expresses the essence of Steiner's thought:

> *Your present surroundings are, in a sense, your creation, in that you are mentally so unemancipated; your nerves and senses convey to you your own perception of life. If you were capable of focusing your ego or daily consciousness within your deeper mind, if in short you trained yourself to pass into a thought compound from which form, as the senses convey it, were absent, the material world would vanish.*

In fact, these words are not by Rudolf Steiner; they are from the "script" written by Myers, and published by Geraldine Cummins as *The Road to Immortality*. It emphasizes Steiner's repeated assertion that it is a mistake to take the "facts" too literally. To do so is to leave out of account a "fifth dimension" that confers meaning on them.

Chapter Seven

Decline and Rebirth

THE SUFFERINGS OF WORLD WAR I HAD THE effect of making thousands of converts to spiritualism—and, paradoxically, of convincing more people than ever before that it was nonsense. The man who must bear a large part of the responsibility for these contrary effects is Sir Oliver Lodge.

In November 1916, Lodge's *Raymond, or Life and Death* was published, and caused an immediate sensation—although not quite the kind Lodge had hoped for. Ever since 1909, when Lodge had produced a book called *The Survival of Man*—admitting his belief in life after death—scientists had felt that he had "let down the side." At least in that book he had discussed the experimental evidence and maintained a rigorous scientific detachment.

But to devote a four-hundred-page book to arguing that his son had come back from the dead looked like emotional self-indulgence. *Raymond* made an easy target for hostile reviewers—particularly a passage in which Raymond explained that the "other side" is not all that different from our earth. Most people, he said, wore white robes, although many would have preferred to wear a suit. They could also eat if they wanted to, or even have a cigar or a whisky and soda. "There are laboratories over here and they manufacture all sorts of things in them." It sounded too silly for words. One psychologist called Charles Mercier was quick off the mark with a thoroughly hostile book called *Spiritualism and Sir Oliver Lodge*. Most scientists felt simply that Lodge had become a little cracked, and that the kindest thing would be to ignore him.

Sir Arthur Conan Doyle encountered the same hostility in 1918 when he confessed his conversion to Spiritualism in a book called *The New Revelation*. During the war, the Doyles had looked after an ailing young woman named Lily Loder-Symonds, who amused herself in her sickbed by practicing automatic writing. The Doyles were convinced that it was simply her subconscious mind speaking. Then one day there came a message: "It is terrible. Terrible. And will have a great influence on the war." On that day, a German submarine sank the passenger liner *Lusitania* and over one thousand passengers drowned, many of them Americans. The sinking prepared the way for America's entry into the war. From then on, the Doyles took the automatic writing more seriously. In April 1915, Conan Doyle's brother-in-law Malcolm Leckie died at Mons. One day, as Doyle was sitting by Lily Loder-Symonds' bedside, watching her produce automatic writing, he was startled to recognize Malcolm Leckie's handwriting. Doyle began to ask questions, and "Leckie" replied. Doyle asked him a particularly difficult question about a private conversation they had had before the war. The reply specified precisely what he and Leckie had discussed. Yet Doyle had mentioned it to no one else—not even his wife. From then on, he had no doubt of the reality of life after death.

His conversion caused even more embarrassment than that of Sir Oliver Lodge. Distinguished friends, such as Lloyd George, Winston Churchill, and King George V, felt that he was displaying a childish credulity. Many people asked mockingly: "What would Sherlock Holmes have said?" In fact, when the final volume of Sherlock Holmes stories, *The Case Book*, appeared in 1927, it received an unprecedentedly cold reception; the middle-class public felt that its idol had revealed feet of clay. The last novel about the great Professor Challenger—*The Land of Mist*—in which Challenger is converted to Spiritualism—was received with widespread derision. Doyle's biographer states that Doyle's support of Spiritualism prevented him from receiving a peerage.[1]

One of the saddest stories of antispiritualist prejudice concerns an architect named Frederick Bligh Bond. In 1907, the ruins of Glastonbury Abbey were bought by the nation, and Bligh Bond was appointed to take charge of the excavations. Bond was a devotee of Catherine Crowe's *Night Side of Nature*, and decided that his task would be greatly simplified if he could contact some of the long-dead monks of the abbey and ask them where to dig. A friend named John Allen Bartlett was able to produce automatic writing. In November 1907, Bond and Bartlett sat on either side of a table, with Bartlett holding a pencil and Bond's hand resting very lightly on top of it. Bond asked questions, and Bartlett's hand wrote out the answers. When Bond asked where a missing chapel had been situated, Bartlett's hand drew a plan of the abbey with the chapel on it. The "communicator" called himself "Gulielmus Monachus"—William the Monk. When Bond's team dug in the position indicated, they found the chapel. His employers, the Church of England, were delighted. They continued to be delighted as Bond made find after find, including another chapel. Bond took care to tell no one that most of his information came from William the Monk and various

1. Charles Higham, *The Adventures of Conan Doyle*, p. 261.

other communicators who called themselves "the Watchers." Finally, in 1917, he decided that his success had justified itself, and told the whole story in a book called *Gate of Remembrance*. The Church was horrified, and Bond found himself out of a job. He was not even allowed within the precincts of the abbey, and the abbey book shop was ordered not to sell his guide book to Glastonbury.

There is an ironic footnote to this story. In 1936, the Archbishop of Canterbury, Cosmo Lang, decided that it was time for the Church of England to make up its mind about Spiritualism. So he appointed a commission to look into it to decide whether the doctrines of Spiritualism were consistent with Christianity. The commission took three years to report. Their conclusion was that not only was Spiritualism not opposed to Christianity—after all, Christians believe in a life after death—but that the evidence for survival was extremely powerful. The archbishop was apparently so embarrassed by these conclusions that he dropped the report into a drawer, where it lay forgotten for more than thirty years. It was finally published in the mid-1970s.

We have already observed this phenomenon: the feeling that there is something morbid and degenerate about a preoccupation with life after death. It is a perfectly valid reaction. Healthy people naturally feel that we should turn our attention to the fascinating problems of life and the physical universe rather than to death. Yet we can also see that such criticism is totally irrelevant where Lodge and Doyle were concerned. Doyle would have been an idiot *not* to be impressed when the automatic writing told him something that was known to no other living person. Lodge would have been a very poor scientist if he had failed to recognize that the Raymond group photograph[2] constituted strong *prima facie* evidence that his son had survived death. It is important to remember that Lodge and Doyle had been members of the Society for Psychical Research for more than two

---

2. See p. 131.

decades before they finally became convinced of survival; the same applied to James Hyslop and Sir William Barrett. Crookes himself only came to accept survival in 1917, after a séance at which he became convinced that his dead wife was speaking to him. These men were convinced by evidence, not by wishful thinking.

This in itself tells us why spiritualism failed to convince the masses. If it took twenty years to overcome the doubts of men who were interested in the problem, it would obviously take centuries to convince those who weren't.

It must also be admitted that Raymond Lodge's remarks about cigars and whisky and soda—not to mention white robes—probably did more harm to spiritualism than the exposure of a dozen fake mediums. In various forms, the problem has continued to be a bugbear ever since. There is a slight element of absurdity in the whole notion of life after death—a touch of the preposterous that was exploited in H. G. Wells' "Inexperienced Ghost" and Noel Coward's *Blithe Spirit*. Most of the books about life after death fail to avoid this touch of absurdity. In 1928, the Rev. Charles Drayton Thomas produced his book *Life Beyond Death With Evidence*, an impressive account of his "contacts" with his deceased father and sister through mediums. But when his father begins to describe the world he lives in, there is an effect of bathos.

> *We have roads, but the surface is unlike the stoned or macadamised roads of England. . . . The appearance is something like natural soil, but without mud or anything disagreeable. . . .*
>
> *We have London, but it is not your London. . . . There is some likeness in the parks and beautiful buildings, but with us they are all finer . . . I have seen no snakes or lions here. . . . We have horses, dogs and cats but very few monkeys. . . .*

After all this, it is difficult to feel the appropriate emotion when the father and sister describe an interview with Jesus, who, predictably, radiates "a great majesty, together with great sweetness and humility."

In the 1930s, a medium named Jane Sherwood began to practice automatic writing, and received lengthy communications from a certain "G. F. Scott," describing the life beyond. These were published as *The Psychic Bridge* and *The Country Beyond.* "Scott" later revealed his true identity—as T. E. Lawrence—and dictated another book about his own personal experiences of life after death. A spirit called "Mitchell," who had taken upon himself the role of Lawrence's mentor, tells Lawrence that he has lived a monk-like existence, and that he ought to go and experiment with all the experiences he has missed on earth. For example, women. "Go on a proper spree." Lawrence is taken on a kind of brothel tour. "These girls are not prostitutes . . . they are women who have missed sexual experiences during their earth life and need to work out this lack before they can progress. . . ." Lawrence, who on earth had shown homosexual tendencies and a taste for being flogged, bursts into lyrical prose: "We two have wandered happily in an enchanted land exploring the delights of an intimate companionship crowned by the magic of union. . . ."[3]

If it were obvious that Jane Sherwood and Drayton Thomas had been deceived—either by their own unconscious minds or by spirits with a penchant for leg-pulling—these passages would not be such an embarrassment. But Jane Sherwood's *The Country Beyond* has been described by Raynor C. Johnson—a leading authority on mysticism—as "one of the best attempts to convey to us valid impressions of the conditions we shall all have to meet some day when we have finished with our physical bodies." Drayton Thomas' book is one of the most impressive arguments for survival ever published; his "father" was able to accurately forecast items he would find in the newspapers the following day—items which (as enquiry revealed) had not even been set up in print at the time.

It seems that these awkward paradoxes are inherent in the nature of spiritualism. Students of the paranormal find them no more off-

---

3. *Post Mortem Journal.*

putting than poetry lovers find Wordsworth's occasional descents into bathos. They are simply another aspect of James' Law. But for many potential converts between the wars, they formed an insuperable barrier to belief. Laboratories and brothels in the sky could simply not be taken seriously.

There were several other causes for the decline of spiritualism in the 1920s and 1930s. The days of the great mediums—such as Dunglas Home, Eusapia Palladino, and Leonore Piper seemed to be at an end. There were still many remarkable mediums—Mrs. Leonard, the Schneider brothers, Helen Duncan—but their achievements were not so spectacular. In the cynical and disillusioned frame of mind engendered by the Great War, exposures and denunciations received far more publicity than successful experiments with mediums. The magician Harry Houdini made a career from attacking spiritualism in the 1920s; his book *A Magician Among the Spirits* denounced mediums as "human vultures." When investigating the American medium Margery Crandon, there is evidence that Houdini cheated by hiding a ruler in a specially designed cabinet, so she could be accused of using it to ring a bell. (Houdini's assistant later admitted that he had hidden the ruler in the cabinet on Houdini's orders, and added: "There's one thing you've got to remember about Mr. 'Oudini—for 'im the truth was bloody well what he wanted it to be.") In fact, even the serious investigators often seemed to be on the side of the skeptics. After a series of experiments with the Austrian medium Rudi Schneider, Harry Price denounced him in a Sunday newspaper instead of simply making an unfavorable report to the Society for Psychical Research. (It became clear later that his motive was pique because Schneider had agreed to work with some rival investigators.) When Helen Duncan was charged with cheating and fined ten pounds, Price wrote a book attacking her. In due course, Price himself would be denounced for trickery in his most famous investigation the haunting of Borley Rectory.

In the Society for Psychical Research, the skeptics became known as the High 'n Dries. In the Society's early days, Frank Podmore had been its only High ‘n Dry. By the late 1920s, some of the Society’s most influential members, including its research officer, E. J. Dingwall, and its librarian, Theodore Besterman, were High ’n Dries. The “wets”—or even the faintly damps—hardly stood a chance. Dingwall went to America to investigate Margery Crandon, and was apparently thoroughly satisfied with her genuineness—large quantities of ectoplasm were extruded from somewhere between her thighs, and reached out to touch Dingwall in the form of a hand—but when he came to write up his investigations six months later, he had changed his mind, and made it clear he thought she was a fraud. The result of such controversies was that the Society was split by internal dissensions, and ceased to perform the task it was founded to carry out. One consequence was that when reports of an amazing Brazilian medium, Carlos Mirabelli—who floated in the air, dematerialized, and reappeared in another room, and caused dead people to materialize in broad daylight—reached the Society in 1927, it was in too much disarray to send a competent investigator. Mirabelli’s remarkable phenomena were never confirmed. The days when the Society could despatch a man like Richard Hodgson to the other side of the world at a few weeks’ notice were long past.

There was one major breakthrough in psychical research or, as it now came to be called, paranormal investigation, in the 1930s. A gambler walked into the office of Dr. Joseph Banks Rhine at Duke University in 1934 and told Rhine he was convinced he could influence the fall of the dice. As the two crouched on the floor, it dawned on Rhine that this might be a method for proving psychokinesis—“mind over matter”—in the laboratory. Eighteen series of statistical tests were conducted over eight years, and they showed one fascinating result: that when people were “fresh,” they *could* influence the fall of the die. As they went on and became tired and bored, they got worse at it. Rhine’s methods may have been dull compared to the experiments of Crookes with Dunglas Home or Richet with Eusapia Palladino, but he effectively proved the paranormal powers of the human mind in the laboratory.

This was undoubtedly an enormous step forward. It demonstrated the correctness of that central argument of Catherine Crowe and Frederick Myers: that the powers of the human mind are greater than we suppose. But it came no closer to answering the question that the Society for Psychical Research was founded to investigate: is there life after death? Then, in the late 1930s, another series of statistical experiments brought this one stage closer.

Dr. Samuel George Soal was a mathematician at the University of London, and he was unimpressed by Rhine's results. In 1936, a well-known photographer named Basil Shackleton walked into Soal's office and announced: "I haven't come to be tested, but to demonstrate telepathy." He could, he claimed, guess his way through a whole pack of playing cards and get most of them right. Soal tested him, but was disappointed; Shackleton's first score was ten out of twenty-five, but after that, he got steadily worse; on the seventh test he only got three out of twenty-five. Shackleton said he needed a drink to get his powers working; but even after a drink, his score was still disappointingly low.

In 1939, a conversation with another researcher, Whately Carington, gave Soal a new idea. Carington had been involved in a series of "picture guessing" experiments, and he had noticed a curious phenomenon: some of his subjects were guessing the next picture. Soal went back and looked at some of his own results. First of all, he looked at the results produced by a London housewife named Gloria Stewart, and found that she had frequently guessed the next card. Soal went on to look through results produced by other subjects, but found nothing very interesting. Then, by chance, he came upon Basil Shackleton's results. Here the "displacement" score was even more striking than in the case of Gloria Stewart. Again and again, Shackleton guessed either the previous card or the next card, instead of the one Soal was asking him to concentrate on. Soal asked Shackleton to take part in another series of experiments. They went on for two years, and demonstrated beyond all doubt that Shackleton was frequently able to guess the next card—a card that Soal himself had not yet seen. So this was not telepathy; it was precognition—the faculty apparently demonstrated by Drayton Thomas's father when he was able to predict what would be in the newspapers the next day.

It is true, of course, that precognition does not "prove" life after death, but if it really exists, it proves there is something fundamentally wrong with our common sense, materialistic view of the universe. We can find room for telepathy and psychokinesis in the scientific picture of reality, but the future has not yet taken place; consequently, there is no possible "scientific" way in which it can be known. To explain precognition, we need to take a leap into some completely new type of explanation: for example, some fourth or fifth dimension, of the kind suggested by Whately Carington in *A Theory of the Mechanism of Survival*. When Soal demonstrated precognition, he had taken the most important step toward proving life after death since the foundation of the Society for Psychical Research.

In 1942, an American researcher, Dr. Gertrude Schmeidler, of Radcliffe College, produced a result that was almost as important. She was testing a group of students for extrasensory perception (ESP), and before the experiment, she asked which of them believed in the possibility of ESP and which didn't. She labeled the "believers" sheep and the "nonbelievers" goats. When she examined the results of the card-guessing tests, she discovered that the sheep had scored significantly above chance. What was even more interesting was that the goats had scored significantly below chance. They were unconsciously "cheating" to support their view that ESP does not exist. In doing so, they were revealing as much extrasensory perception as the sheep, but using it negatively. For years, mediums and psychics had been explaining that their powers often failed to work in the presence of skeptics, and the skeptics had jeered at this as a feeble excuse. Gertrude Schmeidler had demonstrated that skepticism is not necessarily as scientific and detached as it pretends to be.

These results were taken to heart by Dr. Helmut Schmidt, a research scientist at the Boeing Laboratory in Seattle. If people are more likely to show extrasensory perception in a friendly, trusting atmosphere, then it would be a great advantage if the scientist could devise an experiment in which cheating is quite impossible. Then he can relax and try to coax the subject into the right mood for ESP. Schmidt met this challenge by devising a machine that used decaying radioactive material to make various lamps go on and off. Nobody had the least idea when the next radioactive atom would "decay" and shoot out a high-speed particle. Schmidt's subjects had to guess which lamp would be the next to light up, and press a button. Then the machine automatically registered a hit or miss.

Schmidt soon discovered a number of subjects who scored well above chance. Many of these were already psychic—one physicist admitted that he often dreamed of the future. Schmidt also produced a perfect demonstration of Gertrude Schmeidler's "sheep and goats" argument—one extroverted American girl who produced scores well above chance, and one introverted South American whose scores were equally far below chance, demonstrating as much psychic ability as the extrovert, but used in a negative direction. These two subjects were also able to demonstrate psychokinesis (mind over matter) by willing lights to flash on and off in a particular direction. Helmut Schmidt was the first scientist to demonstrate the reality of extrasensory perception and psychokinesis in the laboratory.

These advances were impressive, but anyone who took an interest in psychical research in the 1960s and early 1970s had to admit that it had all become rather boring. Card-guessing games and random-number generators may produce marvelously convincing proofs of the reality of extrasensory perception or precognition, but it is hard for most people to work themselves into a state of excitement about it. This is not quite what Myers and Sidgwick had in mind on that famous starlit walk.

There was at least one researcher who was still working in the older tradition. Dr. Karlis Osis, born in Riga, Latvia in 1917, had worked with Rhine at Duke University on extrasensory perception and precognition before he became research director at the Parapsychology Foundation in New York. Osis was fascinated by the kind of death-bed visions reported by Sir William Barrett—like the case of "Mrs. B"[4] who saw her father and sister in the room as she was dying, although she had no idea that her sister was dead. He called them "Peak in Darien cases," from the last line of Keats' sonnet—a suggestion of reverence and awe. He had the sensible idea of circulating a questionnaire to doctors and nurses, asking them what they had observed about dying patients. Six hundred and forty questionnaires were returned, covering more than thirty-five thousand cases. In 1961, Osis published his observations in *Deathbed Observations by Physicians and Nurses.*

One of the first things Osis discovered was that fear is not the dominant emotion in most dying patients. Discomfort and pain were more common; what was surprising was the large number of patients who were elated at the time of death, even to the point of exaltation and seeing visions. These amounted to about one in twenty. The visions were often of "heaven"—of beautiful cities or a "promised land." A six-year-old boy dying of polio saw beautiful flowers and heard birds singing. Most of these patients were fully awake and in clear consciousness, with a normal temperature. Many patients who were brought back from the dead by medical attention were often unwilling to be revived and expressed sentiments like "I want to go back." One doctor, recalling two personal experiences of near-death hallucinations, suggested that this might be due to oxygen starvation of the brain. He had been close to death by drowning, and also by oxygen starvation when his breathing equipment froze up in an aeroplane; on both occasions he experienced beautiful imagery and a feeling of deep happiness. He resented being revived from drowning. But other medical experts have disagreed, and Osis points out that

---

4. See p. 130.

such visions often occurred in fully conscious patients long before the final slide into the death coma.

In his summary of conclusions, Osis remains cautious. He notes that Barrett was mistaken to believe that all death-bed visions of relatives involve those who are dead. He found that 52 percent were of dead relatives, 28 percent of living relatives, and the remaining 20 percent of religious figures. But the Census of Hallucination taken by the Society for Psychical Research showed that people in normal health saw twice as many living relatives as dead ones. So "predominance of hallucinations of the dead seems to be a real characteristic of terminal cases." In reply to the obvious criticism that dying patients may be sedated or in states of fever, he points out that most of the visions of dead relatives happened to patients who had not been sedated, who had no "hallucinogenic pathology," and who were fully awake and able to respond intelligently to questions. So in its general conclusions, *Deathbed Observations by Physicians and Nurses* backs up the conclusions reached by Barrett in *Death-Bed Visions*: that dying people usually feel no fear of dying, and that they often believe they are being met by dead relatives.

Osis concludes his study by remarking that his observations need verifying, particularly by studies in other cultures. This hint was taken up by his colleague Erlendur Haraldsson, who conducted similar studies in India. It might have been reasonable to expect that, in a totally different culture—particularly one that places less emphasis on life after death—death-bed visions would be of a different kind. Haraldsson discovered this was not so; the death-bed visions of Indians were much the same as those of Americans.

Osis and Haraldsson approached the problem of death in the detached spirit of a Society for Psychical Research investigation. The other major investigation of the 1960s was undertaken with altogether more emotional commitment. Dr. Elizabeth Kübler-Ross had visited the extermination camp Maidanek at the end of World War II, and established a camp for refugees on the Vista River in Poland. In America in the early 1960s, now married to a professor of neurology and pathology in Chicago, she was struck by the American tendency to ignore death and pretend that it does not exist. She often found that doctors would refuse to admit the terminally ill into their wards. She gained nationwide notoriety when she invited a twenty-year-old girl who was dying of leukemia to her classes at the University of Chicago, and *Life* ran an article about the experiment. The death of this girl in 1970 confirmed Dr. Kübler-Ross' feeling that our "death-denying society" needs to have its attitudes changed.

To begin with, her attitude toward life after death was one of skepticism; she was only concerned with the psychological problems involved in accepting death. Gradually, her study of the dying led her to the conviction that both survival and reincarnation are established facts. Her own observation of death-bed visions of the dying confirmed that they often see dead relatives. She noted, for example, that while dying children hope to be with mummy and daddy, they actually tend to see deceased grandparents on the point of death.

Her conclusions, set out in books like *Of Death and Dying* and *Questions and Answers on Death and Dying*, are not presented as systematically as those of Osis and Haraldsson, but their general outline is clear enough. She believes that everyone knows the time of his own death, and that everyone who dies is met by dead relatives or other loved ones. She has also come to accept that dying should be regarded as a climax of living, and perhaps as its most beautiful experience. She is convinced that all human beings have "guides" who continually watch over them, and who can be seen in moments of psychic stress. As to the "world beyond death," she has accepted two major conclusions that are stated repeatedly in the literature of spiritualism: that time in "the next world" is quite unlike time as we know it, and that there is no "judgment" of the dead; they judge—and punish—themselves.

Elizabeth Kübler-Ross' obvious emotional identification with her subject has led to accusations that she has allowed her beliefs to dictate her findings. This may well be so. It is also clear that these findings are based upon the study of hundreds of cases, and that they are basically consistent with those of Barrett, Osis, and Haraldsson.

By the late 1960s, the subject of near-death experiences had begun to attract an increasing number of serious investigators. Two of these, Russell Noyes and Ray Kletti, came upon some long-forgotten work on this subject by a professor of geology from Zurich, Albert Heim. Heim's own near-death experience occurred when he was leading a climbing party in the Alps in 1871. A gust of wind blew his hat off, and as he tried to grab it, he fell seventy feet to a snow-covered ledge. The fall only occupied a few seconds, yet he felt that time had expanded into far more than that.

> *Mental activity became enormous, rising to a hundred fold velocity . . . I saw my whole past life take place in many images, as though on a stage at some distance from me. . . . Everything was transfigured as though by a heavenly light, without anxiety and without pain. The memory of very tragic experiences I had had was clear but not saddening. I felt no conflict or strife; conflict had been transmuted into love. Elevated and harmonious thoughts dominated and united individual images, and like magnificent music a divine calm swept through my soul. I became ever more surrounded by a splendid blue heaven with delicate and rosy and violet cloudlets. I swept into it painlessly and softly and I saw that now I was falling freely through the air and that under me a snow field lay waiting.*

Heim was knocked unconscious by his fall but survived. The exquisitely peaceful quality of the experience led him to begin collecting other people's observations on climbing accidents. He claimed that, over twenty years of research, he had discovered that 95 percent of the victims had experienced similar feelings to his own. Heim's conclusion was that people who had died from falls had experienced the same feeling of peace and reconciliation at the end.

Noyes and Kletti published a translation of Heim's observations, and added much research of their own. Unlike Elizabeth Kübler-Ross, they were unable to accept the view that such experiences provide some kind of proof of survival. Their own conclusion was that when man faces death, he experiences a "depersonalization" which is basically a psychological defense against death. The result is a kind of "death trance" whose purpose is to make death easy. The sensation of seeing the whole of one's past life also seems common to these experiences. Lyall Watson quotes the case of a nineteen-year-old skydiver who fell from a height of three thousand feet.[5] "All my past life flashed before my eyes . . . I saw my mother's face, all the houses I've lived in, the military academy I attended, the faces of friends, everything." In fact, he had a soft landing and broke only his nose. These experiences of heightened memory have obviously a great deal in common with the "flashback" experience discovered by Wilder Penfield when he touched the cerebral cortex with an electric probe during an operation on an epileptic and induced memories of childhood.

In the mid-1960s, when Elizabeth Kübler-Ross was beginning her research into the death experience, a young philosophy student at the University of Virginia, Raymond Moody, was also starting to collect accounts of near-death experiences. One of the men who aroused his interest in the subject was a psychiatrist, Dr. George Ritchie of Virginia, who, as a young soldier, had apparently "died" and then revived. In December 1943, Ritchie had been in a hospital in Texas with a respiratory infection. He began to spit up blood and lost consciousness; when he woke up he saw his own body lying on the bed. Outside in the corridor a ward nurse walked through him; a man he tapped on the shoulder ignored him. He tried to get back into his body but found it impossible. Then Ritchie experienced some kind of religious revelation. The room became "brighter than a thousand arc lights" and a figure he identified as Jesus appeared. After a tour of a great city in which he was shown the consequences of sin, Ritchie woke up in his body, quite convinced he had died. Like so many who have been through the near-death experience, Ritchie insisted that it was quite unlike a dream; it all seemed quite real.

---

5. *The Romeo Error*, p. 63.

For the next eleven years, Moody went on collecting near-death experiences, quite unaware that anyone else was doing so—at this stage he had never heard of Elizabeth Kübler-Ross. Three years teaching philosophy convinced him he would rather be a doctor, and he took a medical degree. Over the years, he collected about a hundred and fifty near-death experiences, was struck by their basic similarities, and wrote a short book about them called *Life After Life*. When his publisher sent a proof to Elizabeth Kübler-Ross, she commented that she might have written the same book herself. *Life After Life* appeared in 1977, and became a national bestseller.

The similarities are certainly striking. There was, first of all, the sense of peace and happiness described by Heim, the Rev. Bertrand, and so many others. There was another experience that appeared again and again: the impression of moving through a dark tunnel, usually with a light at the end. "I was moving through this—you're going to think this is weird through this long dark place. It seemed like a sewer or something. . . . It was like being in a cylinder . . . I entered head first into a narrow and very very dark passageway. . . . Suddenly I was in a very dark, very deep valley."

In case after case, the person emerges from the tunnel to find himself looking at his own body. (There were, however, many cases in which the experience began with the out-of-the-body experience.) A youth who almost drowned saw his body "in the water about three or four feet away, bobbing up and down. I viewed my body from the back, and slightly to the right side." A woman who "died" with heart trouble felt herself,

> *sliding down between the mattress and the rail on the side of the bed—actually it seemed as if I went* through *the rail—on down to the floor. Then I started rising upward, slowly. On my way up, I saw more nurses come running into the room . . . then I stopped, floating right below the ceiling, looking down.*

Compare this with a case described by Kübler-Ross, in which a woman in intensive care went into critical condition, and the nurse rushed out of the room to get help:

> *Meanwhile, this woman felt herself float out of her body. In fact, she said she could look down and see how pale her face looked. Yet at the same time she felt absolutely wonderful. She had a great sense of peace and relief.*

The same thing was described again and again by Moody's subjects: the out-of-the-body experience, accompanied by a blissful sense of timelessness. Another recurrent feature was the perception of the "new body"—shaped like the physical body that had been left behind. Patients often became aware of this new body when they realized they were no longer in the old one—often by trying to communicate with other people. "I tried talking to them but nobody could hear me, nobody would listen to me . . . they would just walk *through* me." The physical senses often seem to be heightened, so that seeing and hearing are far more keen than in the physical body. But the "hearing," when it concerns voices, seems to be a form of telepathy or thought-transfer. (This again is a feature that can be found in records of near-death and after-death experiences since the beginning of psychical research: communication becomes telepathic.) There is often a feeling of awful loneliness, but this is usually dispelled when the "dead" person becomes aware of others like himself: sometimes other people who have died, relatives or friends—and sometimes an entity or spirit he believes to be a guardian angel. One man was told by such a spirit that "I have helped you through this stage of your existence, but now I am going to turn you over to others."

One of the most common experiences was of a bright light—like the "thousand arc lights" described by George Ritchie—which seems to radiate a sense of love and warmth. Christians, understandably, are inclined to identify this with Jesus. There is a sense of direct telepathic communication, without language. "It was like talking to a person, but a person wasn't there." The "light" may ask probing questions about what the person has done with his life. This, Moody found, was often followed by flashbacks, a flood of memories in which the past life is seen in review.

Very often there was a sense of some kind of border or limit—like the big stones described by Wiltse. It may be a body of water, a distant shore, a gray mist, or many other things. The "dead" person experiences a conviction that if he passes this limit, then he is permanently "dead." Until it is passed, there is a choice of returning to the body. Since all Moody's interviewees had returned from the near-death experience, he heard many different versions of how the return to the body was accomplished. "I just fell right back down to my body. The next thing I knew I was in my body again . . . it was just like a swoooosh and I felt like I was drawn through a limited area, a kind of funnel, I guess." But the majority of people simply woke up and found themselves "alive" again.

In a subsequent book based on further research (*Reflections on Life After Life*), Moody observed some other interesting aspects of the near-death experience. There were many glimpses of a heavenly realm, and the phrase "city of light" occurred repeatedly. There was also an experience Moody calls "the vision of knowledge," a flash of mystical insight into the nature of the universe.

> *For a second I knew all the secrets of all the ages, all the meaning of the universe, the stars, the moon—of everything. . . . This all-powerful knowledge opened before me. It seemed that I was being told that I was going to remain sick for quite a while and that I would several close calls. And I did have several close calls after tha. They said some of it would be to erase this all-knowing knowledge that I had picked up . . . that I had been granted the universal secrets and that I would have to undergo time to forget that knowledge. But I do have the memory of once knowing everything. . . .*

When asked what form the knowledge presented itself to him, Moody received the reply: "It was in all forms of communication, sights, sounds, thoughts. It was as if there was nothing that wasn't known. All knowledge was there, not just of one field but everything." Moody asked if spending his life seeking knowledge was pointless. The reply was:

No! You still want to seek knowledge even after you come back here. I'm still seeking knowledge . . . It's silly to try to get the answers here. I sort of felt that it was part of our purpose . . . but that it wasn't just for one person, but that it was to be used for all mankind. We're always reaching out to help others with what we know.

Moody was struck by this notion of "forgetting" this universal knowledge before returning to life, and cites Plato's story of a soldier called Er—from *The Republic*—who was allowed to return from death. Er describes how the souls who were allowed to return to earth had to first drink of the waters of the River of Forgetfulness, and some of them "who were not saved by good sense" drank far too much. Like many of Moody's subjects, Er had no idea of how he returned to life; he simply woke up and found himself lying on his funeral pyre. It is plain that what interests Moody about all this is the question of that barrier of "forgetfulness" that seems to interpose between "the other world" and the present one—and, by implication, the question of why some people seem to have escaped total forgetfulness.

Another of Moody's subjects described his "knowledge" experience as being like a school: ". . . it *was* real . . . you would feel, sense the presence of others being around." Moody compared this with the comment of another subject who, in a near-death experience, felt that he had been into what he called libraries and institutions of higher learning. His present subject agreed enthusiastically:

This is a place where the place of knowledge . . . It's like you focus mentally on one place in that school and—zoom—knowledge flows by you from that place automatically. It's just like you'd had about a dozen speed reading courses.

Another woman told him: "It was like I knew all things . . . I thought whatever I wanted to know could be known."

All this is important because it seems to answer a fundamental objection to the whole notion of survival—the apparent triviality of the preoccupations of the communicators. If we are going to wake up in the next world to the same kind of consciousness we have to put up with here, it scarcely seems worth the trouble of dying. Most of us are obscurely aware that there is something wrong with the quality of everyday consciousness; it is always getting us involved with questions and problems that we know to be unimportant, yet which stick in our heads like some irritating tune. When we experience a sudden surge of happiness or vitality, these problems are whipped away like a leaf in a gale. So if, as most spiritualists seem to agree, death is some kind of an evolution, then we have some kind of vague expectation that it will involve a higher level of vitality, a "bird's eye view" of what life is all about, a greater freedom. The whole atmosphere of séances seems to be irritatingly banal, "human all too human." Even when the communicators claim to be great musicians or writers—as in the case of the psychic Rosemary Brown—what they have to offer seems downright substandard, the kind of thing that would have ended in their wastepaper baskets on earth.

Moody's subjects who experienced "visions of knowledge" seem to be making the point that life after death is not really a continuation of earth life on the same level. Moody emphasizes how often they say things like "it's impossible to explain," or "the words I would use are different because there really are no words . . . ." This may also be regarded as an answer to Rudolf Steiner's objection that "the Spiritualists are the greatest materialists of all." The observations of Kübler-Ross, Moody, and others make us aware that when we study accounts of life after death, we should continually remind ourselves of the "language gap," the problem of trying to translate new perceptions into words that were evolved with a narrower purpose in mind. Our concepts of reality are closely bound up with language, and most accounts of life after death seem to agree that language has become unnecessary.

The effect of Moody's book was to virtually create a new academic industry: the study of near-death experiences (abbreviated as

NDEs). Kenneth Ring, a professor of psychology at the University of Connecticut, attempted a far more systematic survey than Moody had aimed for. He noted that Moody made no claim to present scientific evidence about the experience of dying, much less of life after death. In 1977, the year *Life After Life* appeared, Ring set out to remedy this shortcoming by tracking down and interviewing scores of people who had come close to death, and studying the results statistically. In all important respects, Ring's findings confirmed Moody's. So did those of other researchers: Michael Sabom, Edith Fiore, Maurice Rawlings, and Margot Grey. Edith Fiore (in *You Have Been Here Before*) summarized accounts of more than a thousand near-death experiences. To read some of these books often gives the bewildering impression of reading the same thing over and over again. At least the sheer repetition drives home the fact that Moody's cases were not a random sample, selected because they satisfied his own emotional preferences. Again and again there are the same descriptions of finding oneself in a state of "disembodiment," of passing through some kind of tunnel with a light at the end, of a sense of communication with some benevolent being or beings, of some kind of "review," of an experience of some border between life and death, and of a return to life. (Moody calls this "the core experience.")

It has been repeatedly pointed out that all this "proves" nothing. James Alcock expressed the basic objection in *The Skeptical Enquirer*:[6]

> *I have no argument with people's theology or philosophy. What is bothersome, however, is the necessity these people feel to try to provide "objective" evidence to support their beliefs, and their attempts to fool the layman with their claims of scientific rigour and exactitude. Survival research is based on belief in search of data rather than observation in search of explanation. It is an expression of individual and collective anxiety about death.*

---

6. Spring 1979. Quoted by William R. Corliss, *The Unfathomed Mind, A Handbook of Unusual Mental Phenomena* (1982), p. 584.

This is a perfectly fair objection, but it also seems to overlook the fact that science is based upon *repeated* observation. To ignore something that is repeated by thousands of observers would be a contradiction of the scientific attitude. Kübler-Ross, Moody, Ring, and others are the first to admit that their observations of NDEs *prove* absolutely nothing about life after death. Since these researchers are not concerned with other evidence of survival—the kind of evidence we have been surveying in this book—they make no attempt to argue a logical case for life after death. In the concluding chapter of his own book, Ring has the courage to "remove my white lab coat and describe my own beliefs—for what they may be worth." After emphasizing that near-death experiences prove nothing about survival, he goes on:

> I do *believe—but not just on the basis of my own or others' data regarding near-death experiences—that we continue to have a conscious existence after our physical death and that the core experience does represent its beginning, a glimpse of things to come.*

He goes on:

> *My own understanding of these near-death experiences leads me to regard them as "teachings." They are, it seems to me,* revelatory experiences. . . . *These experiences clearly imply that there is something more, something* beyond *the physical world of the senses. . . . Anyone who makes the effort to inform himself of the nature and consequences of genuine mystical or religious experiences will soon become convinced that the core experience is itself a member of this larger family.*
>
> *Why do such experiences occur? . . . I have one speculative answer to offer, although I admit it may sound not only fanciful but downright playful. I have come to believe that the universe . . . has many ways of "getting its message across." In a sense, it wants us to "wake-up," to become aware of the cosmic dimensions of the*

drama of which we are all a part. Near-death experiences represent one of its devices for waking us up to this higher reality.

Ring's point may be underlined by quoting a passage from a book on recent research into the "mystical experience," Nona Coxhead's *The Relevance of Bliss.* She cites the case of a psychotherapist, Wendy Rose-Neill, whose experience took place when she was tending her garden on an autumn day.

On this particular day I felt in a very contemplative frame of mind. I remember that I gradually became intensely aware of my surroundings—the sound of the birds singing, the rustling of leaves, the breeze on my skin and the scent of the grass and flowers.

I had a sudden impulse to lie face down on the grass and as I did so an energy seemed to flow through me as if I had become part of the earth underneath me. The boundary between my physical self and my surroundings seemed to dissolve and my feeling of separation vanished. In a strange way I felt I blended into a total unity with the earth, as if I were made of it and it of me. I was aware of the blades of grass between my fingers and touching my face, and I was overwhelmed by a force which seemed to penetrate every fiber of my being.

I felt as if I had suddenly come alive for the first time—as if I were awakened from a long deep sleep into a real world. I remember feeling that a veil had been lifted from my eyes and everything came into focus . . . I realized that I was sur rounded by an incredible loving energy, and that everything, both living and nonliving, is bound inextricably with a kind of consciousness which I cannot describe in words.

Although the experience could not have lasted for more than a few minutes, it seemed endless—as if I were in some kind of suspended eternal state of understanding. . . .

Here phrase after phrase echoes what Ring has said of the near-death experience—the feeling of waking up for the first time, the sense of unity with the earth and the universe, the "loving energy," the impression that time had been suspended.

We can see that what is being discussed is, to some extent, right-brain experience. Our left-brain obsession with the present and with survival keeps us trapped in the world of trivial immediacy. It is as though we were surrounded by a thin wall of soundproof glass. As we relax "into the right brain," the glass walls slide silently back, and we suddenly experience contact with the real world. The everyday sense of urgency, of being in a hurry, suddenly disappears; the clock stops ticking frantically, and there is a floating sensation of timelessness.

There is another important point to note. In ordinary consciousness, we are aware of ourselves as spectators of the world around us, as if watching it on film. In these right-brain experiences, there is still a "spectator," but we cease to identify with him or her. There is a feeling that the "spectator" is *not* "you." The "deeper you" feels relaxed and totally alive. So there is an odd sense of being two people at once—or, as Ray Bryant said of his hypnotic regression experiences, of watching a television program and taking part in it at the same time.

The central recognition in these experiences is that they are somehow more "real" than ordinary experience. We are, in fact, observing the world with something more like our "whole being," instead of just a small part of it. So to try to dismiss mystical experience as somehow "one-sided," as Bertrand Russell does in *Mysticism and Logic*, is scientifically inaccurate. Psychologically speaking, right-brain experience is more "complete" than left-brain experience, for it also involves the left. What the poet sees in his "moments of vision" is, in the most precise and scientific sense, "truer" than what he sees when he is running for a bus or having a shave—just as seeing with both eyes is truer than seeing with only one.

This involves the corollary that the insight of the "core experience" is also truer—closer to reality—than the world of our ordinary perceptions. In criticizing near-death studies, James Alcock implies that they are based on vague wishful thinking. The testimony of those who have experienced an NDE contradicts this; they insist that the experience is nothing like a dream: that it is *more real* than everyday experience. It is, course, still possible to argue that NDEs are some kind of illusion or trick of the brain. But if they are taken in conjunction with the other evidence for survival, it seems more likely that they are genuine glimpses of a type of consciousness that is independent of the body.

Margot Grey, the founder of the International Association for Near-Death Studies in Great Britain, makes a clear connection between near-death experiences and mystical insight in a passage she contributes to *The Relevance of Bliss*. She describes how her own interest in near-death experiences began with a personal insight in 1976. In India, she was struck down by a fever that lasted three weeks, and she hovered on the brink of death.

> *At some point during the process of passing in and out of consciousness I became aware that if I somehow urged myself, I could rise up out of my body and remain in a state of levitation up against the ceiling in a corner of the room.*
>
> *At the time this seemed entirely natural and felt very pleasant and extremely freeing. I remember looking at my body lying on the bed and feeling completely unperturbed by the fact that is seemed likely that I was going to die in a strange country . . . but thinking that it was totally unimportant where I left my body, which I felt had served me well and like a favorite worn out coat had at last outlived its usefulness and would now have to be discarded.*

She describes a sense of floating in total darkness, and a sense of being "at one" with infinite space:

> *Later on, I seemed to be travelling down an endless tunnel; I could see a pin-point of light at the end of the tunnel towards which I seemed to be moving. . . . I remember knowing with absolute certainty that I would eventually be through the tunnel and would emerge into the light, which was like the light of a very bright star,*

but much more brilliant. A sense of exaltation was accompanied by a feeling of being very close to the "source" of life and love, which seemed to be one.

The result of this experience was a "mental rebirth." "My mental energies seemed extended and refined by a new consciousness and I determined to study the phenomena that I had experienced, in order to try to discover what other people experienced when apparently on the threshold of death." The work of Ring and Moody was available to her, and she began her own research into the near-death experience in England. When Ring read the typescript of her book *Return from Death*, he felt much as Elizabeth Kübler-Ross felt on reading Moody's *Life After Life*: that, without realizing it, they had been writing the same book.[7] They had arrived independently at the same conclusion: that the real importance of the near-death experience is its aftereffect on those who have been through it. In her conclusion to her book, Margot Grey writes:

In the final analysis, science would seem to be converging with, or at least not conflicting with, what mystics have asserted for millennia when they have stated that access to spiritual reality only becomes possible when consciousness is freed from its dependence on the body. . . . For it is only when one approaches the realm beyond death that one can experience it directly.

It would be a mistake to assume that what Margot Grey is saying is that we would all be better off dead. The last part of her book makes it clear that she feels the real importance of the NDE to be its effect on the lives of those who have been through it. Madame Blavatsky once said that although our earth-realm is the "solidest" and most difficult of all the worlds, it also offers us the most opportunity. This again is a thread that runs throughout world mysticism: the notion that physical life on earth is not some kind of purgatory, to be

---

7. I am grateful to Margot Grey for lending me chapters of the typescript of her book, and of Kenneth Ring's introduction.

patiently endured until we can escape to a higher realm, but some kind of unique opportunity. The main problem of human beings is that "confinement in the present" keeps us in a state allied to sleep or hypnosis, in which we accomplish nothing whatever because we have no idea of what we ought to be doing. The mystical experience and the "core experience" both seem to bring a flash of insight into "what it is all about." This is the insight that emerges clearly from all the writers on the near-death experience, and which Margot Grey states with more emphasis than most.

It could be said, then, that the study of the near-death experience is the most important breakthrough in psychical research since the foundation of the Society for Psychical Research more than a century ago. To the objection that the NDE has nothing to do with psychical research, we can only reply that it seems to have a great deal to do with it. The SPR originated in a starlit walk during which Myers asked Sidgwick:

> *whether he thought that when Tradition, Intuition, Metaphysic had failed to solve the riddle of the Universe, there was still a chance that from any observable phenomena—ghosts, spirits, whatsoever there might be—some valid knowledge might be drawn as to a World Unseen.*

With admirable perseverance, the SPR compiled dossiers on hallucinations, phantasms of the living, apparitions of the dead, out-of-the-body experiences, precognitions, and séance phenomena. Skeptics such as Hyslop, Lodge, Barrett, and Conan Doyle slowly became converted to the belief in survival. Yet there was never a case that was so overwhelmingly convincing that it could be used to confound the skeptics. The apparition of Samuel Bull[8] seems to be as

8. See p. 132.

well attested as a case can be—except that it was all over just before the SPR arrived on the scene. The Cross Correspondences is a watertight case for survival—but is so long and complicated that no skeptic would waste his time on it. Drayton Thomas' *Life Beyond Death* will convince any unprejudiced reader that his father and sister communicated with him after death; but the descriptions of "the world beyond" remain an embarrassing stumbling block. So as far as solving "the riddle of the Universe" was concerned, the SPR was a failure. It provided mountains of data, but no inspiration.

The study of near-death experiences changed all that. From the scientific point of view, it may be irrelevant that *Life after Life* became a bestseller. Yet it meant that one form of psychical research had made the kind of wide general impact the founders of the SPR had dreamed about. Moreover, NDEs are not a rarity, like poltergeist phenomena, nor a specialized subject that can only be studied under "test conditions." Most people probably have half a dozen acquaintances who have had near-death experiences and can verify some aspect of the "core experience." On the day I began writing this book, I bumped into the wife of a friend on my afternoon walk, and mentioned that I was writing about life after death; she immediately told me about her own near-death experience, which might have come straight out of Moody. In the middle of the night, feeling very ill with a serious internal complaint, she went downstairs and sat in an armchair feeling sick and exhausted. Her temperature rose, and she felt consciousness slipping away. Then she found herself being sucked into a long tunnel with a light at the end. She experienced a sense of total relaxation and peace, and all her fear of death vanished. Totally reconciled to the idea of dying, it suddenly struck her that her husband and son would find her body in the chair the next morning; she made an effort to return to her body, and then found herself back in the chair, with her temperature normal again. The experience convinced her that she need never be afraid of death, and she remarked that it had given her the courage to live as well as to die.

Another local resident described how, after a serious heart attack, he had left his body, and found the room full of a blinding light. A voice asked him: "Do you want to live?" and when he replied yes, he opened his eyes to find his mother—convinced he was dead—by his bedside. Elsewhere, I have described my own mother's near-death experience when in the hospital suffering from peritonitis.[9] She also entered a state of relaxation and happiness about the prospect of death, then thought that a man dressed in white "like a biblical character" stood by the side of her bed and read to her from a scroll. He ended by telling her that she could not die yet because she was "needed here." (This proved to be correct; she had to nurse my father through years of cancer.) She insisted that the experience was not at all dream-like.

Does the evidence of the near-death experience provide the "valid knowledge of the World Unseen" that Myers and Sidgwick hoped to uncover? Regrettably, no. It is personally convincing; it brings the individual an overwhelming sense of insight into the riddle of the Universe. As evidence of life after death it is worthless. It is true that thousands of people, of all nationalities and all religious affiliations, have testified to the reality of the "core experience." But it could still be some defense mechanism of the brain when confronting death, perhaps the release of an enkephalin, one of the brain's natural anesthetics.

Now as we have noted, this also happens to be one of the most basic objections to the whole idea of survival. The skeptics have always insisted that it is merely a defense against our fear of the unknown. This was fully recognized by the original members of the SPR. When they could safely dismiss the idea of fraud or faulty observation, they asked whether the phenomena could be explained in terms of telepathy or clairvoyance or the activities of the subliminal mind. Thomson Jay Hudson explained practically all paranormal phenomena as the activities of the subliminal mind. We have seen

---

9. *Mysteries*, p. 615.

that, in fact, there have been a number of cases—the Cross Correspondences, the Chaffin will case, the red scratch case, the red pyjamas case, the Drayton Thomas case, and perhaps a dozen others—where most of these explanations can be ruled out. These are backed by literally thousands of cases that, while not watertight, still strongly suggest the persistence of the personality beyond death. Anyone who is willing to consider this evidence without bias—even if he finds it "logically" unacceptable—is bound to admit that it points towards the reality of survival.

If we can accept this kind of evidence, then there seems to be no sound reason for rejecting the evidence of the near-death experience, for the two seem to point towards the same conclusion: that the physical body is inhabited by another kind of body that can survive death. The near-death experience proves nothing in itself, but when backed up by the testimony of psychical research, it becomes strong supportive evidence.

It is important to make this distinction between primary and supportive evidence; the failure to grasp it has led to much of the hostility to psychical research. When Swedenborg gave the queen of Sweden a message from her dead brother, or when he told the wife of the Dutch ambassador about the secret drawer with the receipt, this was primary evidence—evidence that he was not merely a religious crank suffering from delusions. Swedenborg would insist that his writings on the scriptures are strong supportive evidence of his "spiritual insight," but the rest of us may not agree. We can reject his scriptural discourses without rejecting belief in his psychic powers. We may go further and, like Wilson Van Dusen, believe that his insight into the realm of spirits was valid. Or we may, like Steiner, feel that although he possessed genuine mediumistic powers, he somehow imposed his own rigid scientific outlook on his "spiritual perceptions" and falsified them by dragging them down to a material level: a version of what Whitehead calls "the fallacy of misplaced concreteness." In short, we do not have to accept Swedenborg lock, stock and barrel. The sensible thing is to accept the "primary evidence," and then decide through common sense how much of the supportive evidence is acceptable.

Myers' *Human Personality* is an attempt to present primary evidence for various paranormal faculties. The Cross Correspondences provide some evidence that Myers survived death, but we may or may not feel that this supports the arguments of *Human Personality*. If we decide that the Cross Correspondences are primary evidence for survival, we may still feel that the "Myers" of the Geraldine Cummins scripts is an impostor, or a manifestation of her unconscious mind. Again, *we* decide how much supportive evidence we can accept. A convinced Spiritualist will be able to swallow it all, including Raymond Lodge's heavenly laboratories for making whisky and cigars. We are under no compulsion to do so. But if we are open-minded, we shall agree that the sheer mass of *primary* evidence makes it unlikely that this is all wishful thinking. This amounts to the kind of evidence scientists demand when investigating the laws of nature. Like the evidence they try to gather in the laboratory or the observatory, it tends to form a basic pattern. The next task is to study that pattern, and then look carefully at the vast piles of supporting evidence, and decide how much of it fits the jigsaw puzzle. This is a question of personal choice; you can accept or reject as you feel inclined. But those who reject the primary evidence lay themselves open to a charge of wilful blindness or intellectual laziness.

What are the basic elements of this overall pattern?

The fundamental assumption is that the human being is not some kind of complex robot or computer, who works entirely on impulses that flow from the environment. In *The Selfish Gene*, the biologist Richard Dawkins explains how he thinks life began. First, the action of sunlight on various gases created the basic building blocks of life, the amino acids. The result was a "primeval soup." This soup was, of course, dead. Then, at a certain point, ordinary chemical—and physical—reactions produced a "particularly remarkable molecule," the replicator molecule, which could reproduce itself. He agrees that this is an unlikely accident to happen—as unlikely as a man winning the first prize on the football pools. But if a man lived for millions of years, he would probably win several first prizes. So says Dawkins, the replicator molecule came into existence. The world finally became full of identical copies. But the copying process is not perfect; mistakes will happen. As a result, some replicators become less stable than others, and less fecund. Some become more stable and more fecund.

At which point, Dawkins asks: "Shall we call the original replicator molecules 'living?' Who cares?" Here he seems to be attempting some sleight of hand. The hypothesis of replicator molecules being formed by accident seems dubious enough—as likely as the works of Shakespeare being written by Eddington's monkeys strumming aimlessly on a typewriter. But to then suggest that these self-copiers would be somehow "alive," and therefore, capable of evolution, seems an attempt to play fast and loose with language.

My own deep and intuitive conviction is that there is a basic difference between living and dead matter. So computer experts may try forever to convince me that we might one day build a computer so complex that it would be literally alive, and I shall remain a skeptic. They may as soon convince me that I am not really alive.

What I might be willing to accept is that the basic building blocks of organic matter were created by chance—by the action of sunlight or electrical discharges on ammonia and carbons—and that, when half the work had been done, the force we call life took advantage of the situation to somehow "insert" itself into matter. This seems to agree with my own intuitions about the nature of life, which—in my own case—is a continual struggle of the "alive" part of me to widen the boundaries of the dead or mechanical part, which seems determined to entrap me in the "here and now."

Now if this view is correct, and Dawkins is wrong to believe that life is a mere product of matter, it would also seem to follow that life has its own independent consciousness and sense of purpose. In the

1860s, a philosopher named Edouard von Hartmann wrote a vast work, *The Philosophy of the Unconscious*, largely devoted to examining the amazing manifestations of instinct in nature—all, apparently, so full of purpose, all totally unconscious. He reached the gloomy conclusion that life is full of blind striving toward nothing in particular. But he might just as well have argued that all this blind striving does not begin in a state of blindness. A man who has to walk a mile in the dark without a light is not necessarily lost and aimless. He may have consulted a map before he set out, and know exactly how many yards will bring him to the next crossroads. The incredible complexity in nature, from the amoeba to the giant squid, seems to suggest that although life is "blinded" once it descends into matter, it may have had a very clear sense of direction before it set out for its walk in the dark.

The same argument would apply to Darwin's picture of evolution by natural selection. Darwin, unlike Dawkins, admits that "life" somehow exists apart from matter, but he still sees life as a helpless and passive spectator of the changes brought about by accident and the survival of the fittest. The primitive giraffe may wish it had a longer neck, but it can do nothing about it; millennia will have to pass before its descendants will acquire a longer neck by pure chance. If Dawkins is wrong, the chances are that Darwin was also wrong. Life may not be able to initiate the changes (although even that is not certain), but it may be able to take instant advantage of every accidental change to achieve its own purposes, like a man selecting chunks of stone from a landslide to build his own house. But if he can select stones from a landslide, there seems no logical reason why he should not also be able to make his own bricks. If the study of the paranormal has taught us anything, it is that human powers often seem to be able to defy the "laws of nature." For example, in 1899, a New Zealand magistrate named Colonel Gudgeon went with a group of friends to watch a Maori tribe perform a fire-walking ceremony. They were embarrassed when a shaman held out his hand and invited Gudgeon and his friends to join them. "I confer my *mana* on you." To his surprise, Gudgeon felt no burning heat—just a pleasant, tingling sensation—

and none of them were even blistered. Clearly, it was some form of mind over matter—a form that should be impossible according to the Darwin-Dawkins view of evolution.

The paranormal view, then, presupposes that "life" (whatever that means) can exist apart from matter, and possesses its own consciousness and sense of purpose. In that case, we may assume that when life separates from matter at "death," it returns to a different state of consciousness, involving a higher degree of freedom. In that case, why did it descend into matter in the first place? Presumably to bring the realm of matter under its control—as it may already have brought other realms of "finer" matter—matter whose rate of vibration is higher than ours—under its control.

This view—that life is attempting to establish control over matter—is known as "vitalism," and its two leading exponents in the twentieth century have been the philosopher Henri Bergson and the biologist Hans Driesch. It is significant that both Driesch and Bergson joined the Society for Psychical Research and became its presidents. In his presidential address in 1926, Driesch expressed the basic idea of vitalism: that the development of organisms is "directed by a unifying nonmaterial mind-like Something . . . an ordering principle which does not add either energy or matter" to what goes on. This principle might exist outside time and space.[10] Driesch was violently attacked by his scientific colleagues for his interest in psychical research—as though it displayed a foolish credulity. Yet it can be seen that, *if* the primary evidence for survival can be accepted, then it is a very short step from vitalism to "spiritualism." Their premises are identical.

The problem for Driesch—and for every other psychical researcher in the past century—is that even sound philosophical premises cannot make the paranormal respectable. They *might* succeed if paranormal research confined itself to investigating the unexplored regions of the human mind—clairvoyance, psychokinesis, telepathy, psychometry,

---

10. Quoted from Reneé Haynes, *The Society for Psychical Research, A History* (1882-1982), p. 203.

and so on. But it is practically impossible to do this. The moment the investigator raises the question of whether a medium is genuine, he is raising the question of whether the communications come from the "dead." He may decide that mediumship is really another name for multiple personality, and that the "communications" are based on telepathy or clairvoyance; but if he is honest he will admit that there are cases where neither of these hypotheses cover the facts. To admit the possibility of survival is also to admit the possibility of spirits. At that point, most modern investigators dig in their heels; they feel as if they are being dragged back into the superstitions of the Dark Ages.

This was the problem we encountered at the beginning of this book. Adam Crabtree is a psychiatrist; his job is to cure people with psychological problems. From his personal point of view, it makes no difference whatever whether the problem is due to Freudian repressions, multiple personality, or "diabolical possession." From the point of view of his standing in the scientific community, it would certainly be preferable to dismiss the last hypothesis and to think in terms of orthodox psychotherapy. This corresponded with his own inclination. He has described how, when he was a theology student in Minnesota, he came across a pamphlet called *Begone Satan* by the Rev. Carl Vogel, describing a case that occurred in Wisconsin in the 1920s. A girl named Anna Ecklund began to be plagued with desires to commit "unspeakable sexual acts" and to blaspheme. When she began to show classic signs of possession, Father Theophilus Riesinger, a Capuchin from the community of St. Anthony, decided to do an exorcism. Anna was laid on a bed, and the ceremony of exorcism began. Within moments, Anna's body had flown off the bed, and landed against the wall above the door, where she stuck. She was dragged down by main force and the exorcism continued. Her howls and screams were so loud that people came from all over the town of Marathon to see what was happening.

The exorcism continued the next day and for many days after. Voices speaking in many languages issued from Anna, although her lips remained tightly closed. Her head would expand "to the size of a water pitcher" and her body swelled like a balloon. Her convulsions were so powerful that the iron bedstead bent to the floor. Various entities who announced themselves as demons spoke to the exorcists, and showed intimate knowledge of sins they had committed in childhood. Finally, Anna's deceased father was "summoned," and admitted that he had constantly tried to commit incest with her, and that because she had resisted him, he had cursed her and invoked devils to possess her. The father's ex-mistress also appeared, and admitted to killing a number of her newly born children. During all this time, Anna was deeply asleep, or in trance. Finally, Anna's body shot up off the bed, so that only her heels were resting on it, and as the priest repeated the exorcism, there was the sound of a strange scream, that gradually faded into the distance. Then the girl's eyes opened and she began to cry. The possession was over.

The monk who had translated the German pamphlet was in the same monastery as Crabtree, and he verified the details of the story. Crabtree knew him to be a level-headed, good-humored man; yet he still found the monk's story preposterous.

In due course, Crabtree decided that the monastic life was not for him, and entered psychotherapy in 1969.

> *As a psychotherapist, I fairly quickly came to accept the reality of the less spectacular paranormal phenomena, specifically telepathic and clairvoyant experiences. These seemed to be undeniable from the extensive evidence my clients spontaneously provided from their intuitions and particularly from their dreams. But in those early years I was extremely reluctant to go beyond this minimal acceptance.*[11]

It was not until 1976 that a colleague spoke to him of a patient who seemed to be possessed by a spirit, and Crabtree was able to witness this phenomenon. He still declined to take it seriously, but in the following year, he began to encounter cases of the possession

---

11. Letter to the author, January 1, 1985, quoted with Dr. Crabtree's permission.

type in his own practice (as described in chapter 1). He decided, from the purely pragmatic point of view, to treat them as possession.

Crabtree insists that, as a psychotherapist, he remains a phenomenologist; that is to say, he does not say this *is* possession, but that this patient shows all the signs of possession, and treating it *as* possession will probably be the simplest way to affect a cure. But he is a member of the Society for Psychical Research, and his book makes it clear that he is willing to give serious consideration to the possession hypothesis.

Another psychotherapist, Dr. Ralph Allison, who practices in Santa Cruz, California, has written a book on multiple personality[12] which makes it clear that he has come to accept the real possibility of possession. In 1972, Allison encountered a case of multiple personality. In her teens, Carrie had been the victim of a gang rape, and it was after this that she began to experience blackouts in which another personality took over. Also in her teens, Carrie had been involved in amateur witchcraft, and simply as a therapeutic measure, Allison tried exorcism under hypnosis. It worked, but Allison considered that this had simply been due to suggestion. In subsequent years, Allison encountered cases of multiple personality in which he could not accept that the "other selves" were genuine alter-egos. "An alter personality serves a definite and practical purpose—it is a means of coping with an emotion or a situation that the patient cannot handle." But in some cases, this did not appear to be so. He placed a girl called Elise, who was suffering from multiple personality, under hypnosis, and a male alter-ego who called himself "Dennis" emerged. Dennis seemed to serve no purpose. He insisted that he was "possessing" Elise solely because he was sexually interested in another of her personalities, a girl called "Shannon," who had taken over after Elise had been prostrated by the loss of a baby. When he asked Dennis how he hoped to have sex with Shannon, Dennis explained

---

12. *Minds in Many Pieces* (1980).

that he entered the bodies of men Shannon went to bed with, and so enjoyed making love to her. Allison found this an interesting concept: obviously, Elise's body was the same as Shannon's; but Dennis was not in the least interested in it when Elise was "in" it.

When Allison questioned Shannon, she confirmed all that Dennis had said. Allison was baffled at the idea of an alter-ego entering someone else's body (although if he had read Kardec or any other number of spiritualists he would have found it familiar enough). But Elise's other personalities also insisted this was so. Dennis himself claimed that he had once been a stockbroker, who was killed during a robbery. He claimed that Elise was not the first person he had "inhabited." He also explained that if Shannon would settle down with one lover, he would be glad to enter the man permanently. But she "moved around" too much. Allison admits: "Despite all my efforts, I was unable to find a more plausible explanation for his existence than the spirit theory."

Under hypnosis, another alter-ego emerged, a girl called "Michelle" who insisted that, like Dennis, she was not a subpersonality but a spirit. She also claimed there was a third spirit involved. A few days later, after Elise had experienced some violent convulsions, one of the subpersonalities told Allison that the three "possessing spirits" had now left. Allison was inclined to accept this. "Nothing in the psychological literature could account for what I had seen." Some time later, another of the subpersonalities told Allison that Shannon was herself a possessing spirit—the spirit of Elise's dead baby. Shannon herself confirmed this, and told Allison she was willing to "leave." Elise woke from the session with amnesia; but Shannon never reappeared.

Dealing with another case of multiple personality, a girl called "Sophia," Allison succeeded in fusing most of her alter-egos under hypnosis. But two subpersonalities remained: two women called "Mary" and "Maria." When Sophia was under hypnosis, Allison was told that Mary and Maria were her twin sisters. The doctor who had delivered the triplets was also her mother's lover, and he smothered the first two babies; however, a visit from a neighbor prevented him from killing Sophia. Sophia said that "spirits" of all three babies had been waiting to enter them after each one was delivered. Concerned that the other two might be lonely, Sophia had invited them to share her body with her. Eventually, Allison succeeded in persuading Mary and Maria to leave during a hypnotic session. After this, his attempts to re-invoke them under hypnosis were a failure.

Allison's stories sound preposterous, yet to anyone who has read the rest of this book, they have the ring of authenticity. The underlying theme that has run through psychical investigation since the days of Jung-Stilling and Catherine Crowe has been the notion that human beings consist of bodies inhabited by spirits—personalities already formed, so to speak—and that these spirits survive death. In some cases in chapter six, we have encountered instances in which a spirit has apparently moved from one body to another, so Lurancy Vennum *became* Mary Roff, and Sobha Ram became Jasbir Lal Jat. We may decide that such cases do not constitute proof of reincarnation and possession, but at least we have to recognize the consistency of the underlying theme; that personality is not a mere reflection of the body, a "summation of the different contributions to behavior from the various control units of the brain," but an independent entity which controls the body—and which might be capable of far greater control if it was fully aware of its own status.

This recognition encapsulates the aim of the present book. It is not my purpose to try to convince anyone of the reality of life after death: only to draw attention to the impressive inner consistency of the evidence, and to point out that, in the light of that evidence, no one need feel ashamed of accepting the notion that human personality survives bodily death.

Chapter Eight

Channeling

CHANNELING BECAME POPULAR IN THE 1970S, mainly due to the Seth books of Jane Roberts, and to the writings and television programs of the actress Shirley MacLaine. The actuality of channeling—meaning to write down the words of "spirit entities"—has been known for centuries. In this book we have already mentioned the remarkable Andrew Jackson Davis, who discovered after being hypnotized that he could go into trance and receive teachings from an entity he believed to be Swedenborg. His *Principles of Nature* (1847) went through thirty-four editions in thirty years.

Jane Roberts describes in *Seth Speaks* (1972) how she became a channeler. It began one evening in 1963 while writing poetry.

Suddenly my consciousness left my body, and my mind was barraged by ideas that were astonishing and new to me at the time. On return to my body, I discovered that my hands had produced an automatic script, explaining many of the concepts that I'd been given. The notes were even titled "The Physical Universe as Idea Construction."

Soon after this, she and her husband began experimenting with a ouija board, and the pointer spelled out messages from an entity called "Seth"; then Jane found that she could go into a trance while Seth used her voice.

The Physical Universe as Idea Construction summarizes Seth's basic concept: "You create the world that you know." We create our own reality, and the human race creates the world in which we live.

The idea sounds like Bishop Berkeley, who declared (around 1710) that the sensory world depends for its reality on being perceived. (Asked what happened when there is no one around to perceive it, Berkeley replied that God is always around, so the world continues to exist.)

Seth also declares that the human personality as we know it is only a tiny part of a far greater personality, some of which exists beyond space and time.

Richard Broughton comments in his classic work *Parapsychology, The Controversial Science* (1991): "Modern 'channeled' texts tend to enjoy enormous popular appeal and publishing success, even though more critical observers dismiss the material as bland platitudes derivative of well-known religious teachings."

This does not apply to all channeled texts, for example, Stainton Moses' *Spirit Teachings* (see pages 157–158). As Stainton Moses himself came to accept, many channeled texts are undoubtedly from disembodied entities, not from the subconscious mind of the channeler.

This does not, of course, guarantee their genuineness. One of Jane Roberts' books, *The Afterdeath Journal of an American Philosopher* (1978), purports to be the words of William James.

In fact, it sounds nothing like James—unless he has lost much of his literary talent:

> *Yet, what a rambunctious nationalistic romp, and it was matched with almost missionary fervor by the psychologists, out to root from man's soul all of those inconsistencies and passions that were buried there; and to leash these as well for the splendid pursuit of progress, industry and the physical manipulation of nature for man's use.*

Here we feel that someone is trying to sound vigorous and positive, and only succeeds in sounding self-assertive. I do not know if James ever used the word "rambunctious," but I doubt it. "Leash these as well for the splendid pursuit of progress" is woolly—James would have said simply "and to harness these for the pursuit of progress." (Even "all of those" sounds wrong; a writer accustomed to use the minimum of words would say "all those.")

Clearly, deciding whether a spirit communication is genuine is not an easy matter—although the spirit occasionally makes it easier by making some obvious mistake. In 1973, a book entitled *Bertie: The Life After Death of H. G. Wells* claimed to be channeled through Wells by two ladies, Elizabeth Hawley and Columbia Rossi. But when "Wells" calls a chapter "We Sojourn to Rome," it is quite clear that this is an imposter, since Wells knew what the book's authors and editors obviously did not: that to sojourn means to stay somewhere, not travel there.

So Bertie is certainly a fraud, either intentionally or unconsciously. There are many pages in the Seth books that make a strong impression of authenticity. If Seth is genuine, in the sense of being a spirit, then how do we explain an almost certainly bogus William James channeled by Jane Roberts?

Thomson Jay Hudson, discussed earlier in this book (see pages 92–93), would certainly argue that both Seth and James are brilliant products of Jane Roberts' subjective mind. In *The Law of Psychic Phenomena*, Hudson tells how, probably in the late 1880s, he went to

Boston to see a hypnotic demonstration by Professor William R. Carpenter, and saw him place a young man in a trance, then "introduce" him to Socrates. The young man, at first awe-stricken, gradually gained confidence, and plied Socrates with questions about the universe, then repeated back to the audience the philosopher's words (since Carpenter told him they could not hear the replies). These replies were so brilliant that some of the audience were inclined to believe that the spirit of Socrates was actually in the room. Later, the young man was "introduced" to various modern philosophers, and his exposition of their ideas was equally brilliant and, according to Hudson, profound. But in the case of thinkers with whose work he was unacquainted, the replies bore no relation to the philosopher's actual opinions. The young man's unconscious mind had invented them, as if in a dream. They showed remarkable creativity. (Most people must have heard magnificent music in dreams that is not by any known composer—I once found myself conducting an orchestra in some splendid piece of my own composition.) Hudson writes:

> *He frequently expressed the most profound astonishment at the replies he received. This was held to be an evidence that the replies were not evolved from his own inner consciousness.*

But, says Hudson, that was simply not so.

So, according to Hudson, the works of Andrew Jackson Davis, which had their origin in hypnosis, were simply an expression of his subjective mind—or what we would now call, with our knowledge of split-brain physiology, the right hemisphere of the brain.

Hudson noted that the young man's subjective mind could not produce information that he did not know in his conscious state, such as where a philosopher died. As we have seen, many spirits appear to be able to do this—so that Stainton Moses' "communicator" was able to read aloud from a closed book selected at random on a shelf, and Swedenborg was able to bring back information from "the spirit world" about a secret drawer.

This, of course, goes to the heart of the problem. The world is full of channeled books, from the Bible (which most Christians believe to be "the word of God") to the Seth books and *A Course in Miracles*. How are we to know which are genuine and which are not?

The problem is illustrated by the sad story of Edward Irving, a Scottish preacher who achieved immense popularity in London in 1830, when, after praying for a miracle, members of his congregation began to "speak in tongues." His colleague, Robert Baxter, spoke sentences in Latin, French, Italian, and Spanish, none of which he had studied. Irving and Baxter were told by the voices that they would manifest miraculous powers at the end of forty days—but nothing happened. After several more disappointments, it became clear that the spirits were not to be trusted. Irving was forced to resign, and died two years later.

It is true that Irving belongs to the history of gurus or messiahs rather than channelers; but it is often difficult to draw the line. In 1875, forty-four-year-old Helena Petrovna Blavatsky (whom we have also met earlier) sat in her room on West 47th Street in New York, and covered page after page with handwriting at lightning speed. Her friend Colonel Olcott asked her how she could quote from books she did not possess; she replied that the quotations came to her by inspiration. Olcott describes how she would pause in her writing, and stare into space, as if looking at a blackboard, then appear to be copying what she saw.

Olcott tells a story of how he raised doubts about the accuracy of one of her quotations, and she stared into space, then told him to go and look on a shelf in the corner. There Olcott found the two volumes of the book in question, although he was sure they had not been there a moment before. He checked the quotation—and found that it contained a mistake—then returned the books. A moment later, they had vanished.

The result of her labors was a huge two-volume work called *Isis Unveiled*, which claimed to be a distillation of the wisdom of ancient Atlantis. It became a bestseller and made her famous. Even a modern reader can see why. The range of her knowledge seems extraordinary, from Plato and the Hindu scriptures to nineteenth-century philosophers and scientists. Occasionally, she seems to be pulling the reader's leg, as when she described a huge underground tunnel in Peru, extending from Cuzco to Lima.

The Secret Doctrine (1888) is even more ambitious (if less chatty and readable); it sets out to "string together all the ancient philosophical religious systems,"[1] and Madame Blavatsky claims to be its "writer" but not its author. The author was a being called "Koot Hoomi" (or "Humi"), one of the "secret Masters" who control the evolution of humankind, and live at some unknown location in the Himalayas. Another was called "Djwhal Kul" (pronounced "Jual Kool"), who would become the mentor of Alice A. Bailey.

In 1880, in India, Helena (or HPB as her disciples called her) met a British newspaper editor named A. P. Sinnett, and told him about the Masters. Sinnett was deeply impressed when HPB displayed her psychic faculties in a series of minor miracles: when an unexpected guest turned up at a picnic, HPB ordered someone to dig in a hillside with a table knife, and he unearthed a cup and saucer of the same pattern as the china they were using; when a woman remarked that she had lost her brooch, HPB told the guests to search the garden—the brooch was found in a flower bed wrapped in paper.

Sinnett expressed his desire to correspond directly with the Masters, and a few days later, found lying on his desk, was the first of what became known as "the Mahatma letters." On one occasion, a letter fell out of the air as he sat at dinner. Sinnett went on to write his own bestseller *Esoteric Buddhism* (1883), in which he explained that he had obtained his knowledge from the secret Masters. In 1883, toward the end of a century that had been dominated by scientific materialism, that was exactly what everyone wanted to hear, and it

---

1. See page 610, vol. 1.

became immensely popular; W. B. Yeats read it, and the result was the formation of the Dublin branch of the Theosophical Society.

Alas, her downfall was almost upon her. As described earlier (see page 182), a young man named Richard Hodgson came to investigate her on behalf of the Society for Psychical Research, and a resentful housekeeper convinced him that HPB was a fraud. Her reputation never recovered from his damning report, and she died in 1891. Yet many accounts make it clear that she was a genuine medium. A female companion, a countess named Constance Wachmeister, tells how, after HPB had gone to sleep behind a screen, she was unable to sleep, and tiptoed to the bedside to turn out the lamp. It promptly relit itself—although it was obvious that HPB was asleep, and in any case, would not have had time to light a match. This happened three times, and the third time, as she left the bedside, she saw a disembodied brown hand turn up the wick.

Her follower Charles Johnston, who founded the Dublin branch, tells how he watched HPB idly tapping her fingers on the table top and then raise her hand clear above the table—while the tapping noise continued. She then began to "send" the astral taps on to the back of Johnston's hand, and he felt them as a series of mild electric shocks.

Whatever we think of the ideas expounded in *The Secret Doctrine*, there can be little doubt that, as a medium, Madame Blavatsky was no fraud, and that the implications of Hodgson's report are therefore unfair. In all probability, the Mahatma letters (whose handwriting differs from HPB's) were channeled by her.

Whether mediumship is enough to guarantee the truth of spirit teachings is, of course, an entirely different matter. This is nowhere more obvious than in the strange affair of the "new Bible" called *Oahspe*, first published in 1882.

Oahspe claims, in the words of its title page, to be written in the "words of Jehovih (sic) and His Angel Ambassadors." This huge channeled work of more than eight hundred pages, printed in double columns, claims to be a history of the world over the past twenty-four thousand years, with a glance back to twenty-four thousand years before that.

The work seems to have aroused some degree of interest—as it was bound to in a country as obsessively religious as America in the nineteenth century, when anyone could make some kind of a living by standing on a platform at a street corner and talking about the Will of the Lord.

In a letter written in 1883, the medium—and dentist—John Ballou Newbrough tells how he came to produce the book. It was, he says, "mechanically written through my hands by some other intelligence than my own." From the age of twenty or so (he had been born June 5, 1828, in Springfield, Ohio), Newbrough had been interested in the recent craze called Spiritualism. At meetings, he would find that his hands refused to lie still, and often wrote "messages." Sometimes he went into an involuntary trance and "talked and saw and heard differently from my normal state."

One morning in 1870, Newbrough went to his friend Edwin Augustus Davis, who lived on Sixth Avenue in New York, and told him that he had been awakened at 4 A. M. with a hand on his shoulder, and heard a voice that said it wanted to ask him a question. "Would you like to perform a mission for Jehovih?" the voice asked. Newbrough then saw that the room was full of "beautiful spirits or angels," although without wings. He was told that he had to "live spiritually" for ten years and purify himself, becoming a strict vegetarian (something that was hardly heard of at the time). He was also told to be charitable and to treat poor patients for free.

So for ten years Newbrough followed a strict regime. Then one day in 1880, he was told to buy a typewriter. When he protested that he could not type, the voice told him that his hands would be guided. On January 1, 1881, he sat at his table, and his hands began to pound the typewriter at a speed that amazed him. He was able to sit and watch his hands moving at the speed of a very fast typist. It must have been fast, for he claims that the seven hundred thousand-word *Oahspe* was written in fifty weeks, at a rate of about a quarter of an hour each day, or two thousand words a day. Since it takes a normal person an hour to write a thousand-word letter, this is eight times the usual speed.

He was told not to read what he wrote, and obeyed this injunction. The pages piled up by his typewriter. Meanwhile, the spirits made his bed and tidied his room. On December 15, 1881, the book was finished.

A friend who possessed some pages of the original typescript says that it is beautifully typed, whereas a letter from Newbrough is full of errors.

Newbrough had *Oahspe* printed in Boston and London, presumably at his own expense, and it appeared in 1882. A new and enlarged edition appeared in 1891, and a cheap edition in 1912. So it is obvious that the book had its following. I was able to buy the latest edition (printed in California) without trouble in 1977.

Oahspe has a wider range than other "bibles" in that it speaks of Hindus, Buddhists, Mohammedans, and Zoroastrians as well as Christians and Jews. Thor and Osiris and Zarathustra also figure largely.

A 1978 article by Augustine Cahill, from a magazine called *Odyssey* states:

> *For those interested in the mystery of UFO phenomena, or in the Erich von Daniken thesis that mankind, and advanced human knowledge of earlier civilization, reached this planet from outer space, Oahspe presents its own cosmic viewpoint. The entire universe is populated, not only with human beings on other planets but with their liberated souls entering the astral plane and passing through an infinity of degrees of personal development in knowledge, power, and fulfillment, yet remaining essentially human in fundamental relationship. These enlightened entities travel the universe in spacecraft of many kinds, some small and swift, others as large and populous as floating worlds.*
>
> *Rather a long time before jets and helicopters were thought of on earth, Oahspe had this to say: "The Goddess Arieune slackened the speed of her arrowship to suit that of Hoab's vessel, so onward they sped in a direct line, propelled as a rocket is propelled, by constant emissions from the hulk: the which expenditure is manu-*

> *factured by the crews and commanders, skilled in wielding Jehovih's elements. For as mortals find means to traverse the ocean and raise a balloon, so do the Gods and spirits build and propel mightier vessels through the firmament, betwixt the stars and over and under and beyond the sun.*

This certainly sounds amazing—until we remember that Jules Verne, born in the same year as Newbrough, had written *From the Earth to the Moon* in 1865. Yet even that fails to explain *Oahspe*'s anticipation of rocket propulsion (Verne's voyagers are fired out of a gigantic cannon).

Cahill claims that "*Oahspe* clearly predicts the current decadence of our materialistic civilization," and prophesies a new society will take over that will be "highly spiritual and deeply devotional."

He also points out that *Oahspe* describes a great riverine civilization that flourished in India during the third and fourth millennium B. C., and that the discovery in 1926 of the ruins of Mohenjo Daro and Harappa in the Indus valley confirmed its existence.

So obviously, *Oahspe* is a fascinating enigma, which deserves to be the subject of some major study by a sympathetic critic. Whether he would reach the conclusion that this is a divinely inspired addition to the world's sacred scriptures, or simply the amazing creation of some subjective mind filled with echoes of the Bible, is a matter on which I would not be prepared to venture an opinion.

In 1890, the year before Madame Blavatsky's death, one of the most interesting of her successors was born in Manchester, England into a rigidly religious family. Alice La Trobe-Bateman was fifteen, and staying with an aunt in Scotland, when a turbaned man in European dress walked into the room and told her that it was her destiny to perform important spiritual work. Later, when she saw a picture of HPBs "secret Master" Djwhal Kul, she recognized her visitor.

Alice went to India, married, divorced, and became a member of the Theosophical Society. When she married Foster Bailey, she became Alice Ann Bailey. At this point, Djwahl Kul returned (she refers to him as D. K., or the Tibetan) and proceeded to dictate books to her telepathically—twenty of them, many more than a thousand pages long, with titles like *A Treatise on Cosmic Fire* and *A Treatise on White Magic*. Her fellow Theosophists took umbrage at this undue familiarity with the secret Masters, and she withdrew and formed her own group, with the active help and support of her second husband.

Alice Bailey's writings start from the premise of the existence of the Hierarchy, a group of Masters that meets every quarter of a century to review the evolution of humankind. The Tibetan's purpose is to cause the inner planes of human consciousness to evolve.

The American scholar Arthur Hastings, whose study of channeling—*Tongues of Men and Angels* (1991)—includes two chapters on Alice Bailey, remarks that the scope of her writings is "vast and majestic, with a vision of complex connections and levels, of inner planes and energies." He also complains that the writing "seems technical, but (is) nevertheless vague," and describes many of the volumes as "disorganized and rambling." "Djwahl Kul," he concludes, "was not a master of writing," which "is obviously a different skill from the mastery of the inner planes."

This raises an obvious problem. If these spirit entities are, in some respects, superhuman, how can they be "disorganized and rambling?" You would expect superhuman entities to be far more organized and concentrated than our disorganized species. Also, why is there need for so many thousands of pages? *A Treatise on Cosmic Fire* is more than thirteen hundred pages long, while the *Treatise on the Seven Rays* runs to more than thirty-five hundred. Are so many words essential? Surely any reasonably intelligent person ought to be able to summarize his ideas in less than twenty thousand or so pages?

Much of the writing has a vaguely inspirational tone. We are told in *A Treatise on Cosmic Fire* that an Avatar will shortly come to earth "at the close of this century," a teacher of love and unity who will "work aggressively for unity, cooperation and brotherhood."[2]

Indication of the nearing of this event will be seen in the reaction which will be set up during the next twenty five years (i.e. before 1950) against crime, sovietism and the extreme radicalism which is now being made use of by certain powers to achieve ends contrary to the plans of the Lord. The era of peace will be ushered in by a gathering together on earth of the forces which stand for construction, and development, and by a conscious deliberate banding together of groups in every land who embody the principle (as far as they can vision it) of Brotherhood. Watch the signs of the times, and be not discouraged over the immediate future.

Here it seems clear that the Tibetan is not a particularly good prophet; the events between 1925 and 1950, far from showing a reaction against crime, sovietism, and radicalism, seemed to demonstrate the opposite: a steady rise in crime, a tightening of the grip of sovietism, and an increase in left-wing violence.

Hastings comments that "believing in a hidden Hierarchy can reassure individuals that there is a conspiracy for good." This, of course, is no reason for dismissing the notion. All religion is based on the notion that we are not living in a wholly mechanical universe, and that there is, in fact, some higher form of intelligence that guides evolution.

Madame Blavatsky taught, as the composer Cyril Scott put in in his *Outline of Modern Occultism* (1935), that:

Man is in the process of evolving from comparative imperfection to much higher states of physical and spiritual evolution. Secondly, that the evolutionary process in all its phases is directed by a Great Hierarchy of Intelligences who have themselves reached these higher states.

---

2. See *A Treatise of Cosmic Fire*, page 754.

In a book called *The Intelligent Universe*, cybernetician David Foster has argued for this notion on purely scientific grounds. Cybernetics is the science of control—making a machine behave as if it is intelligent—for example, as the ball in a lavatory cistern cuts off the water before it can overflow. Most people now know enough about computers to know what a "program" is. Foster points out that an acorn may be seen as a program for an oak tree. But a program implies programming and a programmer, and Foster argues that the energies involved in programming a living thing would need to be of a far higher order than any known on earth—of the order, he suggests, of cosmic rays. This, he believes, points to the existence of some universal intelligence.

Skeptics will reply that this is merely a more sophisticated version of the argument of the eighteenth-century theologian William Paley, who declared that a watch makes upon us the impression of something created by intelligence, and that surely the workings of the universe demonstrate this on an even larger scale. Nineteenth-century materialism replied that the evolution of intelligence does not prove that its beginnings were not the result of an accident, and that chance and natural selection can account for everything we see around us. In that sense, the argument has not progressed since the days of Madame Blavatsky.

Most channeled material will certainly not help to settle this question. It begins from the assumption of a spiritual world, and makes no attempt to prove it. So most skeptics are soon driven to irritation by a feeling that they are being railroaded. This may apply even to those who are willing to concede that channeled material may originate in some "higher source."

A Course in Miracles exemplifies the problem. The amanuensis was a woman named Helen Schucman, who regarded herself as an atheist. Born in 1909, she grew up in New York, but felt bored and unfulfilled with her work in her husband's bookstore. In her forties, she studied psychology, and received her doctorate in 1957. She became a member of the Psychology Department at Columbia, where she and her boss, Bill Thetford, often clashed. After a difficult faculty meeting in 1965, Thetford said he felt there must be a better way, and that he would try to change some of his negative attitudes; Helen Schucman said she would help him. Soon after, she rang him to tell her that a voice was ordering her to take notes for "a course in miracles," and Thetford advised her to go ahead and take them. By 1972, a large book had been completed. In 1975, she met psychical researcher Judy Skutch, who was impressed by the "dictated" manuscript, and helped in its private publication. *A Course in Miracles* went on to become an enormous success. Yet Helen Schucman remained skeptical. "l know it's true but I don't believe it."

That is understandable; she was Jewish and an atheist, and *A Course in Miracles* is basically Christian—in fact, the entity who dictated it often seems to identify himself with Christ. The basic problem it sees as fear, a sense of alienation from God, and the book aims at dealienating the student. It talks a great deal about undermining the ego's thought system, and seems aimed at people who feel dissatisfied and frustrated.

It is certainly aimed at a higher intellectual level than fundamentalist Christians. It is still difficult to see how it differs from hundreds of other exhortatory Christian texts:

> *When you have accepted your mission to extend peace you will find peace, for by making it manifest you will see it. Its holy witnesses will surround you because you called upon them, and they will come to you. I have heard your call and I have answered it. . . .*
>
> *Do you really believe that you can kill the son of God? The Father has hidden His Son safely within Himself, and kept him far away from your destructive thoughts, but you know neither the Father nor the Son because of them. You attack the real world every day and every hour and minute, and yet you are surprised that you cannot see it. If you seek love in order to attack it, you will never find it. For if love is sharing, how can you find it except through itself? Offer it and it will come to you, because it is drawn*

to itself. But offer attack and love will remain hidden, for it can live only in peace.

This is the problem with so much channeled material; it sounds as if it might have been written by a computer program that has been instructed to produce variations on love, peace, goodness, mercy, sin, fear, guilt, and so on.

Fear is the expected punishment for our sins, which our guilt demands. . . .

The solution, Arthur Hastings comments, "is to turn to the voice within, called the Holy Spirit, which is our link to and communication with God."

The problem is that this sounds like the unsophisticated religious fundamentalism that can be found in any society as troubled as ours, and which, while it does no harm—and probably does some good—is unlikely to appeal to anyone who sets value on intelligent self-appraisal.

From this point of view, the writing of Shirley MacLaine is more acceptable. In the third volume of her autobiography *Out on a Limb*, she explains why she came to accept the channeled messages of Seth, and in doing so, explains the wide appeal of channeling:

More and more, as I read and thought, the message forced me to reexamine motives, to rethink, or perhaps to think for the first time, about values and aspects of living I had heretofore simply accepted.

She goes on to speak of the kind of dissatisfaction and futility that T. S. Eliot expresses so powerfully in *The Waste Land*:

I had been used to living in a world where, by the very nature of the life we led, it was nearly impossible to get the time to look into yourself. . . . Human contact seemed superficial, striving for meaningful goals, wanting deeper meaning but only talking around it.

She describes how moved she was when, sitting in the back of a mock-up limousine on the set of *Being There*, her fellow actor Peter Sellers told her about his near-death experience. He had had a heart attack while on the set, and had floated outside his body, being taken to the hospital. He was not concerned, since it was only his body that was involved. He watched a surgeon cut out his heart and massage it. Then he saw a white light above him and felt "there was love, real love, on the other side of the light." A hand reached through the light, and at the same time he heard the surgeon say that his heart was beating again. Then a voice from the light said: "Go back and finish. It's not time." Then he found himself back in his body.

MacLaine goes on to tell how, a year and a half later, she was talking with friends in her sitting room when she suddenly knew that something had happened to Sellers; she jumped up and told them what she felt. A few moments later, the telephone rang—it was a reporter telling her that Sellers had died of a heart attack. During this time, she could feel the presence of Sellers in the room.

Sellers always suffered from precisely this sense of meaninglessness that she discusses; he often admitted that although he could slip so effortlessly into various roles, he had no real sense of his own identity. In television interviews, he emerges as awkward, shy, and unsure of himself. This lack of inner security could lead to appalling behavior—selfish, unfeeling, and dishonest. (This becomes very clear in the moving autobiography *PS–I Love You* by his son Michael.) What *A Course in Miracles* says about fear and insecurity certainly applies to Sellers. But its assumption that its audience all suffers from the same problems is rather like that of a doctor who assumes that all his patients are suffering from appalling illnesses, or a psychiatrist who assumes that everyone needs to be psychoanalyzed.

MacLaine's third volume of her autobiography is probably the best general introduction to channeling that exists, and can certainly correct some of the false impressions that arise from books like *A Treatise on Cosmic Fire* and *A Course in Miracles*.

She tells how, in Stockholm, soon after reading Edgar Cayce, she learned that her friends, a husband and wife, intended to spend the evening with a trance medium who channeled an entity called "Ambres." Not sure what she was getting into, she agreed to go. On the way there, she asked several times whether her friends thought that Ambres was really a spiritual entity, and they assured her they did.

The medium, Sture Johanssen, was a carpenter, a sturdily built man who spoke no English. His wife, Turid, was a plump, rosy-cheeked woman, who held his hand when the session began, apparently to provide him with some of her physical energy.

After ten minutes of sitting in a candlelit room, the medium became rigid, then began to speak in a gutteral voice in a language that was apparently ancient Swedish (MacLaine's friend translated for her). This new personality was totally unlike Sture.

The audience began plying Ambres with heavy philosophical questions about the origin of the universe and the birth of worlds. Ambres talked about God as intelligence, and of the need for love. He also spoke about the Great Pyramid, describing it as a "library in stone" (a view, incidentally, also found in *Oahspe*).

When it was all over, and Sture was returning to consciousness, gulping down water, the guests talked quietly. Shirley tried to absorb what she had seen. It had certainly been impressive, and elaborate fraud seemed unlikely.

Back in America, she read the Seth books and other channeled material. (Jane Roberts was then still alive—she died in 1984.) When she told her friend Cat about Ambres, Cat offered to introduce her to an American channeler, Kevin Ryerson. The following evening, Ryerson called on her, a young man who told her he had just married. He told her how, when he had been meditating, a spirit had begun speaking through his mouth. His sister, apparently, had the same ability.

Ryerson explained that several entities spoke through him, and that one of them, who called himself John, seemed the most developed. Then there was an Irishman named Tom McPherson who, like the others, had been through various reincarnations, notably one as an Irish pickpocket.

Ryerson went into a trance, and soon an entity called "John" was speaking through him, in a "raspy whisper which didn't sound in Kevin's vocal range." John told her that "we"—the spiritual entities who spoke through Kevin—had known her in past lives.

John told her: "To understand yourself now you must understand that you are more than what you seem now." This, of course, is one of the basic teachings of Seth. In *Under Ben Bulben*, W. B. Yeats called it the "partial mind":

Know that when all words are said
And a man is fighting mad,
Something drops from eyes long blind,
He completes his partial mind. . . .

In other words, our consciousness is "partial," like the moon in its last quarter. Yet the full moon is there nevertheless—although invisible.

John goes even further. He tells her: "Man is the co-creator with God of the cosmos."

After a while, "Tom McPherson" took over, and spoke with an Irish accent. He demanded tea, then went on to tell her how he had once been a spy for the British. Her doubts about his genuineness vanished when he told her that she had had "floating dreams" in childhood, an experience of which she had never spoken.

Tom likes puns—he is amused by her phrase "solely for the soul." It enters the reader's head that if such an entity decided to dictate a book like so many channeled books, it would not necessarily be a work of primeval wisdom. The fact that a writer happens to be a spirit does not guarantee profound insights.

When John returns, he tells her that she was incarnated several times during the five-hundred-thousand-year period "of the most highly evolved civilization ever known to man," what the Bible symbolized as the Garden of Eden. The time period is certainly startling—

since we are accustomed to think of civilization being, at the most, ten thousand years old; but there is a modern body of opinion that holds it could well be true.

Her doubts about John also vanished when he was able to tell her about her current love life, which she had kept a closely guarded secret, since the man—Gerry—was a distinguished British politician who was already married.

Gerry, apparently, was also married to Shirley in a previous incarnation; at this time he was involved in "cultural exchanges with extraterrestrials." This again becomes a constant theme throughout the remainder of the book—the notion that earth has been receiving visits from extraterrestrials throughout history, and that they are increasing during the present period because humankind is in urgent need of some kind of guidance.

Somehow, the description of this session with Kevin Ryerson is far more convincing than channeled material like *A Course in Miracles* because it is told directly by someone who experienced it, and whose frankness about other matters establishes confidence in her honesty. Entities who can talk indefatigably for a thousand pages somehow exhaust our credulity.

There follows an interesting chapter of the book describing her reading on the subject of reincarnation, which seems to have been wide. The last quarter of the book is taken up mainly with a description of a trip to Peru with a friend named David, in whose company she had an out-of-the-body experience.

She asked a psychic woman in Peru about her friend Bella, who intended to run as the mayor of New York, and was told that a bald man with long fingers—who had not yet declared himself—would win. Back in New York, she saw Bella lose to a man with a bald head and long fingers—Ed Koch. It becomes possible to see why Shirley MacLaine's skepticism about her new experiences was soon eroded.

Shirley MacLaine's views on reincarnation receive support from the work of the Czech psychologist Stanislav Grof, who began to work in the 1950s with the recently discovered hallucinogen LSD in

Prague. Small doses of LSD brought back childhood memories often in startling detail—and sometimes experiences of being in the womb. Although at first inclined to dismiss these as imagination, Grof soon came to recognize that his patients seemed to be showing a knowledge of embryology that went far beyond anything they could have picked up casually. Larger doses of LSD often caused "mystical" experiences in which the bounds of the normal ego seemed to dissolve, apparently confirming Seth's assertion that the self we know is only a small fragment of a larger being.

In *Realms of the Human Unconscious* (1975), Grof has a section on patients who had "ancestral experiences" under LSD. Nadja, a fifty-year-old psychologist, relived a scene which she believed to be from her mother's life. It was 1902 and she was about three or four. She was dressed in a starched, "fussy" dress, and hiding under the staircase. On the porch she could see many relatives. "I felt excluded, ostracized and ashamed."

Nadja approached her mother, telling her she had dreamed of her as a child (her mother would have been shocked by the true explanation), and described the scene. Her mother confirmed it, and went on to add many details that Nadja had not yet had a chance to mention. Her own mother, Nadja's grandmother, had been extremely strict, obsessed with cleanliness, and dressed her daughter in starched clothes. Her description of the house turned out to be remarkably accurate, and her mother described how, on Sundays, many relatives came in for food and sat on the porch.

A patient called Renata experienced scenes from a particular historical period, Prague during the seventeenth century, at the beginning of the Thirty Years War—a period about which Renata knew very little. Yet when Grof looked at books on this period, he discovered that her descriptions of the architecture, the dress, the weapons, and household utensils were all accurate. So was her description of the complicated relation existing at the time between the Czech royal family and the vassals.

Many of her flashbacks were of the life of a young nobleman who was one of twenty-seven executed by the Hapsburgs after the Battle of the White Mountain in 1621. She finally relived the final hours of the nobleman before execution. Renata concluded that he was one of her ancestors. Since, of course, she could not have been a direct descendant (since he was executed, and could not therefore have passed on the memory genetically), it seems more likely that Renata was obtaining glimpses of herself in some previous incarnation. (One of the odd—and apparently absurd—things about the study of reincarnation is that there is so often a connection between present and past incarnations—after all, there is no apparent reason why a Czech patient should have visions of being a Czech nobleman rather than an Icelandic fisherman or a Chinese peasant. Yet it does seem to happen again and again, as do connections between people who were close in past incarnations and are now again thrown together.)

Several years later, Renata's father, whom she had not seen since she was three, conducted research into his ancestry, and told her that their family was, in fact, descended from a Czech nobleman executed after the Battle of the White Mountain.

Renata also experienced a regression to the consciousness of a large prehistoric reptile, basking by a lake in the sun. The therapist seemed to be transformed into a male of the species, and she experienced sexual arousal at certain scales on the side of the monster's head. Grof consulted a palaeontoligist, and learned that some modern reptiles experience sexual arousal at the sight of certain colored areas on the head of the male.

Grof describes patients who claimed to have been able to experience the consciousness of animals, and even of plants.

There is also an interesting description of a man who, under LSD, felt a sense of total freedom, of transcending space and time, and found himself walking into his parents' apartment on the other side of the world. A clock outside showed the correct time difference. The sense of the apartment was so real that he was tempted to take down a picture off the wall, just to confirm the experience scientifically. As he reached for it, he experienced a feeling of danger, and "the uncanny influence of evil forces." He recalled warnings of the danger of toying with "mystical" powers before overcoming ego limitations. He also experienced a sense of fear at the feeling that, if the experiment was successful, his ordered universe would collapse, and he would "find myself in a state of utter metaphysical confusion." So he resisted the temptation to transcend space and time.

Grof's experiments seem to leave little doubt that the apparently rigid limitations that surround us are an illusion—or perhaps, as Seth says, a joint creation. But can experiences that happen with the aid of LSD be taken seriously? Grof mentions many examples of confirmation—similar to Renata's discovery that she was a descendant of the executed nobleman. One man felt himself to be in a parallel dimension, surrounded by discarnate beings. One of them communicated with him telepathically, and asked him to contact a couple who lived in Kromeriz, Moravia, and to tell them that their son Ladislav was well. He was given the name, address, and telephone number. Grof tried ringing the telephone number and asking for Ladislav. The woman who answered began to cry, and said that Ladislav had died three weeks ago.

LSD, of course, can be an extremely dangerous substance to take, and can lead to the sense of disorientation and "metaphysical confusion." Grof decided to see whether its effect could be duplicated with less risk. In *The Adventure of Self Discovery*, he describes how he and his wife Christina developed techniques of breathing—often hyperventilation—and massage that could duplicate the effects of LSD, and produce what he called "holotropic," or nonordinary states of consciousness.

Finally, this book would be incomplete without some reference to the work of Robert Monroe, a Virginia businessman involved in radio, who in 1958 began to have out-of-the-body experiences.

These may well have been connected to experimenting with sleep learning devices involving the use of different sounds in the ears. One day, Monroe found himself floating out of his body. Panic-stricken, believing he was dead, he succeeded in diving back into it.

It began to happen with increasing frequency, until one day he realized that he could do it at will. He could float off and see what his friends were doing—and what he saw would be verified later by the friends.

He did not enjoy moving in our physical world; it was hard work, like swimming underwater. However, he soon found that there was another world—which he called Locale 2—where he felt quite at home. It was, he said, the natural environment of the astral body (or spirit body), and is the place to which we move after death. In his classic book *Journeys Out of the Body*, he says that Locale 2 seems to interpenetrate our world, and that the easiest way to understand this is the idea of vibrations, "an infinity of worlds all operating at different frequencies, one of which is this physical world."

Monroe's descriptions of Locale 2 make it sound as if it is the "parallel dimension" experienced by Grof's patient.

Oddly enough, Locale 2 does have some physical objects; but Monroe says these are created by thought—a notion that may have some bearing on the paradoxical behavior of UFOs, and their apparent ability to appear and disappear in a manner that seems to defy our laws of space and time. In fact, in another of his books, *Far Journeys*, Monroe states that UFOs and their inhabitants come from this "parallel dimension."

Monroe went on to develop techniques for enabling anyone to leave the body, and these are taught at his Monroe Institute in Virginia. (He died in 1995.) Training starts with sounds played through earphones, the purpose being to "balance" the two halves of the brain, which are normally "out of sync." Scientific investigation has shown that Monroe's claims can be substantiated in the laboratory. The majority of people can learn the techniques of out-of-the-body experiences in a fairly short time.

In fact, it seems that the American military has been aware of this for years. During the Cold War, the army recruited psychics to conduct spying missions against the Russians, and also in antidrug operations. One of these, a soldier named David Morehouse, began to have out-of-the-body experiences after a bullet had penetrated his helmet and knocked him unconscious. When he reported these to the medical officer, he was immediately recruited for the "remote viewing" program. There he was only one of many who were being taught to collect intelligence by "astral projecting" and proceeding to different targets.[3] One of his targets was a new type of Soviet landing craft, which he was able to describe in detail.

Amazingly, this "remote viewing" could also be applied to the past. Morehouse was asked to find out whether the Korean airliner shot down by the Soviets in 1983 was on a spying mission, and he concluded that the copilot had deliberately allowed it to drift off course over Russia, looking for holes in the radar coverage.

He always felt that using his powers for military purposes was wrong, and finally, against strong and sometimes frightening opposition, resigned from the army.

So it seems clear that human beings possess powers that few of us suspect. In recent years, an American professor named Robert Jahn has proved this beyond all doubt. Jahn, who works at Princeton, invented a machine called a Random Events Generator, which is, in effect, an automatic coin-flipper. Then he brought in ordinary people from the street to make them try to influence the coin flipper to make it produce more "heads" than "tails." The success rate was amazing, proving you did not have to be a psychic to demonstrate mind over matter.

3. Morehouse describes precisely how this is done in his book *Psychic Warrior* (1997), which the American military made determined efforts to suppress.

Even more astonishing was an experiment in remote viewing. While one woman sat in a television studio, another went to downtown Chicago to a randomly selected location. It proved to be the Rockefeller Chapel, and the woman in the studio described it with precision and accuracy.

This sounds like telepathy, but it was not. The woman in the TV studio was asked to describe the location half an hour before the other woman arrived there. She was describing an event that would happen in the future.

All this may seem to justify the hope that the gap that existed between science and the paranormal during the nineteenth century is steadily being closed.

In 1983, in a book called *Mindsteps to the Cosmos*, the astronomer Gerald Hawkins (perhaps best known for *Stonehenge Decoded*) proposed that humankind periodically goes through what he calls a "cosmic mindstep," a new, revolutionary change in man's perspective on the universe. He is talking about mindsteps in astronomy, but they could apply just as well to the whole field of human evolution.

To begin with, says Hawkins, man was little more than an animal, stuck firmly on earth. Then he began to take notice of the heavens, and to invent myths in which the heavenly bodies are gods—he demonstrates that the Babylonian *Epic of Gilgamesh* is about gods who are also the sun, moon, and planets. This was Mindstep 1. Then came the Greeks, who studied the heavens, and tried to explain the movements of the heavenly bodies—Mindstep 2. Since Ptolemy placed the earth firmly at the center of the universe, his scheme was impossibly complicated. It was not until Copernicus placed the sun at the center of the solar system that the next great mindstep took place. The invention of printing also brought about a "knowledge explosion."

The next step was the age of space, when man began looking to other galaxies, and finally began to grasp the size of the universe. This was Mindstep 4.

The next mindstep? Could it be some totally new technology, enabling us to explore the universe? Or perhaps contact with extra-terrestrial civilizations?

Or could it, perhaps, be an awareness of this vast new realm opened up by scientists like Stanislav Grof and Robert Jahn, and investigators like Robert Monroe? If so, then there seems little doubt that it is our most important mindstep so far.

Chapter Nine

Postscript

In 1968, I went to Cambridge to interview the philosopher C. D. Broad for a color supplement article. Broad, a kindly and modest soul, was rather irritated at the time because his college—Trinity—had just made him kitchen steward, at the age of eighty, and he was looking forward impatiently to completing his present duties and getting back to his beloved Scandinavia.

After talking about his philosophical ideas and his views on the younger generation, we turned to psychical research; Broad had joined the Society for Psychical Research in 1920, and had twice been its president. He made the interesting comment: "If these facts of psychical research are true, then clearly they are of immense importance—they literally alter *everything*." I reminded him that, in his autobiography,[1] he had remarked: "So far as I can tell, I have no desire to survive the death of my present body, and I should be considerably relieved if I could feel much surer than I do that no kind of survival is possible." Broad insisted there was no contradiction here:

> *I've been terribly lucky in this life . . . I've achieved all the success I could probably want—probably far more than I deserve—so I don't like the idea of taking a chance in another world. I'd rather just come to an end.*

Broad was underlining a point that we have touched on repeatedly in this book. To *know* there was life after death would certainly "alter everything." Yet in another sense, it would alter nothing. A baby opens its eyes on a complex, baffling, and rather frightening universe. It soon develops the conviction that the grown-ups know all the answers. It is rather disconcerting to achieve adulthood and realize that this is not true. Kierkegaard wrote:

> *Where am I? Who am I? . . . How did I come to be here? What is this thing called the world? . . . How did I come into the world? Why was I not consulted? . . . And if I am compelled to take part in it, where is the manager? I would like to see him.*

To say, "Don't worry—there is life after death" is no answer. It is true that if death *was* the end of the individual, it would deepen that sense of pointlessness and futility. But to be told that we shall go on living in another world leaves us facing the same question. William James expressed it: Why is there existence rather than non-existence? To answer that question, we would presumably need to get "outside" existence, and that seems clearly impossible.

This explains why Spiritualism has not made a greater impact on the modern world. When it was launched in Rochester in 1850, its

---

1. *The Philosophy of C. D. Broad* (1959).

followers had no doubt they were helping to found a new religion. But a religion is an attempt to explain man's place in the universe. Spiritualism was not based on some mystical insight about the relation of man to God; it was based on the assertion that dead human beings are not really dead at all, but continue to live in a world not unlike the present one. That leaves the question about man's place in the universe precisely where it was before. No wonder Roman Catholic theologians joined with agnostic scientists in denouncing it as boring, shallow, and irrelevant.

I was forcefully reminded of these objections a few months before I began to write this book. A correspondent told me that he had just learned of the existence of one of the most remarkable mediums of all time. I shall refer to her as Martha. She was, said my correspondent, a "materialization medium," and during her séances, perfectly solid people would appear out of thin air and walk about the room. They would behave exactly like normal people, replying to questions, allowing themselves to be touched and sitting down at the side of members of the audience. In short, there was no mystification; it was all as straightforward as a tea party.

I immediately wrote to Martha, explained that I was about to write a book on life after death, and asked if I could come to one of her séances. I received a friendly reply saying that I was welcome at any time.

Not long after, I happened to be in the provincial town where Martha lived, and I telephoned to ask if I could come to a meeting. She explained that this was impossible at the moment, because the friends in whose house the séances took place were away on holiday, but she invited me to have tea at her home.

Martha proved to be a rather attractive woman in her thirties. I was introduced to her husband, Bill, and to her son and his girlfriend. What they told me sounded impressive. Martha had been an actress, but since she had been married to Bill—an engineer—she had given up the stage. (Her son still worked in the theater as a lighting engineer.) They had discovered her powers accidentally one day when she had become exasperated with a friend with whom she was having an argument. She touched a small table, and it shot across the room. When she placed her hands on it, it rocked from side to side. The table answered questions by means of the usual code. They all became fascinated by it, and began spending their evenings asking questions. (Martha emphasized that she had previously had no interest whatsoever in such matters—in fact, she was a Catholic.) One day, she fell into a trance, and a spirit spoke through her mouth. When she woke up, she apologized for falling asleep, having no memory of what had happened. At later séances, spirits "materialized."

A woman with a strong Scottish accent, who identified herself as the medium "Helen Duncan," soon became Martha's "control." One day, a small boy appeared—let us call him "Jeremy"—and described how he had died a few years before from an accident. He gave his name and address, and told them that at this very moment, his father was sitting at home alone, because his mother was away for the night. On the ceiling above him, said Jeremy, there was a red admiral butterfly.

It was late at night, but they decided to test Jeremy's story. They found the telephone number, and a man's voice answered. Bill said: "Look, I'm going to ask you a silly question. Is there a red admiral butterfly on the ceiling in that room?" The man answered with astonishment: "My God, so there is! But how did you know?" They answered: "Because your son just told us. . . ." The father confirmed all that Jeremy had said about his death. The next day, both parents arrived, and there were tears of joy as they hugged and kissed their "son."

It was an impressive story. In fact, I found Martha and Bill altogether convincing. They seemed a charming couple, completely natural and down-to-earth, and if their story could be confirmed, then there seemed no doubt whatsoever that Martha was the most remarkable medium since Daniel Dunglas Home. I had little doubt that it would be confirmed, for they assured me that I would not only be able to talk to Jeremy and Helen Duncan, but touch them as well.

At the first opportunity, I hurried back to the suburb where Bill and Martha lived. It was still impossible, for some reason, to hold a séance at the home of their friends; but they offered to do it in their own sitting room. I was invited early for tea—in fact, a large meal with hot sausage rolls and all kinds of cakes and scones—and I was told a great deal more about their contacts with the "other world." It seemed that Martha was having problems with various bloody-minded skeptics, and one of these had accused her of fraud in a well-known spiritualist journal. I found all this surprising; if Martha's phenomena were half as convincing as they sounded, it was hard to understand why anyone should want to denounce her.

After about two hours, the séance began. Rather to my surprise, Bill and Donald (their son) began covering the windows with sheets of thick black plastic. They explained that even the slightest ray of light could cause harm to the medium. Martha sat in an armchair; I sat on the settee with Donald and his girlfriend; Bill sat opposite Martha. A tape recorder with popular classical music was switched on, and the lights were turned off, leaving us all in total darkness. The music, they explained, helped to create the right atmosphere. Soon there were several loud raps on the table, which, Bill explained, meant there were thirteen spirits present. Then a small boy's voice sounded, and Jeremy was there. I was introduced to him, and I asked if he would mind if I recorded his voice. He gave permission, and I switched on the recorder I had brought. Then we all went on talking—it was very casual, very normal, like a fireside chat. Jeremy had a rather high-pitched voice, with something oddly muffled about it, as if he was speaking with some object in his mouth. After a few minutes, Jeremy asked: "Can you hear Laura?" The music had been switched on again—Placido Domingo singing "I wouldn't be without you"—so I couldn't detect the newcomer. Bill greeted her, and again I was introduced. Laura took my hand in both of hers she felt like a perfectly normal human being. Laura also sang along with the music; she had a pleasant voice, but again with something odd about it—I can only describe it as a slight wobble. At this point, a flashlight was produced, but it had a red sock over the end, so that it showed practically nothing, even in that total darkness. It was held close to Laura's bare feet, and I could see them dimly against the rug.

Suddenly a voice with a Scottish accent said: "Hello there! It's lovely t' see you all tonight." Bill greeted her: "Hello Helen. "I expect, Colin, that you're gettin' a bit of a shock?" She asked Bill to turn down the music, and explained: "We need the music because Martha's afraid o' the dark. There's just enough so her unconscious mind can hear the music." She went on to introduce herself to me and welcome me "from the bottom o' my heart." She'd heard I was a man of many words, and she was a woman of many words.

After a few more minutes of this, Bill decided it was time for a break. The music was played; then the lights were switched on. There was Martha, sitting in her armchair in her track suit, gradually waking up and asking: "Did anything happen?" We assured her it had.

After a break of five or ten minutes, the séance began again. There was a great deal more chatter from Jeremy, then Helen offered to do an "experiment." This amounted to taking the torch and showing me her feet, then her knees. Once again, it was practically impossible to see anything but the faint glow of flesh in the dim red light.

Helen was, as she had said, a woman of many words; she talked a great deal. I interrupted her at one point to ask if she recalled a friend of mine, Leonard Boucher, who had attended one of her séances during her lifetime. She said she did, and asked me what had happened to "Len." I said he was now in Zimbabwe. "Is he?" said Helen with surprise, "I thought he was in Rhodesia." We had to explain that they were the same place. She asked me to remind Leonard about Portsmouth.

After more talk, I asked her if she could tell me anything about the nature of poltergeists. "I will explain," said Helen magisterially, but she did not explain. Instead, she told us that poltergeists had never harmed anyone, and that there was no need to be afraid of them. "The living can do you far more harm than the dead. . . ." For the next quarter of an hour or so, she rambled on, saying nothing in particular—certainly nothing about the nature of poltergeists. It became clear that she either knew nothing about poltergeists, or preferred to keep it to herself. I was not sorry when Bill announced it was time for another break. By this time, my tape had run out.

Bill had told me that Sir Oliver Lodge's son Raymond usually appeared at their séances, so I asked whether I might meet him. In fact, I had already listened to a recording of an earlier séance with "Raymond." Eventually, after more conversation, Raymond arrived and introduced himself to me. It was at this point that my vague doubts began to become insistent. This Raymond sounded nothing like the voice I had heard on tape. He spoke in a rather slow voice, with an upper-class accent, and a slightly feminine intonation, like Ella Shields as "Burlington Bertie."

I asked him if it was true that spirits could see in the dark, and he confirmed this—in fact, he told me that when a friend of mine from the Society for Psychical Research had attended one of Martha's séances, he had astonished him by telling him how many fingers he was holding up. He added that the room had been full of wires at the time, and that the spirits had proved their ability to see in the dark by avoiding them.

This seemed an invitation, so I asked Raymond whether he could tell me what expression I was wearing on my face at the moment. I pulled a horribly distorted face and thrust out my lips. Raymond asked hesitantly: "You mean if you've got your mouth open, or something?" Quite suddenly, I knew beyond all possibility of doubt that Raymond could not see in the dark. I said yes, that was what I meant. Raymond replied promptly that "he didn't do that any more." Why not? I asked, and he explained that it convinced no one. "But it would convince me," I told him. "For example, if you could tell me how many fingers I am now holding up." I held up two fingers. "We don't do that any more," said Raymond irritably. "Why not? Wouldn't you like to convince me?" Raymond explained that if I left the house, and stated in print that Raymond had been able to count my fingers, no one would accept this as proof. They would accuse

Martha of using infrared light or something of the sort. I explained again that it was not a question of convincing other people, but of convincing me. If he could tell me how many fingers I was holding up, I would accept that he was a spirit. If not, I wouldn't.

At this, Raymond became very waspish. They had already given me all the evidence I should need, he said. They had allowed me to touch the spirits, and to see them by the light of the torch. I pointed out that the torch showed nothing that could be regarded as evidence—not even whether Martha was still sitting in her armchair. While it was true that someone had taken my hand and allowed me to touch her arm, I could certainly not swear that it was not Martha herself.

It became very clear that seventy years in the spirit world had not eliminated Raymond's ordinary human characteristics; it was obvious that he was finding it hard to control his temper. They had given me proof, he insisted. That should be enough. I insisted that he only had to tell me how many fingers I was holding up to remove all my doubts. "We don't do that kind of thing any more. . . ." I noticed that as he became angry, the voice seemed to become more feminine.

It seemed pointless to continue, and I said so. The music was played, and the lights turned on. It was a very awkward moment. I was as certain as I could reasonably be that Raymond was a fraud, and it seemed to follow that the whole séance had been a fake. Martha woke up sleepily and asked what had happened; Bill explained that Raymond and I had a disagreement. I thanked them and took my leave quickly, anxious to avoid further embarrassment.

As soon as I arrived home, I wrote to Leonard Boucher in Zimbabwe, and asked him whether Helen Duncan had known him as "Len," and whether he had seen her in Portsmouth. His reply, when it came, was much as I expected. They had been on formal terms—no first names. (In any case, I had never heard anyone call him Len; it was always Leonard.) He also had not seen her in Portsmouth but in Scotland.

The correspondent who had first told me about Martha was furious when I sent him my report on the séance. He had no doubt whatsoever that she was genuine, and if I disagreed, then it must be because I had joined the ranks of the willfully blind. I explained that I was not certain that Martha was a fraud, but that I was a hundred percent certain that Raymond was. This failed to mollify him. Nothing would convince him that I had not gone over to the "enemy."

The whole episode only served to underline what I had known all along: that communications with alleged spirits can teach us nothing about the nature of reality. The basic task of human beings is to learn about the nature of reality. Even if Raymond had been able to count my fingers and read the expression on my face—even if he had been able to read my mind—it would have made no real difference. It would merely have confirmed what I already believe to be true: that such things are possible. When I listen to the tape recording of that séance, I am seized by an uncontrollable desire to yawn, and by the conviction that spirits have nothing to add to the sum total of human thought—even genuine ones.

What, then, do I believe can be learned from the evidence of psychical research?

I would suggest that one of its most important insights concerns the personality. We all take personality for granted. I am I, and that is all there is to it. Cases of multiple personality reveal that the truth is infinitely more complex. If I allow myself to become completely defeated by life, I may develop a subsidiary personality that *can* cope with its problems. "Christine Beauchamp" (Clara Fowler) was timid and fearful, so the cheerful and mischievous "Sally" took over. Louis Vivé was passive and apathetic, so a more aggressive and assertive "Louis" took over. Billy Milligan was about to commit suicide by jumping off the school roof when a subpersonality displaced him and took over. The obvious deduction is that we already contain many potential personalities, all, so to speak, waiting in the wings and ready to be activated. In normal, healthy people, they blend with the basic personality without disrupting it. We meet someone we haven't seen for two years, and realize that he had become "another person," more confident and efficient. We do not feel that he had been "taken over" by a stronger personality, only that he has become *more himself.* Elsewhere[2] I have even suggested that every human being contains a whole ladder or hierarchy of "selves." At the bottom rung there is the baby who opens his eyes on a strange world, then the child who begins to develop a mind of his own at about the age of three, then the first "completed" personality at the age of seven, then the adolescent who develops new sexual and emotional potentials, then the young adult who integrates all the previous levels. This is not the end of development. In "great men" we can easily trace the development of new levels so that, for example, we speak of the various "periods" of a Shakespeare or Beethoven. We can also see plainly that even the Shakespeares and Beethovens were incomplete human beings; if they had lived longer and continued to struggle they might have developed to still higher levels.

This explains why we reject the notion that personality survives bodily death. We can see that personality grows and develops, like the body, which argues that it dies, like the body. Yet in cases of multiple personality, we can also see that there is a "basic self" that forms the foundation of the personality. Mystical ecstasy seems to dissolve the personality. Some mystics have even compared this sense of escaping their individuality to a spirit rising out of a rotting corpse; yet they still remain fully alive and conscious. If anything survives death, it is this basic substratum of the personality. If reincarnation is a reality, this is also what reenters the newly born child.

Perhaps "substratum" is the wrong word here. In *Mysteries* I have suggested that the "ladder" of selves is not a normal ladder with parallel sides, but something more like an inverted "V." The higher we move, the shorter the rungs become, and the more effort of "compression" we have to make if we are to move up from a lower level. (On

---

2. *Mysteries*, Introduction.

the other hand, it is easy to fall *down* a rung, as in a nervous breakdown.) Perhaps the "ultimate self" lies at the top of the ladder.

I began this book by discussing Adam Crabtree because some of his cases seem to illustrate that this "development" mechanism also seems to leave room for what used to be called possession. According to Kardec, spirits can wander in and out of us as they feel inclined (and Ralph Allison's "Dennis" case seems to provide support for this view). They can, to some extent, influence our thoughts, but they cannot, under normal circumstances, take control, or even exert any real influence on our actions. This sounds, of course, like the grossest kind of medieval superstition, but the evidence of psychical research suggests that we should at least accept it as a working hypothesis.

Perhaps the most interesting aspect of psychical research is the recognition that we seem to possess all kinds of powers of which we are consciously unaware—from telepathy and psychokinesis to astral projection and precognition of the future. Yet I believe these powers are less important than we might assume. All the major religions have recognized them as a byproduct of "spiritual development." The Hindus say that a yogi who takes the trouble to walk on water is still in an early stage of development.

The alternative—the striving towards God or Ultimate Reality—strikes most of us as uninviting or unreal. This may be simply because we are attaching the wrong meaning to the words. The French psychologist Pierre Janet insisted that the measure of mental health is a faculty he called "the reality function." He was not speaking about some mystical reality, only about the everyday reality that surrounds us all. Repressions, miseries, guilts—above all, preposterous fears and doubts—prevent us from responding directly and healthily to this reality. Human beings are the only creatures who spend 90 percent of their time in a dream world inside their own heads. We are too *subjective.* Our basic problem is to learn objectivity—to achieve what might be called "objective consciousness."

In fact, objective consciousness is less rare than it sounds. We only have to walk outdoors on a sunny morning to experience a sudden sense that life is delightful and boundlessly interesting. If we could maintain that sense all the time the world would become a kind of paradise—no more war, no more crime, no more meanness and pettiness and resentment. Our problem is that we lose this insight so easily. Fatigue lowers our sharpness of perception, and the petty fears and anxieties come swarming back into our minds like rats from the sewers. Everyone must have noticed that when they subject themselves to physical stress, there comes a point at which the level of misery and anxiety suddenly increases steeply. (An easy way to test this is to go jogging, or try digging the garden much harder than usual.) All our slightly repressed mistrust of life suddenly comes welling up from the subconscious. (Not the unconscious, the subconscious—that realm just below the threshold of ordinary consciousness.) The only way to change this is to deliberately set out to drive the rats from the sewers, to subject the fears and anxieties to the scrutiny of the conscious mind and the light of reason. We can "re-program" the subconscious, so it is no longer a health hazard.

We are, in fact, approaching the problem of vitalism (discussed in the last chapter) from a different angle. Vitalism, as we have seen, is the belief that life is engaged in a struggle to conquer matter by "inserting more freedom" into it. So—as T. E. Hulme expressed it—the amoeba could be regarded as a tiny "leak" of freedom, fishes are bigger leaks, animals bigger leaks still, and humans the biggest leaks so far (at least on this planet). *Our* task, according to vitalism, is to make a deliberate, conscious effort to enlarge the leak.

Whether or not we happen to be vitalists, we can all recognize the kernel of truth in this view. When a man is driving a car at ninety miles an hour, he feels "more alive." When he gets excited as he watches a football match, he feels more alive. These are fairly crude methods of feeling more alive. When a reader becomes totally absorbed in the fictional world of a novel, when a music lover is "swept away" by a symphony, they experience a certain internal widening of consciousness that seems quite different *in kind* from mere physical excitement. The football fan knows that his excitement depends on the game; but the person who is carried away by imaginative excitement feels that this experience is somehow *within his own control*—that he or she could conjure it up again by an act of imagination. It seems quite clear to those who have a capacity for intellectual or imaginative excitement that *this* is the key to the deliberate "enlargement of the leak" of freedom.

Schopenhauer was one of the first philosophers to think in terms of a "life force"; he was followed by Edouard von Hartmann, and later by Shaw, Bergson, and Driesch. They all thought of life as a blind, instinctive force, clumsily groping its way towards self-expression. But, as we have seen, Bergson and Driesch later changed their minds. This was for two reasons. First, that if such powers as telepathy and clairvoyance exist, then the forces of life must have far greater control over matter than we suppose. This control seems to be limited by our inability to "tune in" to these powers—or our tendency to actually resist them. (Rosalind Heywood's "Orders" often struck her as absurd, yet obeying them usually turned out well.) Still, the "unseen forces" seem to behave as if they possessed an intelligent purpose, or as if they were "above" ordinary consciousness. Second, if life after death is a reality, then the "other world" seems to exist on an altogether less "solid" plane of matter than our own—perhaps a plane where matter exists at some far higher rate of vibration. This suggests that life has already conquered this plane, and is using it as a base to make forays into our more difficult and inhospitable territory. Gurdjieff once said our earth is the cosmic equivalent of outer Siberia; a better comparison might be a Wild West or darkest Africa, still awaiting colonization and conquest.

As we have seen, the great problem seems to be that when life descends into solid matter, it *loses its memory*. It could be compared to a child who has been sent out on an errand, but who has forgotten his instructions halfway. For human beings, this "forgetfulness" leads to the feeling of being trapped in a dreary world of matter, and to Sartre's conviction that "it is meaningless that we live and meaningless that we die."

Under the circumstances, it seems quite plain that the basic problem for the "life force" is how to prevent us from forgetting our instructions, and wandering back home with nothing accomplished—or, as in the case of a Hitler or Jack the Ripper, leaving the world a great deal worse than we found it.

Let us consider this problem as though we were Higher Intelligences—or Angels—sitting up in heaven, looking down on human beings, and wondering how we can find a permanent solution to this problem of "forgetfulness."

The one thing on which we all agree is that the purpose of life is to increase its power over matter, to "enlarge the leak" of freedom. So the last thing we want is a race of creatures who feel that life is pointless and futile, and that the sooner they can escape from "this dim vast vale of tears," the better. Ideally, we want creatures who feel that life is immensely interesting and exciting, and that no problem need remain permanently insoluble. We want creatures with an enormous "appetite for reality."

The trouble with these human beings is that they all *start out* full of the feeling that life is going to be marvellous, and that the world is "apparelled in celestial light," but end up bored, disillusioned, and defeated. What makes it more annoying is that they are now *so close* to achieving their objective. For hundreds of thousands of years, they have fought grimly against cold and starvation and predators. Again and again, they have missed extinction only by the skin of their teeth. Then they began to use their intelligence to make weapons to hunt for food, and build weatherproof shelters, and from then on, life began to improve steadily. They created civilization, and although this involved two undesirable byproducts—war and crime—they refused to be deterred, and gradually learned to make life more and more worth living. Then they took one of their greatest steps forward, and created art and literature; the first steps toward the conquest of the world of the mind. At last, it began to look as though they were close to achieving their basic purpose—an impregnable bridgehead in the world of matter.

Then a new and unexpected problem arose. They began to grow *bored* with the civilization their ancestors had built with so much labor. The trouble, of course, was that it had all happened too quickly. They had spent millions of years struggling for survival, and then achieved the security of civilization overnight. It left them bewildered and confused. Instead of struggling for more consciousness, they began to choose the road of least resistance, and to waste their lives looking for immediate satisfactions.

Now in the remote past, the Higher Intelligences had kept in touch with the human race through certain individuals who were highly sensitive "receiving sets." These people—called prophets and messiahs—could be *shown* the purpose of life through mystical revelations, and then they used their enormous powers of persuasion to induce everyone to live as if the purpose of life was to earn a passport to heaven. For thousands of years, this method of preventing human beings from "forgetting their instructions" was immensely successful, and the great religions kept man working at the central aim of increasing human optimism and intelligence (for that, in the last analysis, is what it amounts to). But the development of his intelligence caused man to outgrow his religions. The complexity of civilization created more and more "drop-outs," people who took it for granted that life is totally meaningless—a brief sojourn in prison, followed by oblivion. There actually came a point, in the nineteenth century, when the steady increase in human knowledge led man to the conclusion that matter is the only reality.

It was at this point that a subcommittee of Angels decided to try out the idea of a more direct form of communication, to convince humans that there *was* a life after death. This experiment started in the 1840s, and in the form of a religious movement known as Spiritualism, it spread across the world. Unfortunately, it tended to attract the wrong type of person—feeble-minded sentimentalists—and the scientists and philosophers remained aloof. Later, another committee of Angels suggested the increasing use of the near-death experience as a "teaching method," and this also achieved some success—but on far too small a scale to do much good. Moreover, the whole Spiritualist project was undermined by the constant interference of mischievous "earth-bound spirits"—the criminals, layabouts, and juvenile delinquents of the "other world"—who succeeded in creating widespread confusion. On the whole, the Spiritualist experiment is not regarded by the Higher Intelligences as one of their more outstanding successes.

Which, of course, leaves us with the original question: how *can* human beings be prevented from "forgetting their instructions" and wasting their lives? This, we recognize instinctively, is the central question of human existence, the Life Question. It is this instinctive recognition that explains why the evidence of spiritualism has made such a surprisingly small impact on the human race. You would expect it to be a matter of passionate interest to every human being. Dostoevsky wrote in *The Diary of a Writer*: "There is only a single supreme idea on earth: the concept of the immortality of the human soul; all other profound ideas by which men live are only an extension of it." Yet in the century and a half of its existence, spiritualism has made no real progress; it has merely marked time. This is because we all feel, deep down, that the Death Question is of far less importance than the Life Question.

One thing is clear: that this matter of the Life Question is no longer a problem that concerns only the Higher Intelligences. For more than a century now, human beings have also been applying their own intelligence to its solution. (As we have seen, the Society for Psychical Research began when two philosophers asked whether the evidence for the paranormal might help to solve the "riddle of the Universe.") Kierkegaard, Tolstoy, Dostoevsky, Nietszche, Shaw, Jaspers, Camus, and many others have made the Life Question—the *Lebensfrage*—the central issue of their work. (Even I have succeeded in making a small contribution.)

The outline of an answer is slowly beginning to emerge. It is this: Human beings have no problem maintaining a high degree of purpose when faced with emergencies or difficulties that threaten their existence. When this happens, we become aware of the actual mechanism of "enlarging the leak" of freedom. Whenever I am faced with some sudden challenge or danger, its first effect is to undermine my vitality. Adrenalin rushes into my bloodstream, and my confidence drops several points. Then I "steel myself" to meet the problem; I summon energy, and discipline myself to face the challenge. In the moment I overcome the challenge, I experience a deep satisfaction, and a delightful sense of freedom. I have, in fact, "enlarged the leak." If I could spend my life facing interesting challenges, my self-control and my freedom would steadily increase. As far as the Higher Intelligences are concerned, I would have done a thoroughly satisfactory job of widening the bridgehead.

In *A Criminal History of Mankind*, I speak of that initial response to a challenge—the rush of adrenalin—as "Force T," the "T" standing for tension. The response to that challenge I call "Force C"—the "C" standing for control. *This* is the central issue of human existence, the essence of the Life Question, increasing Force C to overcome Force T. That is how we "enlarge the leak." That explains, of course, why our most fundamental human impulse is to seek challenges. When we lived in caves, or on the great African savannas, the problem never arose, for we had more than enough challenge to keep us up to the mark; this is why man has become the most successful creature on earth. When he began to build cities, he already experienced the problem that was to become the greatest obstacle to his progress: "challenge-starvation." He responded to it by inventing war, which made his blood tingle and his heart beat faster. In the succeeding six or seven thousand years, man has become the most aggressive and murderous creature the earth has ever seen—even in comparison with the flesh-eating dinosaurs and the saber-toothed tiger. He has also developed many less harmful ways of responding to challenge-starvation: climbing mountains, exploring the unknown, conquering nature. But his enterprise has had precisely the effect he was trying to avoid: to make life less challenging. When life loses its challenge, it also loses its savor, and we begin to feel suffocated and bored. The instinctive response—in adults as much as children—is to look around for some mischief to get into. Boredom releases the destructive urge. This is why one of the chief problems of Western civilization in the last quarter of the twentieth century is the apparently "motiveless" crime, ranging from vandalism and football hooliganism to mass murder.

Yet when we apply intelligence to this problem, the answer is plain enough. It is mere force of habit that makes us crave a physical stimulus. Think what happens when I face some interesting challenge. I concentrate and set out to arouse my sleeping energies; then I set out to discipline these forces. There is, in fact, nothing to stop me from "arousing" Force T by the same effort of concentration and will, and then setting out to control it. In fact, saints and ascetics have always known this trick. They have created their own challenges—fasting, meditating, tormenting the body—in order to strengthen the will. Such exercises seem wilfully perverse until we recognize their purpose—to arouse Force T and subject it to Force C, thereby increasing the sense of freedom and widening the range of consciousness.

The methods of the saint strike most of us as disagreeably crude and painful. This is partly because we sense that they are unnecessarily strenuous. The past two or three centuries have seen the development of a power with which our ancestors were barely acquainted: imagination. Modern humans take it for granted because they have been exercising it since they were babies: reading comic books, going to the cinema, watching television. It is almost impossible for us to realize what life was like for a man of the fifteenth century. From the moment he opened his eyes in the morning, his mind was fixed on the purely practical world; by comparison with modern humans, his power of imagination was as feeble as a baby's hand compared with that of a grown human. He had almost no "mental life." In this respect, humans have increased their freedom enormously in the course of a few centuries. (The invention of the novel in the eighteenth century was one of the most influential events in human history.) Nowadays, almost every child is familiar with the experience of becoming so totally absorbed in a story that he feels as if they are *living* in the Africa of *King Solomon's Mines* or the France of *The Three Musketeers.* Whenever we experience that same absorption, we know that this is the basic solution of the Life Question. Imagination, properly directed and controlled, is a far more efficient means of arousing Force T and Force C than the self-flagellation of the saint, or the self-chosen discomforts of the round-the-world yachtsman.

Most people will feel doubtful about this statement. This is because we tend to think of imagination as another name for daydreaming or fantasy—in other words, telling yourself lies. This is an error. Imagination is, in fact, basically the power of *escaping the present moment.* This may sound an equally dubious activity, until we give it a little thought. The central problem of human beings is that they are *trapped* in the present moment; their horizon is limited by "close-upness." When a child is utterly bored, he feels that the present moment is somehow unchangeable, that it will go on forever. Although they ought to know better, adults are also subject to the same curious delusion. Experience should have taught them that they are stronger than the matter that surrounds them—that, as Wells says, "if you don't like your life, you can change it." Yet the moment they become bored, they become subject to that familiar sense of being trapped, like a fly stuck on flypaper. They *know* that this is absurd, that the future will bring all kinds of changes. Yet they still allow themselves to be bullied and discouraged into a state of passivity by the sheer "immediacy" of the present moment, like a six-foot teenager giving way to a bully half his size because it has become a habit.

In fact, we are always catching glimpses of our real power over the present. I may be involved in some boring task when a fragment of music creeps into my head, and induces the "absurd good news" feeling. A smell encountered as I walk down an unfamiliar street—of newly baked bread or roasting coffee beans—may evoke my childhood and induce a surge of sheer joy. These moments—Proust devoted a twelve-volume novel to them—are difficult to explain until we can grasp how far we are normally entrapped in the present moment. It squeezes us and suffocates us, and we have become so used to the feeling that we take it for granted as part of the "human condition." What the fragment of music or the unexpected smell does is to remind us that the past seemed just as oppressively real as the present—yet it is long gone. These moments tell us: *You are freer and stronger than you think.* Hence the surge of pure delight.

When we think about it, we can see that what we call happiness is nothing more than this sense of *not* being trapped in the present moment. That is why we enjoy holidays and excitement and romance, just as the early balloonists enjoyed soaring up above the ground, and seeing the world from a "bird's eye view." Excitement gives us a bird's eye view of life itself, and seems to neutralize that strange force of gravity that keeps us stuck in the present.

Now this, in fact, is the real purpose of imagination: not to create fantasies, but to make us aware of *other times and other places.* When it actually happens, we realize that "imagination" is a totally inadequate word for this faculty that can lift us like a rocket out of the present moment, and make us aware that we are, in some curious sense, citizens of eternity. That is why I have elsewhere coined the term "Faculty X" for the ability to suddenly *grasp the reality* of other times and places.[3]

At the moment, it refuses to work to order; it operates fitfully, when it feels inclined. Yet when it *does* work, it does so easily and instantaneously, like switching on a light. Quite suddenly, some moment of the past has become totally real, as real as the present: and we realize that it is as real as the present—or rather, that the present does not have some special status of super-reality, just because it

3. See *The Occult*, chapter 2.

happens to be here and now. We were intended to be the masters of time, not its slaves.

The ease with which this faculty operates suggests that it is somehow encoded in our genes, like our power to walk upright, or the bird's power of flight. This is why Faculty X brings the feeling of "absurd good news." It makes us realize that we *already have it.*

At this point, we may recollect the main thesis of *Human Personality and Its Survival of Bodily Death*: that there is extremely powerful evidence that human beings possess all kinds of unusual faculties of which most of us are unaware, from the extraordinary powers of calculating prodigies and mnemonists (people who can glance at a page of a book and then recite it word for word) to telepathy, clairvoyance, and astral projection. These powers may, in fact, be closely related to Faculty X—for example, the erratic power of "projecting" one's doppelgänger, so it can be seen by other people in distant places. (In the case of the Rev. Mountford,[4] we have seen that this included the ability to "project" a horse and cart as well.) Myers' book is a plea for a new form of psychology to investigate these unknown powers. When Professor Heim saw his whole life flash before his eyes as he fell down the crevasse, he was discovering something about his brain that he had never even suspected. The same applies to the Rev. Bertrand as he lay frozen on a ledge and followed the progress of his students to the top of the mountain. When Sarah Hall saw her own "double" standing by the sideboard, and when Rosalind Heywood split into "Pink Me" and "White Me," they were encountering an aspect of human personality that is at present unknown to science. When Joseph Rodes Buchanan discovered that certain people can "read" the history of an object by holding it in their hands, he was demonstrating that the unconscious mind has access to "hidden" information. When Alfred Russel Wallace placed a schoolboy under hypnosis, then made him "taste" things by putting

---

4. See p. 148.

them into his own mouth, he was proving that the unconscious has access to other minds.

Perhaps the most interesting discovery of psychical research is that we can develop these powers simply by wanting to. The psychologist Abraham Maslow made a similar discovery about the "peak experience," the moment of sudden overwhelming happiness. He discovered that when he talked to his students about the peak experience, they not only recalled many half-forgotten peak experiences, but also began having peak experiences far more frequently. Thinking and talking about the peak experience had "reprogrammed the subconscious mind," and the subconscious mind did the rest.

This suggests that the chief problem confronted by the human race is not some appalling form of original sin, some deep and justified anxiety about our place in the universe, or recognition of our fundamental weakness and helplessness. It is simply the problem of a badly programmed subconscious.

Most of us have allowed the subconscious to become messy and untidy, like a disused playroom that has become a repository for old junk. It smells rather unpleasant because there are a few ancient fish-paste sandwiches and half-eaten apples lurking under the one-eyed teddy bears and mildewed copies of nursery classics. Every time we catch a glimpse of the mess through the half-open door, we shudder and hurry past. Yet it would only take half an hour with a broom and mop to make it one of the nicest rooms in the house.

The whole history of psychical research has been a series of demonstrations of the apparently "absurd" powers of the human mind. For the scientist, this has always been at best an embarrassment, at worst a scandal. It now begins to look as though this may be because he is the slave of his old fashioned idea of the nature of science. More than three centuries ago, René Descartes established the method of modern science and philosophy; he called it "radical doubt." The philosopher, says Descartes, should sit in his armchair and contemplate the universe around him. He should then proceed to doubt everything that can be doubted. Does the sun really go around the earth, as it seems to do? If we question it, we may arrive at the truth. As to the question: "How do you prove your own existence?" Descartes replied: "I think, therefore I am." Having established this apparently unshakable foundation, he felt able to relax in his armchair and turn his telescope on the universe outside his window.

The investigator of the paranormal has no doubt that "I think, therefore I am," but he is inclined to add the disconcerting question: "You are *what*?" For this is clearly the question that Descartes overlooked: Who precisely *am* I? He assumed naturally enough, that he was René Descartes; that is what it said on his birth certificate. But every mystic has had the curious experience of realizing that he is not who he thinks he is. In moments of visionary intensity, his identity dissolves and he becomes aware that it is no more than a mask. Instead he is looking into the depths of an inner universe that bears strange resemblance to the external universe. The question "Who am I?" can only be answered by pointing his telescope inside himself.

In that moment, he realizes that the apparent limitation of his powers is due to the limitation of his picture of himself. In order to expand those powers, he has to expand his knowledge of himself. He merely has to turn the telescope the other way.

Bibliography

Allison, Ralph, M. D. and Ted Schwarz. *Minds in Many Places.* Rawson, New York: Wade Publishers, Inc., 1980.

Baird, A. T. *Richard Hodgson.* London: Psychic Press Ltd, 1949.

Barnes, Rev. E. W., F. R. S., and others. *The Mysteries of Life and Death.* London: Hutchinson & Co., London, n.d.

Barrett, Sir William F., F. R. S. *On the Threshold of the Unseen.* London: Kegan Paul, Trench, Trubner & Co. Ltd, 1920; E. P. Dutton & Co. New York, 1920.

——. *Death-Bed Visions.* London: Methuen & Co. Ltd., 1926.

Bennett, Sir Ernest. *Apparitions and Haunted Houses.* London: Faber & Faber Ltd, 1939.

Bozzano, Professor Ernest. *Animism and Spiritism.* London: Arthur H. Stockwell Ltd., n.d.

Crabtree, Adam. *Multiple Man.* Ontario: Collins Publishers, 1985.

Crowe, Mrs. Catherine. *The Seeress of Prevorst.* London: J. C. Moore, 1848.

——. *Spiritualism and the Age We Live In.* London: T. C. Newby, London, 1859.

——. *The Night Side of Nature.* London:George Routledge and Sons, London, 1845.

Cummins, Geraldine. *Swan on a Black Sea.* London: Routledge and Kegan Paul, 1965.

——. *The Road to Immortality.* London: Psychic Press Ltd, 1967.

Davis, Andrew Jackson. *The Philosophy of Spiritual Intercourse.* Boston: Colby & Rich, Banner of Light Publishing House, 1890.

Doyle, Arthur Conan. *The Vital Message.* London: Hodder & Stoughton, 1919.

Flammarion, Camille. *Death and Its Mystery*. 3 vols. London: T. Fisher Unwin, 1923.

Gowan, John Curtis. *Operations of Increasing Order.* California: published by author, 1980.

Graves, Tom and Janet Hoult. *The Essential T C. Lethbridge.* London: Roudedge & Kegan Paul, 1980.

Green, Celia. *Out-of-the-Body Experiences.* Oxford: Institute of Psychophysical Research, 1968.

Green, Celia, and Charles McCreery. *Apparitions.* London: Hamish Hamilton, 1975.

Guirdham, Arthur. *The Cathars & Reincarnation.* London: Neville Spearman, 1970.

——. *We Are One Another.* Jersey: Neville Spearman, 1974.

Hall, Trevor H. *The Strange Case of Edmund Gurney.* London: Gerald Duckworth & Co. Ltd., 1964.

Hart, Professor Hornell. *The Enigma of Survival.* London: Rider & Company, 1959.

Haynes, Renée. *The Hidden Springs: An Enquiry into Extra-sensory Perception.* London: Hutchinson & Co., 1961.

——. *The Seeing Eye: The Seeing I.* London: Hutchinson & Co., 1976.

——. *The Society for Psychical Research, 1882-1982: A History.* London: Macdonald & Co., 1982.

Head, Joseph and S. L. Cranston. *Reincarnation.* New York: Causeway Books, 1967.

Heywood, Rosalind. *The Infinite Hive.* London: Pan Books Ltd., 1964.

——. *The Sixth Sense.* London: Pan Books Ltd., 1959.

Hudson, Thomson Jay. *The Law of Psychic Phenomena.* London and Chicago: G. P. Putams Sons, 1902.

Inglis, Brian. *Natural and Supernatural: A History of the Paranormal, from the Beginnings to 1914.* London: Hodder & Stoughton, 1977.

——. *Science and Parascience. A History of the Paranormal, 1914-1939.* London: Hodder & Stoughton, 1984.

——. *The Paranormal: An Encyclopedia of Psychic Phenomena.* London: Granada, 1985.

Jaynes, Julian. *The Origin of Consciousness in the Breakdown of the Bicameral Mind.* Boston: Houghton Mifflin Co., 1976.

Jung, J. H. (Jung-Stilling). *Theory of Pneumatology.* London: Longman, Rees, Orme, Brown, Green and Longman, 1834.

Kardec, Allan. *The Spirits' Book.* Lake, Livraria All Kardec Editora Ltd, Sao Paolo, translated in 1972.

——. *The Mediums' Book.* London: Psychic Press Ltd., 1971.

Lodge, Sir Oliver, F. R. S. *The Survival of Man.* London: Methuen & Co. Ltd., 1909.

——. *Raymond or Life and Death.* London: Methuen & Co. Ltd., 1916.

Long, Max Freedom. *The Secret Science Behind Miracles.* California: DeVorss & Co., 1981.

Lorimer, David. *Survival? Body, Mind and Death in the Light of Psychic Experience.* London: Routledge & Kegan Paul, 1984.

Moody, Jr., Raymond A., M. D. *Life After Life.* New York: Bantam Books, 1975.

——. *Reflections On Life After Life.* London: Corgi Books, 1977.

Moore, R. Laurence. *In Search of White Crows.* New York: Oxford University Press, 1977.

Moreil, André. *La Vie et l'oeuvre d'Allan Kardec.* Paris: Sperar, 1961.

Moses, William Stainton. *Spirit Teachings.* London: Spiritualist Press, 1949.

Moss, Peter and Joe Keeton. *Encounters with the Past.* London: Sidgwick & Jackson, 1979.

Murphy, Gardner and Robert O. Ballou. *William James on Psychical Research.* London: Chatto and Windus Ltd., 1960.

Myers, Frederic W. H. with Edmund Gurney and Frank Podmore. *Phantasms of the Living.* 2 vols. London: Trubner & Co., 1886.

Myers, F. W. H. *Human Personality and Its Survival of Bodily Death.* New York: University Books Inc., 1961.

Osis, Karlis. *Deathbed Observations by Physicians and Nurses.* New York: Parapsychology Foundation, Inc., 1961.

Owen, Robert Dale. *Footfalls on the Boundary of Another World.* London: Trubner & Co., 1860.

——. *The Debatable Land Between This World and the Next.* London: Trubner & Co., 1874.

Podmore, Frank. *Modern Spiritualism: A History and a Criticism.* 2 vols. London: Methuen & Co., 1902.

Rhine, J. B. *The Reach of the Mind.* London: Penguin Books, 1948.

Richet, Charles, Ph.D. *Thirty Years of Psychical Research.* London: W. Collins Sons & Co. Ltd., 1923.

Ring, Kenneth, Ph.D. *Life at Death: A Scientific Investigation of the Near-Death Experience.* New York: Coward, McCann & Geoghegan, 1980.

Sabom, Michael B., M. D., F. A. C. C. *Recollections of Death: A Medical Investigation.* New York: Harper & Row, 1982.

Saltmarsh, H. F. *Evidence of Personal Survival.* London: G. Bell & Sons Ltd., 1938.

Sherwood, Jane. *Post-Mortem Journal.* London: Neville Spearman, 1964.

——. *The Country Beyond.* London: Neville Spearman, 1969.

Sidgwick, Eleanor Mildred. *Phantasms of the Living.* Including *Phantasms of the Living* by Edmund Gurney, Frederic W. H. Myers and Frank Podmore. New York: University Books Inc., 1962.

Smith, Susy. *The Mediumship of Mrs. Leonard.* New York: University Books, 1964.

Smith, W. Whately. *A Theory of the Mechanism of Survival.* London: Kegan Paul, Trench, Trubner & Co. Ltd., 1920; New York: E. P. Dutton & Co., 1920.

Steiner, Rudolf, Ph.D. *An Outline of Occult Science.* London: Theosophical Publishing Society, 1914; New York: Rand McNally & Co., 1914.

——. *Reincarnation and Immortality.* New York: Rudolf Steiner Publications, 1970.

——. *Rudolf Steiner: An Autobiography.* New York: Steinerbooks, 1977.

Stevenson, Ian, Ph.D. *Twenty Cases Suggestive of Reincarnation.* New York: American Society for Psychical Research, 1966.

Thakur, Shivesh C. *Philosophy and Psychical Research.* London: George Allen & Unwin, 1976.

Thomas, Rev. Charles Drayton. *Life Beyond Death with Evidence.* London: W. Collins Sons & Co. Ltd., 1928.

Toynbee, Arnold, Arthur Koestler and others. *Life After Death.* London: Weidenfeld & Nicolson, 1976.

Tyrrell, G. N. M. *The Personality of Man.* London:Penguin Books, 1947.

——. *Science and Psychical Phenomena.* New York: University Books, 1961.

Van Dusen, Wilson. *The Natural Depth in Man.* New York: Perennial Library, Harper & Row, 1972.

——. *The Presence of Other Worlds.* New York: Harper Row, 1974.

Völgyesi, Ferenc András. *Hypnosis of Man and Animals.* London: Baillière, Tindall & Cassell, 1966.

Vyvyan, John. *A Case Against Jones: A Study of Psychical Phenomena.* London: James Clark & Co. Ltd., 1966.

Walker, Benjamin. *Beyond the Body.* London: Routledge & Kegan Paul, 1974.

Wallace, Alfred Russel. *Miracles and Modern Spiritualism.* London: George Redway, 1896.

——. *My Life in Two Volumes.* London: Chapman & Hall, Ltd., 1905.

West, D. J., M. B., D. P. M. *Psychical Research Today.* London: Gerald Duckworth & Co. Ltd., 1954.

Wilson, Colin. *Access To Inner Worlds.* London: Rider & Company, 1983.

——. *Mysteries.* London: Hodder & Stoughton, 1978.

——. *The Occult.* London: Hodder & Stoughton, 1971.

——. *Poltergeist!* London: New English Library, 1981.

——. *The Psychic Detectives.* London: Pan Books Ltd., 1984.

Index